DISCIPLINE:

POLICIES AND PROCEDURES

DISCIPLINE:

POLICIES AND PROCEDURES

James R. Redeker

The Bureau of National Affairs, Inc., Washington, D.C.

Library of Congress Cataloging in Publication Data
Redeker, James R., 1941–
    Discipline—policies and procedures.

    Includes index.
    1. Labor discipline—Law and legislation—
United States.   2. Arbitration, Industrial—United
States.   3. Labor discipline—United States.
I Title.
KF3540.R4 1983   344.73'012598   83-6053
ISBN 0-87179-394-6   347.30412598
ISBN 0-87179-399-7 (pbk.)

Printed in the United States of America
International Standard Book Number: 0-87179-394-6 (hardbound)
0-87179-399-7 (paperback)

To Nancy, Rebecca,
Eric, and Tricia

Contents

Introduction

The idea for this book first took shape during a luncheon meeting with an old friend and client. I had known Dick for many years, first when he was the personnel director of several different plants of a large multinational chemical company and now as the corporate Manager of Industrial Relations. Our luncheon had a dual purpose. Dick had just become Director of Human Resources for the company's European operations and we had met to say a temporary farewell and to review the overall labor relations of the company. Most of the time, however, we reminisced about the Labor Board proceedings in which we had been involved together around the country, grievance arbitrations reaching back to his days as a personnel director, and collective bargaining sessions of some special note. As we began to talk about the differences in handling the problems of unorganized plants as opposed to unionized plants, a single theme kept reoccurring: the need for quality supervisors and a truly effective discipline system.

It gradually became obvious to us both that well-trained supervisors and a fair discipline program were often the only discernible differences between a well-run, productive plant and one which seemed to limp from problem to problem, crisis to crisis. Dick recalled the many times he and his supervisors would meet to discuss whether a particular situation warranted discipline or discharge and how the same issues and mistakes always seemed to be present. Just as one problem was solved and the supervisors seemed to recognize the principles involved in the solution, another arose which was simply a variation of the first, and the same principles had to be reviewed all over again. Just as one instance of incorrect or imprecise discipline was set straight for one supervisor, another would make the same mistake, sometimes in the very same facility.

I suppose the realization of this waste of time and energy spawned our discussion of how to provide a simple guide for discipline which first-line supervisors could use, on the job, day in and day out. As we spoke, the idea of a desk manual on discipline seemed more and more to be a reasonable and necessary addition to every supervisor's work area.

Perhaps fortuitously, after our luncheon, I returned to my office and encountered a recurring problem for my clients, low productivity of employees. In the immediate situation, the client had asked for my analysis of the company's personnel relations with a special eye turned toward increasing overall productivity. What the client was considering, in part, was a system of participatory management with the employees. The owner had read an article which extolled the high productivity of Japanese workers, attributing their high productivity to the degree to which they participated in the operation of their plants and the quality of work life. Without any thought about historic and cultural differences between the employees, the client was considering a wholesale reorganization of his personnel relations.

Certainly, the productivity of the American worker and the quality of the goods produced, when compared to that of competing foreign countries, is alarming. Recently released figures, for instance, indicate that a subcompact automobile in Japan requires 111 hours to make at a direct labor cost of about $7.75 per hour. In the United States, a subcompact automobile requires 200 hours to make at a direct labor cost of about $17.50 per hour. As a result, American auto companies start with a point of production disadvantage of over $3,000 per car due solely to direct labor costs.

Setting aside the incredible wage differential, why does it take an American worker 1.8 times longer to make the same product as a Japanese worker. Is it all attributable to a higher level of technology, use of robots, etc.? To what extent is it due to the workers themselves? Can the elements which make Japanese workers more productive be instilled in American workers? If so, how can that be done? Is the historic method of operating U.S. companies contributing to the productivity problem? Must there be drastic changes to the structure of our industries to enable us to compete in the world market?

I suppose I am old-fashioned in some respects, but I believe that much can be done to fine tune the structures we have which will materially improve employee productivity. In this respect, I do not ascribe to the philosophy that American businesses must completely reorganize their systems of dealing with employees, but I do believe they must modernize our historically successful methods. To a great degree, this means going back to the basics. We should examine our current methods of operations to see what we can do to correct the errors in our system, before we overreact in desperation and embrace entirely different systems.

Clearly, paying higher wages and increasing nonproductive paid leave time is not the answer. Paying U.S. automobile workers 2.25 times what Japanese auto companies pay their workers has not made U.S. workers more productive. If it had, the time for production of a single automobile would be at least the same or better than in Japan. The key must lie somewhere else in the dungeon and, perhaps, it is guarded by an entirely different dragon than the one seen by the quality-of-worklife people.

In my opinion, where an employer's discipline system provides a clear and understandable matrix for employees and where it is administered in a manner which produces industrial due process, employee productivity will be increased. I have not arrived at this opinion by ascending to some academic height; rather, I have witnessed numerous companies achieve dramatic productivity increases by strengthening and improving their discipline systems. In addition, these companies increased employee morale in direct proportion to their efforts.

Assuming competitive wages and benefits, discipline often becomes the proving ground in which an employer demonstrates its attitude toward employees. In fact, discipline becomes the proof itself in many cases. Employee perceptions of an employer's fairness and of the quality of the workplace frequently appear to have their bases in how well or how poorly the discipline program operates. From the point of view of the employees, the discipline system may be the most obvious and objective evidence they have of the employer's opinion of their worth as individuals. From the employer's perspective, the discipline program is often the basic and, perhaps, the only tool used to achieve a well-ordered and productive workplace. For this reason, disciplining employees frequently becomes a central focus for both employees and employers, albeit for vastly different reasons. To achieve both party's objectives, the discipline system must be fair in construction and fair in operation.

This book seeks to help both employers and employee representatives to achieve fairness and predictability in discipline.

Part I discusses the basic principles involved in the development and operation of a successful discipline program and how these principles can be translated into specific plans. Part I is directed primarily toward those who construct discipline programs, whether as an employer or employee representative. It is intended to assist these upper management and union officials in the development of fair and effective discipline systems.

As mentioned earlier, the principles, programs, and patterns which are discussed in Part I have not been conceived within the ivory towers of academia. Nor have they been developed by a personnel manager with practical experience only in a limited number of workplaces. Rather, the principles are analyzed and explained from the perspective of someone who has dealt directly with numerous approaches to discipline, implemented in many different types of companies in a multitude of industries and situations. Moreover, they are drawn from the experience received through trying hundreds of arbitration cases and seeing firsthand which discipline systems work, which do not, and why.

Part II of this work seeks to provide all levels of supervision, including first level, with a detailed examination of the primary causes for discipline. It is a "guidebook" to the relevant principles generally accepted as operational in each subject area. The purpose is to give to supervisors and employee representatives a ready and workable understanding of what must be present in any factual circumstance before discipline will be considered appropriate and for "just cause."

One of the most frequent experiences I have had is that of the employer representative who contacts me to determine whether a particular set of facts warrants the discipline or discharge of an employee in administration or degree. At these times I am asked to analyze the facts and apply them to what my research and experience has indicated are the generally accepted conceptions of "just cause." Because the system within which the concept of just cause is given some momentary meaning is that which normally ends in final and binding arbitration, I believe the best sources for discipline principles are actual arbitrator decisions. Consequently, in my practice, the rules I apply to various factual circumstances presented by clients are those which have been derived predominantly from these opinions. The discernment of these rules, however, is often extremely difficult because arbitrators are not bound by any precedents; view each case individually; and, I fear, have some difficulty in reading the decisions of other arbitrators. Consequently, arbitrator decisions may be found to support almost every type of fairly reasonable proposition. Occasionally, the unreasonable is also supported.

To be able to answer questions from clients, I have learned to carry in my mind certain checklists of what elements must be present before discipline or discharge will be sustained by an arbitrator, at least by an arbitrator in the mainstream of arbitral thinking. These mental checklists are the products of reading as well as of litigating many discipline arbitrations. However, they are rarely put into some structured document, unless as a part of a brief which, of course, is limited to the principles relevant to a single set of facts. As a result, I have not until now, recorded principles of discipline in a format constructed for general application.

Occasionally, I have found it helpful to put a checklist for a single cause for discipline into some abbreviated form so that it can be given to a client as a guide. From time to time I have also used lists of principles governing various causes for discipline as teaching tools in supervisory training programs. Never, however, have these lists been made for all the major causes for discipline.

My intent with Part II, consequently, is to set forth the principles and rules used most frequently by arbitrators to resolve issues encountered in the sixteen most common causes for discipline. The purpose for doing this is to provide employer and employee representatives with an easy reference guide with which consistent discipline judgments can be made. Even in unorganized situations where final and binding arbitration is not the culmination of the grievance procedure, the same general principles of discipline may be applied. The common elements of fairness and justice are essential to the operation of any discipline system, regardless of the presence of a bargaining representative.

It is anticipated that this portion of the book will be most useful when employed as a desk manual by supervisors to be consulted frequently as a guide to see if discipline or discharge is warranted. However, the discussion and surveys of arbitration cases in each area will be valuable also for employee representatives, as they attempt to determine whether an employer's action was warranted in a particular case or whether it should be challenged in arbitration; for lawyers and other individuals charged with the responsibility of presenting and arguing a case before an arbitrator; and for arbitrators themselves as they seek to determine whether a particular employer action was for just cause.

For ease of reference, the discussion of each cause for discipline follows the same pattern, *i.e.*, a statement of the issue (Issue); a statement of the general principle and elements which must be present before discipline or discharge will be considered as for good cause (General Principle); a list of relevant matters to be considered before a decision to discipline can be made (Relevant Considerations); a general discussion of the cause and principles of discipline, including an analysis of leading cases (Discussion); a list of key points and guidelines if the discipline or discharge is to be sustained (Key Points; Guidelines); a series of hypothetical cases to illustrate the Key Points and Guidelines (Examples); and a list of cases which are relevant to the points mentioned (Relevant Cases).

As the reader will note from the table of contents, some common causes for discipline have not been included in this Part, *e.g.*, theft, assault and battery on a supervisor, willful destruction of the employer's property. The reason for excluding these causes is that they are generally accepted as justifying summary discharges and the only issue is that of proof, a subject not within the primary purpose of this book. The only causes included, therefore, are those where there are some questions as to either whether discipline should be imposed at all or, if given, what degree of discipline would be appropriate.

In preparing these sections, an effort has been made to review all published arbitrator decisions to determine the consistent elements and facts which arbitrators have found to be most significant. These elements have been listed in their most frequently expressed form. The principles stated, therefore, are drawn from many decisions and, consequently, are not applicable to every specific situation. Nevertheless, I believe that, in a particular case, where most or all of the Relevant Considerations listed are satisfied and the Keypoints are present, the discipline will be justified.

The reader should be aware that not all cases reviewed have been listed as a "Relevant Case." In this respect, there has been no attempt to make the case lists totally complete. My purpose has been to list only those cases which appear to be most instructive or illustrative of the subject or point being discussed. The cases listed do not always confirm the principle for which they are cited and, in fact, may contradict the stated rule. The reason for including these contradictory cases is to provide the reader with as complete and fair a discussion as possible. Consequently, no person should blindly string-cite the cases listed as standing for, or supporting, the principle for which the cases are shown. Sorry.

A special note of caution about the Examples. **The examples are not recitals of actual cases, even though they appear as if they had been decided by arbitrators.**

The Examples are intended only to be illustrative of situations which I believe to be most common. They are in the format of case decisions because I believe they take on a more beneficial and understandable nature when put in that fashion. The sources for the Examples, however, are real cases which have either been reported or in which I or my partners and associates have been actually involved. For this reason, the Examples are realistic, although hypothetical. Unfortunately, reported cases could not be used exclusively because all the variations necessary for a complete illustration of any point simply could not be found.

To repeat: the Examples cannot be cited as authority because they do not recount what arbitrators have actually done. Indeed, what I have set down as what an arbitrator would have decided in a particular example may be a source of dispute. Others may come up with different results and, since we are dealing with the amorphous concept of just cause, such differences of opinion are expected and common. It is hoped, however, that most arbitrators will agree with my suggested solutions and that this book will assist in achieving a higher level of consistency among arbitrators and employers in the treatment of employees. Employer and employee representatives may even agree that the solution reached by the mythical arbitrator will resolve their real-life dispute, and arbitrations can be avoided.

While written primarily from the point of view of the employer, a conscious effort has been made to create a work which would be helpful to employee representatives as well, whether they are business agents who take cases to arbitration or stewards who must file and prosecute grievances at the earliest steps. It is hoped that when both union and management representatives agree on what facts or elements must exist before a particular discipline would be appropriate, both sides will be willing to settle and not arbitrate the disputes. This work is intended, therefore, to serve as a resource for both sides to use as a tool for agreement and to promote a peaceful and productive workplace.

I especially would like to thank several people who have assisted me in reviewing arbitrator opinions and in finding the patterns of discipline discussed in Part II. The work of my associates, Thomas Heimbach, Esq., Wayne Weisman, Esq. and Frederick Strober, Esq., law clerk Laurie Johnston, and law students Sophia Hayes and Christine Levin has been invaluable. I appreciate the efforts of all of these talented people.

James R. Redeker

April, 1983

1

Discipline: Policies

1

Employer/Employee Rights and Responsibilities

Management personnel, for the most part, have an acute sense of the employer's rights and expectations in connection with employees. This sense may be either conscious or unconscious, developed or instinctive. When employees either disregard these perceived employer rights or fail to fulfill the employer's expectations, then management personnel react. This reaction is most often in the form of what management calls discipline. The extent to which the employer's rights and expectations have been consciously and intelligently developed and defined may often be reflected in the type of reaction or discipline which occurs. Where the sense of employer rights is instinctive, the disciplinary reaction probably will also be instinctive. The system of discipline, if it can be called that, will have logic and internal consistency only by chance.

Similarly, employees develop a sense of their own rights and expectations. They react, rationally or irrationally, to what they perceive to be employer failures. Moreover, the extent to which employee rights and expectations have been defined and intelligently developed may well dictate the nature of the employees' response to these perceived employer shortcomings. Employee reactions may be as ill-considered and irrational as some employer discipline.

Unfortunately, many employers and employees have little more than the most primitive understanding of their own responsibilities toward each other. Yet, an understanding of their mutual responsibilities may be more important to labor peace than all the laws heretofore devised to govern the employment relationship. Indeed, employment contracts and collective bargaining agreements are frequently no more nor less than written statements of these understandings. For this reason, the most successful leaders of business and labor often seem to be those who recognize the responsibilities as well as the rights of both management and labor and who strive to maintain a balance to insure that the expectations of each are fulfilled.

3

In this respect, it can be argued that the extent to which employers and employees each perceive the efforts of the other to fulfill expectations and honor the rights of the other is in direct relation to the productivity of the business enterprise and the existence of labor peace. It is noteworthy that the perception of the labor/management effort may be more important than the actual fulfillment of any expectations. Consequently, much of what will be discussed later will have to do with the perceptions, as well as the realities, involved in the labor/management relationship.

While the nature of the industry, the area in which the company is located, and the type of person who is employed may result in the emphasis of one element over another, the basic categories of rights, responsibilities, and expectations of labor and management remain fairly constant.

Management has the right to expect employees to be on time; to attend regularly; to put in a full day's work; to be physically and mentally prepared for the tasks to be performed; to respond positively to direction; to learn the job at hand, as well as new jobs; to adjust to change; to get along with fellow employees; and to know and to follow the rules and regulations of the plant.

Employees have the right to expect sound management of the business to insure the continued existence of employment; information concerning the performance of the business; safe and healthful working conditions; fair and predictable treatment; responsible and humane supervision; decent pay for work performed; appreciation for services; fair promotion and transfer procedures; and adequate job training and orientation. Most of all, they have a right to be treated as people of dignity and substantial worth, with responsibilities that extend beyond the workplace.

When an employer offers work for pay and an employee accepts pay for work, a contract is established which consists of the perceptions of each of the other's rights and expectations and an acceptance of the responsibility to fulfill those expectations. If the commitment or understanding of either party is lacking, mistaken, or incomplete, the contract is destined for breach, and an unproductive and antagonistic atmosphere is almost a certainty.

Consequently, the establishment of a harmonious and productive relationship would seem to depend, in the first instance, upon the conscious awareness of each party of the expectations, responsibilities, and rights of the other. Such an awareness is produced most frequently by the clear statement and delineation of these rights and responsibilities in either written company policies or a negotiated labor agreement. The absence of such writing leaves to chance the true nature of the bargain struck at the time the employee is hired.

Discipline

Nowhere is the nature of the relationship between an employer and an employee so dependent upon clear understandings than in matters having to do with discipline. It is through discipline that the employer forcefully establishes the parameters of its expectations and reacts to what it believes are failures of the employees to conduct themselves in accordance with those expectations. By the same token, the employees' response to discipline gives the employer certain knowledge of the employees' beliefs as to the extent and nature of their rights and responsibilities and of their willingness to fulfill the employer's expectations. It is in this atmosphere of action and reaction that employers and employees define for each other the nature of their relationship. Where a written statement of expectations in the form of a handbook or contract does not exist, the process of definition may be confused and erratic and the resulting confusion may breed a nonproductive antagonistic workforce. The primary action tool for an employer is discipline. How it is used may determine whether the employment relationship will be positive or negative.

In his classic work *Employee Discipline*, Lawrence Stessin stated:

> Employee discipline is the real drama of labor relations. It is the panorama of industrial conflict. It is the nerve center of a network of interrelationships between management and employee. Here are no small issues. . . . On a broader canvas employee discipline is a process of control. It is a method for the maintenance of authority by management. . . . A reprimand, a layoff or a discharge are the prerogatives which management uses as a control to keep these objectives in focus. . . .[1]

The employer clearly has the right to discipline and discharge employees to achieve employee cooperation in the performance of their responsibilities. To be sure, that right is limited by laws protecting employees in various protected classes from discipline, including discharge, due to concerted activities, race, religion, national origin, sex, or nonjob related handicaps. Where a collective bargaining agreement is in force, that right may be further limited by a clause permitting discipline, or discharge, only where just cause exists. Generally, the law does not require just cause to exist prior to the exercise of the employer's right to discipline employees.[2] In the absence of a contract and so long as the discipline is not administered for an unlawful reason, the employer is free to exercise this right at will.

While the employer has a right to discipline, the employee has a right to react to discipline; when the discipline is perceived as unjust, the employee may withhold his or her services, either individually or in concert with other employees. Since this right is clearly one which also damages employees by causing economic loss, withholding services is neither an adequate nor acceptable reaction to an unjust exercise by the employer of its right to discipline, except in the most extreme cases. Consequently, employee reactions to unjust discipline are more frequently of a lesser magnitude and of a character calculated to cause or to result in disharmony in the plant and/or reduced productivity. These reactions are in the nature of protests, and skilled managers are sensitive to the signs produced by these protests.

Consequently, the successful manager of a productive plant reads the signs of protest and heads off difficulty by taking corrective action. Most of all, the successful manager recognizes up front that employees have a right to a discipline system which is fair and appropriate, if for no other reason than to avoid reactions which may adversely affect the employees' productivity. This employee right to fair discipline is itself a composite of various elemental rights, all of which must be satisfied by the employer, if it is to obtain, and maintain, a productive atmosphere in the plant. The following principles contain the realistic, if not the legal, expectations of employees and the responsibilities of management. These principles, or rights, comprise what is coming to be popularly called "employee" or "industrial" due process.

Employee Rights/Employer Responsibilities

- *Employees have a right to know what is expected of them and what the consequences of not fulfilling those expectations will be.*

One of the most frequent inquiries of labor arbitrators deciding discipline cases is whether the employee actually knew that what he or she did fell short of what the employer expected.[3]

To be sure, certain offenses are so clearly contrary to acceptable conduct that discipline is readily accepted or justified upon review regardless of whether there was any prior communication or warning to the employee. These acts are few, however. They include theft, intentional destruction of company property, total refusal to perform safe work, and gross or intentional endangerment of the safety of coworkers. All other acts normally demand some kind of prior notice before terminal discipline will be viewed as justified. The seriousness of the act, however, will often determine the kind of notice required. Occasionally, the nature of the act may be so egregious that even though the offense would normally call for some notice prior to discharge, summary action may be appropriate.

For instance, excessive absenteeism may be just cause for discharge only after a series of lesser penalties have been used to impress on the employee the unacceptability of his or her conduct and to warn the employee that continued similar conduct will result in the ultimate punishment. On the other hand, gross insubordination may warrant discharge after only a single warning, or in an extreme case, it may even justify summary discharge.

Various methods of notice are available to employers and the one chosen may vary according to the sophistication of the employee involved. At one end of the spectrum is a simple clause in the contract or company policy manual which states that employees will be disciplined only for just cause. This type of notice carries added responsibilities for management, because it must further define what "just cause" is for that plant. Since "just cause" defies definition in a vacuum, the concept must evolve on a case-by-case basis, as instances demanding discipline arise.

In this manner, a code of conduct gradually emerges. However, the code will only develop to the extent that specific cases occur, and the employer's response and concept of appropriate behavior is communicated to the employees. The extent to which a single employee who is disciplined is actually aware of a specific rule, therefore, depends upon the employee's personal experience. The extent to which the employees in general are aware of the employer's expectations depends upon what they have observed of the employer and upon the folklore of the workplace.

Obviously, while giving to the employer great flexibility, this method also presents the greatest possibilities for misunderstanding and employee resentment. It also creates difficult evidentiary problems when the discipline must be justified to an arbitrator or to the employee.

At the other end of the spectrum is the contract or policy manual which details at great length the twenty-five or so common acts which will result in discipline, replete with specific punishments for each. Carried to the extreme, there will be gradations of punishments depending on established variables. While having the advantage of complete notice, this technique locks the employer into rigid rules which must be applied regardless of the personal circumstances of the employee, and the system lends an aura of a military camp to the workplace.

Obviously, a system which provides adequate notice to employees, but still maintains employer flexibility, is preferred and will generally lie somewhere between the two extremes. Precisely where on the continuum the proper balance will be achieved depends upon the nature of the employer, the employees, and the workplace in general. The various types of notice and how they can be achieved will be described in detail in a later section. For the moment, it is sufficient to only mention that some kind of notice of employer expectations must exist prior to discipline, if the employees are to receive due process and if the system is to have widespread employee acceptance.

- *The employee has a right to consistent and predictable employer responses to violations of rules.*

Almost as important to the employee as knowing that a particular act may result in discipline is the certainty that the discipline will actually take place. Arbitrator Dallas M. Young stated this principle as follows:

> When a man's job is involved; when a company's investment in the employee is about to be lost; when the future relationship between a management and its employees is at stake—a supervisor is dealing with an extremely serious matter. Arbitrators and Arbitration Boards have consistently held that essential to making discharges stand up are: (1) very clear instructions; and (2) even more explicit statements about the penalty for failure to comply.[4]

If discipline is to have its desired effect, it must be both rehabilitative and a deterrent.[5] The deterrent value increases as the predictability increases. Consistency and predictability, however, do not preclude the individuality of the discipline. However, even in individualizing discipline there must appear to be a consistency in the principles of application. Above all, the employees in the plant must readily perceive that the employer is dispensing discipline according to some defined policy and that the employees are treated the same, according to their individual circumstances.[6] Consistency in discipline requires that obviously similar employees be treated in obviously the same manner. Predictability in discipline requires that the employer always react in the same fashion when presented with the same stimulus.

For instance, an employer may be consistent in its discipline even though a junior employee with a record of disruptive behavior may be given a suspension for insubordination, while a senior employee with an unblemished record is merely warned. However, when two junior employees with similar records are given different types of discipline for the same offense, the employer will be viewed as erratic and possibly vindictive. Fear of the unknown will then breed resentment, distrust, and disharmony. The result of this employee reaction is often an unproductive atmosphere.

• *The employee has a right to fair discipline based on facts.*

Nothing is more vital to an effective discipline system than the process of gathering facts before judgments are made.[7] Employees appear to be quick to perceive or imagine ulterior motives. However, they are as quick to accept a decision based on recognized facts. Employees are often more knowledgeable of what really happened in a given situation than they are given credit for. Rarely, however, do they come forward and reveal those facts when the employment of another is at stake. Nevertheless, most employees appear to want justice done and dislike those among them who do not perform in accordance with their responsibilities. However, the revered American tradition that an authority must prove its case without the aid of the accused, and to a great extent the general citizenry, also pervades the workplace. The law of the shop seems to be consistent in that the employer commonly must discover the facts in any given case without the aid of the rank and file. The degree to which the employer is able to ascertain these facts, in spite of the "conspiracy of silence," may often be the measure of the employees' esteem and respect for management.

To operate an effective discipline system, then, the employer must establish methods for fact-finding which are dependable and free from personal prejudices. To a great extent, this depends upon well-trained supervisors. Supervisors are most often the only direct source of information regarding employee conduct. They must be schooled in methods of ascertaining the facts necessary to permit the employer to make and substantiate conclusions upon which discipline decisions depend. Countless discharge and discipline cases, which should not have gone to arbitration, have been reversed or modified simply because management's judgment was based on supposition, assumptions, wishful thinking, or unwarranted jumps in logic. Clearly, an employer must train all first line supervisors to recognize and to obtain all of the elements of an employee's offense before discipline can fairly follow from the facts.

The most important element in the process of fact-finding is a detailed record keeping system. Discipline for absenteeism; tardiness; falsification of records, or excuses; or for repeated offenses of the same kind, all depend upon the ability of the employer to document the violations. These records must be more than mere notations of occurrences. They should include enough description of the events to assure that anyone reading the record can conclude that the offense occurred or reoccurred. As sad as it may seem, the employer must maintain records on every employee, as if it will some day have to justify the employee's discharge.

If the employees are aware that whenever discipline is administered the employer can establish that a violation occurred and that the employee disciplined was the proper person, confidence and trust are established in the absoluteness of the employer's system, as well as an awareness that the employer is not to be abused.

Of course, all of this may be of little value if the discipline administered is not appropriate for the offense or for the circumstances. Appropriateness is relative. What may be shockingly severe to one group of employees may be routine to others. As stated earlier, the key to employee acceptance appears to be consistency. While many cases can be cited where an arbitrator has modified discipline for being too severe, there are none where an employer presented evidence that the same offense resulted in comparable discipline in other cases and an arbitrator modified the disciplinary action. In fact, such an action by an arbitrator might be cause for overturning an arbitrator's award.[8]

The importance with which arbitrators view comparable treatment is demonstrated by the fact that they will rarely, if ever, reduce the penalty of an employee, where it is proven that the degree of discipline given was the same as that given other employees on prior occasions for the same cause. This will be true even where the arbitrator may believe the punishment was too severe. In *Rohn Industries, Inc.*, for instance, an employee was discharged for sleeping on the job. The arbitrator, clearly affected by the union's argument that the penalty was too severe, nevertheless sustained the discharge, because the employer had discharged up to eight other employees previously for the same reason.[9] The arbitrator quoted Arbitrator Whitley P. McCoy, in *Stockham Pipe Fittings Co.*, as follows:

> Where an employee has violated a rule or engaged in conduct meriting disciplinary action, it is primarily the function of management to decide upon the proper penalty. If management acts in good faith upon a fair investigation and fixes a penalty not inconsistent with that imposed in other like cases, an arbitrator should not disturb it. The mere fact that management has imposed a somewhat different penalty or a somewhat more severe penalty than the arbitrator would have, if he had had the decision to make originally, is no justification for changing it.[10]

- *The employee has a right to question the facts and to present a defense.*

In great measure, the plant is a microcosm of our society, and many of the rights employees believe to be theirs are drawn directly from the principles by which our society operates. It is, perhaps, for this reason that many theoreticians in this field speak in terms of the constitutional concepts of due process.

Arbitrator Carroll R. Daugherty eloquently stated this proposition as follows:

> . . . Every accused employee in an industrial democracy has the right of "due process of law" and the right to be heard before discipline is administered. These rights are precious to all free men and are not lightly or hastily to be disregarded or denied. The Arbitrator is mindful of the Company's need for, equity in, and right to require careful, safe, efficient performance by its employees. But before the Company can discipline an employee for failure to meet said requirement, the Company must take the pains to establish such failure. Maybe X was guilty as hell; maybe also there are many gangsters who go free because of legal technicalities. And this is doubtless unfortunate. But company and government prosecutors must understand that the legal technicalities exist also to protect the innocent from unjust, unwarranted punishment. Society is willing to let the presumably guilty go free on technical grounds in order that free, innocent men can be secure from arbitrary, capricious action. (2) The Arbitrator then has only two alternatives: (a) reinstate X with pay for all time lost; and (b) reinstate him without such pay. (3) In the light of all the instant facts, the Arbitrator is of the opinion that the proper decision here is to reinstate X as of the date of his discharge but without back pay. The Company is now so directed.[11]

Unfortunately, the academicians, and some arbitrators, confuse these noble principles with the economic realities of plant operations: A company is not a precise mirror image of our society, because it is not fashioned as a democracy, or even a limited democracy. Such ivory-towered thinking is in the forefront of the movement toward the conversion of economic entities into social entities, with the result that American businesses are being crippled by the massive amounts of nonproductive time required to meet government regulations. Nevertheless, the concepts of self-worth and dignity are carried into the shop, even if self-determination may not be. Star Chambers simply do not work. Employees believe that they have a right to a "day in court," and they react strongly when this is denied.

While it is debatable in the practical world of a production facility whether an employee's right to defend himself or herself arises before or after the employee has been disciplined,[12] the right itself is not open to question. Arbitrator Theodore K. High stated the right in this fashion:

> I find it completely unacceptable that the Company feels it adequate to simply take disciplinary action and then

wait for the employee to file a grievance before getting the employee's side of the story. The whole purpose of an investigation and giving an employee an opportunity to present his case is so that it will have an effect upon the Company's disciplinary action, if any, which it finds appropriate under the circumstances. In other circumstances, I would find that this failure to provide sufficient due process to Grievant would be sufficient to nullify the Company's disciplinary action.[13]

The central role of industrial due process is to provide an effective opportunity for an employee to be heard and to mount a defense. While widely recognized, this employee right is one which can be satisfied at various times in the procedure. A denial at an early stage will not void otherwise appropriate discipline, where the right is granted at sometime prior to the administration of the disciplinary action. This precise issue was raised in *University of Missouri*.[14] In that case, the grievant argued that a denial of an evidentiary hearing before termination was a denial of due process, which should void the discharge. Arbitrator Yarowsky, in refusing to give credence to the argument, stated:

He is entitled to these protections [substantive and procedural due process] in any case and independent of the University's Grievance Procedure. But the Board finds that C____ was not denied due process of law because he has no guarantee of a full due process hearing before termination. [Citing *Arnett v. Kennedy*, 414 U.S. 632, 6 FEP Cases 1253 (1974)] C____ does not question whether he has been afforded a full due process hearing before this Board. Such a claim would not be plausible from any perspective in view of the fact that the hearing before this Board was totally adversarial, witnesses were sworn, examination and cross-examination of witnesses were fully and freely permitted and a recording of the two-day trial was made, transcribed and made available to both parties. "As an untainted trial *de novo*, the proceedings before the Joint Council (this Board of Arbitration) cured any prior deprivation of appellants' (Grievant's right to a full and fair hearing)." *Perry v. Milk Drivers' Union*, 656 F.2d 536, 108 LRRM 2570 (9th Cir. 1981).[15]

In the context of the workplace, the right to substantive and procedural due process includes the employee's right to know the charges and to be presented with the facts substantiating those charges. It also takes into account the unevenness of the odds. Managers, no matter how benevolent, may overlook the truly threatening atmosphere of a meeting between employer and employee. The employee, often alone, is faced with a judge and jury, all in one. Even if the discipline given is eminently fair, the employee may be left with feelings of being alone and intimidated—feelings which sometimes vent themselves in obstinant resentment. If discipline, short of discharge, is to have a beneficial effect, the process must avoid those things which can cause this kind of reaction. A right does not exist unless it is effective.[16]

One example of how proper discipline had a negative result is the recent case of a pro-company employee who for years had voted in several representation elections against the petitioning union. After changing his vote in the last election, he felt obligated to explain his about-face. In a conference with the personnel director, he recalled an instance several months previous in which he had been disciplined for negligent work performance. He admitted that the discipline had been fair and deserved. However, he added that when he was called into the personnel director's office for his hearing, he was met, not only by the director, but also by his foreman, the second line supervisor, the production manager, and a secretary to take notes. Five to one. While treated fairly, he felt so completely outnumbered that he decided he had to do something to even the odds.

Clearly, if the discipline system is to achieve its purpose of producing a responsive and productive workplace, it cannot emasculate the employee, and the employee must have the right to effectively make a defense. In unorganized plants this may take the form of simply evening the numerical odds or of having another rank-and-file employee present to assist the accused either as an ombudsman or as a friend.[17] In an organized plant, this function is performed by the shop steward. Either way, the employee must be given not only the chance to defend herself or himself, but an atmosphere and opportunity to mount an effective defense must exist. Absent that element, the employee may feel railroaded and oppressed and may react by voluntarily, or unconsciously, holding back.

- *The employee has the right to appeal the disciplinary decision.*

Our system of society has established a healthy distrust of single, no-recourse proceedings, and this too carries into the plant. The initial proceeding, which results in the administration of the disciplinary action, has too much chance of being colored by personal bias and by the feelings of the moment. Besides, the confrontation is simply over too soon to leave the employeee with any confidence in its objectivity. Even if not used, the employee should know that, if he or she believes the treatment to have been unfair, there is a possibility that some person in greater authority will examine the facts and make a dispassionate decision removed from the effects of the moment and the personalities involved.

The basic right of appeal, however, is often difficult to transform into a reality. In an organized plant it is easy, inasmuch as an arbitration process is built into most contracts. As will be seen later, even unorganized plants can attain some of this type of security. However, the unorganized plant must always prove to its employees that the appeal process is, in fact, fair and honest. This is a heavy burden to satisfy.

- *The employee has the right to progressive discipline.*

Another frequent inquiry of arbitrators is whether the employee was given a chance to improve his or her performance or behavior before discipline was administered. Except in the few cases enumerated earlier which will justify a summary discharge, arbitrators and employees believe in second, third, and sometimes, fourth chances. It is seen as essentially unfair to summarily discipline someone— to take away his or her livelihood—without giving the employee prior opportunities to conform to the expectations of the employer or to correct a mistake. Indeed, a recent study by Professor Malinowski concludes that a large majority of the employees who have been reinstated by arbitrators have continued in their employment satisfactorily.[18] Consequently, the concept of "another chance" appears to be founded in fact, and its use as a management tool is justified, not only to preserve the employment of a worker, but also to preserve the employer's training investment.

Progressive discipline systems will be discussed later in detail. Essentially, such systems demand warnings of progressive forcefulness and provide assistance to cure errant conduct as well as an opportunity to clear the record of offenses which are too old to be useful in determining the pattern of an employee's conduct. The employee must be given the opportunity to pay his or her debt to the employer, to be punished, and to be done with it. An employer's overly long memory exists as a destructive cloud over employees, which destroys their confidence in the fairness of the employer and which can cause resentments to build.

- *The employee has a right to be considered as an individual.*

As noted earlier, consistency in discipline does not require that the employee's personal circumstances be ignored. Any effective discipline system must consider what is appropriate for that particular employee. As stated by Arbitrator Roger I. Abrams, "A system which accounts for individual differences and considers each case of discipline fairly, on its individual merits, is not unreasonable."[19] The employee's prior service, performance, discipline record, and even his or her psychological state are, therefore, all proper conditions to be considered in determining whether the employee should be disciplined and, if so, the degree.

In its early stages, discipline in the workplace exists to bring about future conformance to the rules. Discipline which fits the violation but which does not fit the individual may be counterproductive. While caution must be exercised to avoid wide disparities in treatment which may be viewed by others as discrimination, an employee's prior records and performance must be rewarded with a fitting discipline. When disparate treatments of employees are based upon demonstrable considerations, such distinctions are rarely protested with much vigor. Here, too, the value of well-maintained records is utmost.

Summary

While discipline is essentially a negative tool by which conduct is conformed to pre-determined standards, successful management views discipline as an affirmative tool of its profession. Properly constructed and administered, the discipline system can produce trust and reliance on the good faith and strength of the employer. Discipline systems are accepted by employees as necessary to maintain order in the plant. Most employees welcome a system that will eliminate or rehabilitate employees who will not or cannot fulfill their responsibilities either to the employer or to their co-workers. If the system is designed and operated in a manner which incorporates the rights of employees as detailed here, the discipline system becomes a constructive instrument to enhance productivity rather than a purely negative tool of control.

One of the best summaries of these principles is that of Arbitrator Carroll R. Daugherty and his opinion is worth extensive quotation.[20]

Tests Applicable for Learning Whether Employer Had Just And Proper Cause For Disciplining An Employee

Few if any union-management agreements contain a definition of "just cause." Nevertheless, over the years the opinions of arbitrators in innumerable discipline cases have developed a sort of "common law" definition thereof. This definition consists of a set of guidelines or criteria that are to be applied to the facts of any one case, and said criteria are set forth below in the form of questions.

A "no" answer to any one or more of the following questions normally signifies that just and proper cause did not exist. In other words, such "no" means that the employer's

disciplinary decision contained one or more elements of
arbitrary, capricious, unreasonable, and/or discrimina-
tory action to such an extent that said decision constituted
an abuse of managerial discretion warranting the arbitrator to substitute his judgment for that of the employer.

The answers to the questions in any particular case are
to be found in the evidence presented to the arbitrator at
the hearing thereon. Frequently, of course, the facts are
such that the guidelines cannot be applied with slide-rule
precision.

The Questions

1. Did the Company give to the employee forewarning
or foreknowledge of the possible or probable disciplinary
consequences of the employee's conduct?

Note 1: Said forewarning or foreknowledge may
properly have been given orally by management or
in writing through the medium of typed or printed
sheets or books of shop rules and of penalties for
violation thereof.

Note 2: There must have been actual oral or written communication of the rules and penalties to the
employee.

Note 3: A finding of lack of such communication
does not in all cases require a "no" answer to Question No. 1. This is because certain offenses such as
insubordination, coming to work intoxicated, drinking intoxicating beverages on the job, or theft of the
property of the company or of fellow employees are
so serious that any employee in the industrial society
may properly be expected to know already that such
conduct is offensive and heavily punishable.

Note 4: Absent any contractual prohibition or restriction, the company has the right unilaterally to
promulgate reasonable rules and give reasonable orders; and same need not have been negotiated with
the union.

2. Was the company's rule or managerial order reasonably related to the orderly, efficient, and safe operation
of the Company's business?

Note: If an employee believes that said rule or
order is unreasonable, he must nevertheless obey
same (in which case he may file a grievance there-
over) unless he sincerely feels that to obey the rule
or order would seriously and immediately jeopardize
his personal safety and/or integrity. Given a firm

finding to the latter effect, the employee may properly be said to have had justification for his disobedience.

3. Did the company, before administering discipline to an employee, make an effort to discover whether the employee did in fact violate or disobey a rule or order of management?

Note 1: This is the employee's "day in court" principle. An employee has the right to know with reasonable precision the offenses with which he is being charged and to defend his behavior.

Note 2: The company's investigation must normally be made before its disciplinary decision is made. If the company fails to do so, its failure may not normally be excused on the ground that the employee will get his day in court through the grievance procedure after the exaction of discipline. By that time there has usually been too much hardening of positions.

Note 3: There may of course be circumstances under which management must react immediately to the employee's behavior. In such cases the normally proper action is to suspend the employee pending investigation, with the understanding that (a) the final disciplinary decision will be made after the investigation and (b) if the employee is found innocent after the investigation, he will be restored to his job with full pay for time lost.

4. Was the Company's investigation conducted fairly and objectively?

Note: At said investigation the management official may be both "prosecutor" and "judge," but he may not also be a witness against the employee.

5. At the investigation did the "judge" obtain substantial evidence or proof that the employee was guilty as charged?

Note: It is not required that the evidence be preponderant, conclusive or "beyond reasonable doubt." But the evidence must be truly substantial and not flimsy.

6. Has the company applied its rules, orders, and penalties evenhandedly and without discrimination to all employees?

Note 1: A "no" answer to the question requires a finding of discrimination and warrants negation or modification of the discipline imposed.

Note 2: If the company has been lax in enforcing its rules and orders and decides henceforth to apply them rigorously, the company may avoid a finding of discrimination by telling all employees beforehand of its intent to enforce hereafter all rules as written.

7. Was the degree of discipline administered by the company in a particular case reasonably related to (a) the seriousness of the employee's proven offense and (b) the record of the employee in his service with the company?

Note 1: A trivial proven offense does not merit harsh discipline unless the employee has properly been found guilty of the same or other offenses a number of times in the past. (There is no rule as to what number of previous offenses constitutes a "good," a "fair," or a "bad" record. Reasonable judgment thereon must be used.)

Note 2: An employee's record of previous offenses may never be used to discover whether he was guilty of the immediate or latest one. The only proper use of his record is to help determine the severity of discipline once he has properly been found guilty of the immediate offense.

Note 3: Given the same proven offense for two or more employees, their respective records provide the only proper basis for "discriminating" among them in the administration of discipline for said offense. Thus, if employee A's record is significantly better than those of employees B, C, and D, the company may properly give A lighter punishment than it gives the others for the same offense; and this does not constitute true discrimination.

Notes to Chapter 1

1. Stessin, *Employee Discipline* (Washington, D.C.: The Bureau of National Affairs, Inc., 1960), p. viii.

2. *But see* the discussion of the errosion of this concept in Chapter 4, Part I of this book.

3. *See General Elec. Co.* (Abrams), 74 LA 847; *New Castle Hosp.* (Witney), 74 LA 365; *Prismo-William Co.* (Jedel), 73 LA 581.

4. *Arco Precision Gear & Mach. Corp.* (Young), 31 LA 575, at 579–560. *See also Babcock & Wilcox Co.* (Dworkin), 41 LA 862.

5. *See* Alexander, "Concepts of Industrial Discipline," *Management Rights and the Arbitration Process*, Proceedings of the Ninth Annual Meeting of

the National Academy of Arbitrators (Washington, D.C.: The Bureau of National Affairs, Inc., 1948–), pp. 76, 79–81.

6. *See General Elec. Co.*, *supra*, note 3.

7. *See Grief Bros. Cooperage Corp.* (Daugherty), 42 LA 555; *Decor Corp.* (Kates), 44 LA 389; *Wolf Mach. Co.* (High), 72 LA 510.

8. *See Norfolk Shipbldg. & Drydock Corp. v. Local No. 684*, 671 F.2d 797, 109 LRRM 2329 (CA 4, 1982).

9. *Rohn Indus., Inc.* (Sabo), 78 LA 978.

10. *Stockham Pipe Fittings Co.* (McCoy), 1 LA 160.

11. *Grief Bros. Cooperage Corp.*, *supra*, note 7, at 557.

12. *Compare* Summers, "Individual Protection Against Unjust Dismissal: Time for a Statute," 62 VA. L. REV. 481, 504 (1976), which concludes that arbitrators have generally held that the "employee is not entitled to a hearing before discipline is imposed. . .," with the opposite finding in, Jennings & Wolters, "Discharge Cases Reconsidered," 31 ARB. J. 164, 178 (1976).

13. *Wolf Mach. Co.* (High), 72 LA 510, at 512.

14. *University of Mo.* (Yarowsky), 78 LA 417.

15. *Id.*, at 421.

16. *See also Plantation Patterns, Inc.* (Dallas), 78 LA 647.

17. Littrell, "Grievances Procedure and Arbitration in a Nonunion Environment: The Northrop Experience," *Arbitration Issues for the 1980s*, Proceedings of the Thirty-Fourth Annual Meeting of the National Academy of Arbitrators (Washington, D.C.: The Bureau of National Affairs, Inc., 1948–).

18. *See* Malinowski, "An Empirical Analysis of Discharge Cases and the Work History of Employees Reinstated by Labor Arbitrations," 36 ARB. J. 31 (1981).

19. *General Elec. Co.*, *supra*, note 3, at 850.

20. *Grief Bros. Cooperage Corp.*, *supra*, note 7, at 557–559.

2

Progressive Discipline: The Traditional System

The traditional approach to discipline is based upon the theory that various standards of conduct and productivity can be achieved and maintained through a system of ever-increasing degrees of punishment.[1] In theory, when an employee finally demonstrates that he or she is no longer an acceptable member of the workforce through repeated refusals to adhere to established standards, the employer is justified in terminating the employment. Arbitrator Harry J. Dworkin, in *Babcock & Wilcox Co.*, described this approach to discipline in a case involving a discharge for excessive absenteeism as follows:

> The arbitrator acknowledges that an employee may be subject to discipline, including discharge, for chronic absenteeism where he has failed to respond to more moderate disciplinary procedures. Where the company issues warnings and suspensions, which prove to be ineffectual, management is then free under proper circumstances to consider termination of employment. Where an employee continues to disregard his attendance obligations, just cause may be presented for discharge. The employer has the right to anticipate that its employees will observe the regular scheduled hours of work, and dereliction in these respects may present just cause.
>
> Employers generally will utilize other available methods for correcting chronic absenteeism before discharge penalty is invoked. Discharge is warranted only in such cases where corrective measures appear to be futile. In the instant case, the arbitrator does not feel that the grievant was accorded the proper corrective disciplinary procedures.
>
> The arbitrator subscribes to the principle of progressive discipline. This concept is referred to by Professor Law-

rence Stessen in *Employee Discipline*, page 142, citing *Bell Aircraft Corp.*, 17 LA 230 (Arbitrator Joseph Shister): ". . . What progressive discipline does mean is that progressively more severe penalties may be imposed on each given employee each time any given offense is repeated. Progressive discipline also means that after a specified number of offenses, regardless of whether the offenses are identical or not, the company may have the right to discharge the given employee. Both of these latter interpretations of progressive discipline avoid the inequitable meting out of discipline, and at the same time serve the dual purpose of progressive discipline, namely, the discouragement of repeated offenses by employees and the protection of the right of the company to sever completely its relationship with any employee who by his total behavior shows himself to be irresponsible."[2]

As indicated in Chapter 1, for any discipline system to have credibility, the standards of conduct or performance must be clearly established so that all employees are, at least theoretically, aware of the employer's expectations. Discipline, then, is used to achieve employer expectations by compelling compliance with company rules through punishment or the threat of punishment.[3]

The traditional approach, often called corrective or progressive discipline because the purpose is to correct behavior through progressively more severe penalties, has developed into a fairly set formula. This formula consists of a series of steps, one or more of which may be eliminated or added. However, it is rare for the number of steps to be fewer than three or more than five. The following four steps are involved most frequently:

1. An employee who has committed an infraction is verbally warned and told that if the same infraction occurs again within some specified period the degree of disciplinary action will be increased.
2. If the employee again commits the same or a similar violation within the specified period, the employee will be given a written warning which will be placed in his or her personnel file. The employee will be told that, if his or her conduct is repeated within a specified period, the employee will be disciplined again, but more severely.
3. If the employee again transgresses in the same manner and within the specified period, he or she will be suspended from employment for a period of time without pay and will be given a final warning. This warning will clearly specify discharge as the result of another such infraction within a stated time.
4. If the employee again violates the same rule within the specified time, the employee will be discharged.

Because the system progresses through ever-increasing levels of severity, it is assumed that the employee will learn what type of conduct is acceptable and will be given an opportunity, or be compelled, to conform. However, to really work, this traditional approach must contain two additional and essential elements. Without them, an arbitrator may still find the discipline to have been unfair. These elements can be stated briefly as follows:

1. The system must provide due process to the employee;
2. All employees must be treated the same or advanced through the steps of the system in the same fashion without discrimination.

Due Process

The concept of due process is as elusive in employee-employer relations as it is in the law. The primary elements of employee due process were described in Chapter 1. Essentially, arbitrators appear to conclude that due process exists where the employee is made aware of the nature of his or her violation of company rules or standards; the employee is not punished unless the violation is shown by the weight of credible evidence; the employee is allowed to know all of the facts supporting a finding of a violation; and, the employee is given an opportunity to defend himself or herself. In addition, arbitrators often find that employers must have forfeited the element of surprise prior to their implementing disciplinary action. That is, an employee must know that certain acts, if committed or continued, will result in some kind of punishment, usually the kind actually administered. Indeed, industrial "due process" is inextricably involved in the similarly evasive concept of "just cause." This was recognized by the U.S. Court of Appeals for the Eighth Circuit in *Local 878 v. Coca-Cola Bottling Co.*, as follows:

> . . . arbitrators have long been applying notions of "industrial due process" to "just cause" discharge cases. As Professor Summers noted, "[o]n the bare words 'just cause' arbitrators have built a comprehensive and relatively stable body of both substantive and procedural law." Summers, *Individual Protection Against Unjust Dismissal: Time for a Statute*, 62 Va. L. Rev. 481, 500 (1976) (footnote deleted). Professor Summers also commented that the retention of the bare "just cause" language in newly negotiated agreements is an indication of the widespread acceptance of arbitrators' due process interpretations. Id. at 505. To a similar effect are the comments of Professor Getman:

> To enhance its chances of winning at arbitration, a
> company needs to establish careful disciplinary pro-
> cedures consistent with arbitration awards defining
> the concept of just cause. Arbitrators generally insist
> on equal punishment for the same offense, and they
> require that employees be given advance notice of
> company rules *and a chance to explain their behavior
> before they are disciplined.* Getman, Labor Arbitra-
> tion and Dispute Resolution, 88 Yale L. J. 916, 921
> (1979) (footnote deleted, emphasis added). *See also
> Combustion Engineering, Inc.*, 42 Lab. Arb. 806 (1964)
> (Daugherty, Ar.).[4]

Where an employee's defense is built upon proven surprise or lack
of knowledge, discipline is rarely found to be appropriate.[5] Consequently, the first, and perhaps the most important, element which
must be shown to exist in any discipline case is that the employee
knew, or should have known, that his or her conduct would produce
a disciplinary response. In fact, the progressive or corrective discipline system is built upon the principle of employee awareness,
thereby eliminating any element of surprise. As employees move
through each step, they receive actual notice that their behavior is
in violation of specific rules or standards. For this reason, some
personnel directors refer to the operation of the system as an employee's self-discipline. That is, employees who knowingly subject
themselves to punishments of increasing severity are, in effect, disciplining themselves. The obvious key, here, is the word "knowingly." If an employee is unaware of a rule or does not know that
specific conduct will violate a rule, the employee can hardly be found
to have knowingly subjected himself or herself to discipline. A corollary to this principle is that an employee does not receive the
benefits of progressive discipline when an employer administers increasing degrees of punishment regardless of the nature of the rule
which has been violated. For instance, an employee who is warned
for excessive absenteeism, suspended for carelessness, and discharged for abusive language cannot be found to have had due process. Movement through the steps of the progressive discipline system
only occurs when that movement is occasioned by violations of the
same rule or type of rule.

For adequate notice to have been made to employees, however,
two things must exist: (1) a publication of standards of conduct and
(2) a publication of the discipline system itself.

Such publications should be of two kinds in all cases, general and
specific. Although arbitrators rarely overturn otherwise appropriate
discipline because of the absence of a general publication, they will
almost always find that a specific publication must exist, particu-

larly in cases involving discharge or suspension. A general publication occurs when the employer distributes to all employees a standard set of rules and regulations. Distribution can be achieved by incorporating the publication into a union contract or an employee handbook or by posting the document on a bulletin board. A publication is general if it is distributed to all the employees in the same manner at a time not directly associated with any specific event.

A specific publication usually is written in response to a particular event or situation, is addressed to an individual employee or to a group of employees smaller than the entire workforce, and is intended to communicate a rule of management. This type of publication usually is written during the course of the discipline, and its contents are communicated when the individual employee is told the nature of the unacceptable conduct, why it was unacceptable, and what will result from continued actions of the same kind. Specific publication is essential to a finding of due process where the discipline is of an advanced degree. Arbitrators have found specific publications to be acceptable where: (1) an employee admits to specific knowledge of the allegedly broken rule; (2) an employee admits to being aware of the degree of discipline required by the discipline system for the particular infraction; and, (3) the employer can document the transmittal of this information.

To sustain discipline which will cause an employee to suffer some economic loss, therefore, employers are frequently required to document, or otherwise prove by the weight of the credible evidence, that the employee received specific publication of the rule and that his or her act was in violation of that rule. In addition, an important issue to arbitrators seems to be whether the employee was able to predict what the results of his or her actions would be prior to the disciplinary action.[6] The element of predictability in the discipline system is discussed in Chapter 1.

Four recent cases demonstrate various aspects of the notice requirement. In *Montague Machine Co.*, an employee was discharged for poor work performance.[7] The company presented evidence that several warnings had been given to the employee prior to the event which precipitated the discharge. One of these warnings had been in writing. The arbitrator found that the verbal warnings could be best characterized as "casual conversations," and since they could not have been perceived by the employee as warnings, the verbal warnings should be disregarded as ineffective. The written warning, while effective as a warning for poor work performance, did not state that a future similar occurrence would result in discharge. Consequently, the arbitrator held that the employee had not been given adequate notice of the seriousness of the situation and should not have been discharged. By failing to give the employee adequate notice of the consequence of his continued poor performance, the employer was perceived as not really trying to rehabilitate the employee.

In *Watauga Industries, Inc.*, an employee was discharged for smoking marijuana on the employer's premises in violation of a specific company rule.[8] Finding that the employer had condoned the possession and smoking of marijuana in the past, the arbitrator reinstated the employee. The arbitrator's reasoning was that the employee had not been given notice that the rule against the possession and the use of marijuana in the plant was going to be enforced.

In a somewhat similar case, *Gill Studios, Inc.*, the employee was also reinstated for lack of adequate, specific notice.[9] In that case, the employee had been discharged for having received three reprimands in six months. Although the rule had been generally publicized, the employer had not told the employee after his second reprimand that another, within a specified period of time, would result in discharge. This employer, also, was found to have made an inadequate effort to rehabilitate the employee.

By way of contrast, the arbitrator in *Lucky Stores, Inc.* sustained the action taken against an employee who had been discharged following an absence for a concededly legitimate illness.[10] In that case, the employee had received prior warnings and had been suspended once for chronic absenteeism. The suspension letter threatened the employee with discharge for any further absences, regardless of the reason for the absence. The discharge was sustained, even though the employee's record had improved and the absence was caused by a legitimate illness. The arbitrator found that the absenteeism, although improved, was still excessive and that the employee had been given adequate notice that his next absence, regardless of cause, would result in discharge.

The second requisite of due process is that the charge be factually accurate. Often, this depends on documentation. Without proof of each of the essential elements of the offense, an arbitrator cannot and will not sustain the discipline. Nowhere is this more obvious, and most often lacking, than in "accumulation" cases. A common query of employers is whether disciplinary action taken against an employee will be sustained upon challenge, where the violative act of the employee is claimed to have been "the last straw." Upon close examination, however, the other "straws" rarely exist, except in some supervisor's vague memory. Other than the fact that the discipline would be extremely hard to justify to an arbitrator because of the absence of proof, it could be nearly as difficult to justify it to the employee involved and to the employee's coworkers. This latter consideration is especially important where the employees are not represented by a union and where the propriety of the discipline may be important to many more people than the union's business agent and an arbitrator.

In this regard, a common misconception, which appears to lead many employers astray, is that verbal warnings need not be recorded or written. Where the verbal warning is not recorded, a supervisor must depend exclusively on memory, a notoriously defective disciplinary device. For this reason, many employers have found it advisable to abandon the traditional rubric of initiating disciplinary action with a verbal warning, replacing it with a procedure involving a first and a second written warning. Whatever the system's formal requirement may be, the first warning must at all times be recorded in some fashion to insure that the event is documented and becomes a part of the employee's record.

As noted above, the value of documentation is most critical in cases of cumulative causes for discipline, such as absenteeism, tardiness, negligence, or poor production. The most reliable source for this type of documentation is frequently the foreman's or supervisor's log book in which all facts which may be, or may become, relevant to the operation of the department are recorded on a daily basis. In this respect, most supervisors must face the unpleasant reality that, no matter how good employees may seem, the supervisor must be prepared to keep records to be able to justify any disciplinary action which may be required at some time in the future.

The third requisite of due process is that the employee be allowed to know all of the facts of the charge against him or her. Arbitrators attach an importance to the use which an employer makes of the evidence upon which the discipline has been based. Whether a union is involved or not, this evidence cannot be held in secret but must be shown to the employee for examination. It is only after the employee has had a full and free opportunity to examine the case that the employee can be expected to acknowledge and learn from his or her mistake or to mount a legitimate defense. Even if the employee does not seek to examine the evidence but appears to acquiesce to the disciplinary action, the employer should take steps to ensure that a recital of the facts is documented and placed in the employee's file. Only then will both the employee and the employer be assured that the discipline given is appropriate under circumstances where the employee's work history may be relevant.

Finally, due process requires that employees have an opportunity to defend themselves in an established review procedure. Discipline in a vacuum is rarely found to be appropriate, because it is inherently suspect. An opportunity to defend means more than some *pro forma* meeting at which a supervisor politely listens to an employee's excuses. Again, records are important to document the fact that the employee was shown the evidence upon which the discipline was based and that opportunity was given for the employee to provide explanations or to prepare a defense. The employee's defense should be examined carefully and any factual disputes resolved before the discipline becomes final or before the next step in the appeals process is employed. Just as the employee could make a mistake, so also could the supervisor.

In the progressive discipline system, natural plateaus exist, at which opportunities are presented for employees to mount a defense. These occasions change in character as the discipline increases in severity. For instance, at the warning stage, meetings with the first and second line supervisors and the employee are held. At these meetings, the facts are revealed and discussed; for an initial disciplinary measure, this is usually sufficient. However, at the suspension and discharge levels when an employee is about to suffer more tangible economic loss, the conference with the employer usually assumes a more formal atmosphere, like that of a hearing. Usually present at these hearings are the employee, the immediate and second line supervisors, as well as the manager of industrial relations, or some other similarly placed individual in authority.

Surprisingly, it is often in the hearing aspect of the discipline system that due process is denied. This is due primarily to the fact that supervisors are rarely given the training necessary to handle disciplinary meetings: Notes are not kept; things are left unsaid; facts are not revealed, or sometimes, are concealed; and employees are not given an adequate opportunity to tell their side of the story. Often, what results from these meetings is a failure to give adequate specific notice, a loss of a valuable opportunity to effect a real rehabilitation, and an employee who may be confused, embarrassed, and resentful rather than one who has been helped. This is unfortunate, since the disciplinary conference may well be the single most important element in the system's operation. Indeed, it is the disciplinary conference which is central to the affirmative system, emphasized and discussed in Chapter 3.

In *Plantation Patterns, Inc.,* for example, the discharge of an employee for dishonest misrepresentation was reduced to a suspension, solely because the employer had denied the employee due process.[11] In this case, the employee had requested his supervisor to falsify his time card to allow payment for time away from the job. The employer's grievance system provided for an evidentiary hearing with the employee and, subsequently, a third step grievance meeting. While the evidentiary hearing was conducted, the employee was not allowed representation, and the third step meeting was not held. After reviewing the evidence, the arbitrator stated:

> So where are we? Where we are is at a juncture wherein the arbitrator is abundantly satisfied that D ＿＿＿ was guilty of dishonest misrepresentation designed to defraud the Company.
>
> However, the story doesn't end here. The Union charges correctly that the grievant was denied Union representation at the *one* meeting that was held after his escapade.

This was a meeting of three Company officials, *i.e.*, Kathie Shirah, Donnie Lowe, and Rocky Stiff and the grievant. This presumably was an investigation, but this is not the way to conduct an investigation. First of all, the Company should have asked D ____ if he wanted Union representation, it should not have been denied him. Also, common decency dictates that you don't "tape" the proceedings of such a tribunal without the knowledge and the express aproval of the accused. This was not done.

In addition, there never was a convening of the parties via the grievance procedure. Shortly after the convening of what the Union describes as a Kangaroo Court the Company discharged the grievant. Section 2, Article XVI of the labor contract specifies that if a non-probationary employee files a grievance within a five day period, "the matter *shall* be taken up at a meeting of the Grievance Committee as provided in Step Three of the Grievance Procedure, which meeting shall be held within five (5) working days of the suspension." [Emphasis added.] Obviously, there was no third step meeting in this case, although it was mandated.

What we have here is a case where an employee is clearly guilty of a serious misdeed, but in his defense, the Company has blatantly and illegally subverted the due process rights of the aggrieved.

What is the arbitrator to do? Well clearly, the grievant should not be applauded and made scotfree for his excesses. But equally seriously, the Company should be rebuked for its behavior.

Award

The discharge of the grievant is reduced from discharge to a suspension without pay for two months. He shall be reinstated to his former or equal position, his seniority shall be restored, and he shall be made whole for that portion of his unemployment which the arbitrator has found to be improper.

The arbitrator retains jurisdiction in this matter for the purposes of the remedy.[12]

Another example is to be found in *Texas International Airlines, Inc.*[13] The employee had been discharged for sleeping on the job. Apparently, the employee had pulled two chairs together in the employee lunchroom during his lunch period and had covered them with a blanket; he had then proceeded to fall asleep. This had been noted by a supervisor, who allowed the employee to continue to sleep past the time he was due to report back to work. When the employee failed to return to his workstation, the supervisor discharged him. The arbitrator noted that the employee had not been allowed to give his side of the story or otherwise defend himself and found that the company had denied him due process. The discharge was overturned, and the employer was ordered to reinstate the employee with full backpay. As in *Gill Studios, Inc.*, central to the arbitrator's reasoning was the concept that the employer is obligated to make reasonable efforts to rehabilitate an employee and to assist the employee in avoiding future acts which will result in discipline.[14]

An employee's ability to adequately raise a defense at a hearing may depend on the presence of another person, a steward, an ombudsman, or an appointed supervisor who can speak on the employee's behalf. This is apparent from the list of participants in the disciplinary meetings described above. Unless represented by some other person, the lone employee, in this type of situation, is expected to face three or four managerial personnel in a closed hearing. In this kind of atmosphere, it would be impossible for most rank-and-file employees not to feel intimidated, let alone mount an effective defense.

Nevertheless, the opportunity and ability to respond to charges and to raise mitigating circumstances is essential to industrial due process. Due process cannot be denied in fact, or in effect, if the discipline is to be positive rather than negative. The progressive discipline system presents several opportunities to employers to satisfy this right, and they must make special efforts to develop and to realize these opportunities. Of all the elements in the progressive discipline system, employer efforts seem to be lacking most frequently. The reason for this, perhaps, is that the employer's efforts, in this respect, represent an element which is not a self-activating principle of the discipline system. Notice, for example, usually occurs as a natural consequence of the progression of the system, as does the increasing severity of penalties. The content and value of disciplinary conferences, however, are totally dependent on the human element. The give-and-take required in conferences cannot be formulated in an office or satisfied with written procedures. Effective management of conferences can only be achieved through the training and retraining of supervisors.

The basic unfairness of a discipline system which denies an employee the right to have someone speak for and defend him or her was the central issue in *Fort Wayne Community Schools*.[15] In that case, an employee's request for representation in the hearings preceding her discharge was denied. This denial was held by the arbitrator as a denial of due process, and the employee was ordered reinstated with backpay, even though she had been found to have committed the acts upon which the discharge was premised.

Equal Treatment

Probably the most troublesome element in any discipline system, particularly one based on the traditional concept of punishment, is that of equal treatment. The difficulty lies in the shifting sands of equality and the inevitable question of what constitutes sameness. The standards and the punishment can be absolutely equal as written, but employees are never equal. Each employee's work record, background, and psychological make-up is different, and the struggle frequently comes over the fact that the same treatment, mechanically applied to all employees, is often unfair. Nevertheless, any discipline system that is effective must maintain the appearance of fairness to all. Absolute, quantifiable equality in treatment, however, is not necessary, except in the most restrictive and battle torn workplaces. In such places, employers are forced into a mechanical application of the rules, regardless of the inevitable special circumstances of employees, and in the name of equal treatment, employers must dispense periodic injustices.

Nevertheless, the standardization of expectations and discipline is essential to the employer's ability to sustain penalties for just cause.[16] Within this standardization there may be room for the exercise of judgment and for individual treatment. However, whenever these judgments deviate from the norm to such an extent that the appearance of fairness is called into question, the system is in danger of collapse. While the employer may believe it is constructively treating employees as individuals, the employees will, in fact, suspect favoritism or discrimination. Consequently, unless the basis for any specialized treatment outside the general rules of the system is readily apparent to all employees, the employer is at risk.

The key to maintaining equality in the administration of a discipline system is, again, record keeping. An employer can only be assured that discipline cases will conform to the desired pattern by keeping track of the specific causes for disciplinary actions. This is especially true when the degree of punishment to be administered is involved. Because no system, no matter how detailed, can take into account every fact-mix, it is impossible to prescribe precise penalties for all cases. Moreover, to attempt to do so would result in a many-paged document reminiscent of a prison camp. Often, the best way to develop sensible penalties is simply to allow them to evolve—all previous, similar cases should be taken into account, and a penalty should be administered appropriate to each case.

Employees are less likely to feel that a discipline system is being operated unfairly if the only differences from case to case are in the severity of the penalty, not in its occurrence. This is most frequently seen in discussions over what is called mitigation of the penalty.[17]

For example, an employee's tardiness, even though caused by an extremely difficult home situation, must still be disciplined. The employer may take the employee's special circumstance into account when determining the severity of the discipline.

The traditional, punishment-oriented systems allow little flexibility for individual treatment of employees. This may not be a fatal defect, however. The inherent danger, in allowing individual judgment or discretion to enter into the discipline system, is that any such allowances will be perceived by other employees as favoritism or unfairness. In a work environment where all subjective decisions are disputed, the employer often has to resort to complex and mechanical rules, which may produce more suffering and injustice in the long run, but which are still acceptable to the employees.

Summary

While perhaps the oldest and most widespread of contemporary discipline systems, corrective or progressive discipline continues to be often misunderstood and misapplied by employers, with the result that employee due process is often denied. The beauty of the system is to be found in the ease with which it can be understood and communicated and the almost automatic manner in which it can operate. Its failings are to be found in those areas which rely on the affirmative exercise of human judgment and participation. The frequency of its failures is due to the fact that many employers do not understand that the system is not entirely self-effecting and that supervisors must be trained in its operation. Unless supervisors are schooled in the objectives and procedures of disciplinary conferences, the elements involved in various types of rule violations, and in the differences between equal and same treatment, the progressive system can be just as oppressive and destructive of a productive work environment as having no system at all.

Notes to Chapter 2

1. Situations such as theft, assaulting a supervisor, intoxication on the job, etc., which call for summary discharges and are considered serious enough that the employer is grieved of any responsibility to attempt corrective discipline, have been excluded from this discussion.

2. *Babcock & Wilcox Co.* (Dworkin), 41 LA 862, at 866.

3. Presumably the company rules are reasonably related to the expectations of the employer. Irrelevant, confusing, or unnecessarily complicated rules are destructive to the credibility of the entire personnel program.

4. *Local 878 v. Coca-Cola Bottling Co.* (1980), 613 F.2d 716, 103 LRRM 2380, at 2383. *See also Rochester Methodist Hosp.* (Heneman), 72 LA 276.

5. *See Werner-Continental, Inc.* (LeWinter), 72 LA 1; *General Elec. Co.* (MacDonald), 72 LA 809; *Wilson Paper Co.* (Rose), 73 LA 1167; *A. P. Green Refractories* (Williams), 64 LA 885; *Canron, Inc.* (Marcus), 72 LA 1310; *City of Toledo* (Heinsz), 70 LA 216.

6. *See, e.g., Bethlehem Steel Co.* (Fishgold), 74 LA 507; *Witco Chem. Co.* (Light), 71 LA 919; *Alameda-Contra Costa Transit Dist.* (Koven), 76 LA 770; *Pickands Mather & Co.* (Witt), 76 LA 676; *Northrop Worldwide Aircraft Serv.* (Mewhinney), 75 LA 1059. *But, see, e.g., City of Detroit* (Coyle), 75 LA 1045; *Dravo Doyle Co.* (Jones), 73 LA 649.

7. *Montague Mach. Co.* (Bornstein), 78 LA 172.

8. *Watauga Indus., Inc.* (Galambos), 78 LA 697.

9. *Gill Studios, Inc.* (Goetz), 78 LA 915.

10. *Lucky Stores, Inc.* (Darrow), 78 LA 233.

11. *Plantation Patterns, Inc.* (Dallas), 78 LA 647.

12. *Id.,* at 649.

13. *Texas Int'l Airlines, Inc.* (Dunn), 78 LA 893.

14. *Gill Studios, supra,* note 9.

15. *Fort Wayne Community Schools* (Deitsch), 78 LA 928.

16. *See, e.g., Arkansas Glass Container Corp.* (Teple), 76 LA 841; *Carborundum Co.* (Millious), 71 LA 828; *Niles, Shepard Crane & Hoist Corp.* (Alutto), 71 LA 828; *Sun Furniture Co.* (Szollosi), 71 LA 929; *General Mills Fun Group* (Martin), 72 LA 1285; *Boise Cascade Corp.* (Richardson), 66 LA 1302.

17. *See, e.g., Varbros Tool & Die Co.* (Kabaker), 42 LA 440; *Johns-Manville Perlite Corp.* (Traynor), 67 LA 1255; *Menasha Corp.* (Roumell), 71 LA 653; *Safeway Stores, Inc.* (Winograd), 75 LA 430.

3

Affirmative Discipline: A New Approach

As noted in Chapter 2, the traditional or progressive approach to discipline is a system of ever-increasing penalties. An employee knows that what he or she is doing is contrary to acceptable levels of conduct, and the employee is given multiple opportunities to conform to the company's rules. Consequently, the progressive discipline system's hallmark is punishment, and in this, it closely parallels the discipline of children in the home. The progressive system is subject to the criticism that it is constructed on an illogical premise, *i.e.*, if an employer treats its employees progressively worse, they will get progressively better. When stated in this fashion, the inherent defect in the system is brought into sharp focus.

Reacting to what has been perceived as the less than total success of these punitive systems, some employers have instituted what is termed an "affirmative" or "constructive" approach. This approach capitalizes on a major difference between being a member of a workforce and being a member of a family, *i.e.*, membership in a workforce is voluntary and essentially contractual, while membership in a family is, at least for many years, involuntary and the relationship cannot be dissolved. Consequently, an employer has one advantage over the head of a household: The employer can legally expel an individual from the employment family. The corollary to this is that the employee has a legitimate fear that expulsion from the employment family can actually happen.

To pursue the analogy, a child's fear of expulsion from the family for wrongdoing is normally dissipated in the early years and does not reappear again until the late teens. In the critical, and sometimes seemingly interminable intervening years, parents are left with a punitive system as their final recourse. Why not, argue the proposers of the affirmative approach, build a system dependent upon the employees' recognition of their need to consciously accept and conform to company standards if they are to remain members of the employment family? That is, since employment is essentially a contract between employer and employee, why not place employees in a position of actually and knowingly accepting their responsibility to abide by various rules, and when they transgress, require them to reaffirm this commitment as consideration for continued employment.

To a great extent, this premise places in proper perspective the real objective of any discipline system—the development of productive employees. It discards as inappropriate the attitude of some employers that once an employee starts down the road to discipline, the best thing to do is to accelerate the employee's downward progress to the point where he or she can be legitimately discharged. This attitude looks at discipline soley as a form of punishment for an offense and not as an instrument for correcting a problem. On occasion, therefore, it is not uncommon for an employer to express almost a sense of regret that a disfavored employee has actually straightened out. Under the affirmative approach, both the employer and employee are required to periodically affirm their desire to maintain their relationship.

The constructive approach also seeks to preserve the psychological well-being of an employee, who theoretically will accept affirmative discipline positively and punitive discipline negatively. This argument may be more sophistry than substance, since both approaches can produce positive or negative employee feelings, depending upon the attitude and manner of the disciplinarian. Nevertheless, the reaffirmation of the employer/employee relationship after each transgression has occurred can be seen to have some attitudinal value. In fairness, however, this psychological effect also can be achieved in the traditional, progressive system.

Probably the most sensible argument for the "affirmative" approach has to do with the administration of the discipline system by supervisors. As a rule, supervisors dislike disciplining employees. It places them in direct conflict with a subordinate, with the risk that this conflict will somehow make it more difficult in the future for the supervisor to deal with the employee. The supervisor, fearing employee hostility or the breach of a relationship, puts off disciplining the employee for minor infractions and, then, overreacts when the employee goes too far. The result is a major confrontation, and the employee can reasonably argue that there has not been adequate notice that his or her behavior was errant. Most frequently, this can be seen in tardiness cases. For example, take the employee, whose habitual tardiness has been tolerated for a significant period of time. He is suddenly disciplined severely for a single occurrence, which the supervisor feels is "just going too far." The supervisor had let the minor occurrences slide, until they had become a major problem. Now the supervisor must face the employee and explain why three minutes late can be tolerated, but ten minutes late cannot, and must inform the employee that the next time he or she is late by one minute, disciplinary action will be taken. It is no wonder that the employee becomes confused and resentful. As noted in Chapter 2, it is precisely at the point where supervisors must become involved on a personal level in the administration of the disicpline system that the system frequently breaks down.

Affirmative disciplinarians reason that, if the discipline system could be made relatively painless for both supervisor and employee, the supervisor would be more apt to call minor infractions to the immediate attention of the employee. While pain can be blunted, the unfortunate fact is that under either discipline system the supervisor must still confront an employee with an infraction, and, regardless of what term is used to describe the confrontation, natural supervisory reaction is avoidance.

From another point of view, the affirmative approach does eliminate what may be the greatest inhibitor to a productive discipline system: the concept of payment through punishment. The progressive system, based as it is on increasing levels of punishment, has as its operating principles the ideas that an employee must "pay for the crime" and then receive "total absolution" from the employer. From this, it follows that employees can easily form the attitude that once they have paid the penalty imposed by the employer, they are then released from any further expectations from the employer on that particular issue. The punishment next time may be more severe, but the employee will feel that he or she has been absolved of any prior wrongdoing. This attitude is clearly counter productive. Moreover, the punishment may be viewed by the employee with resentment and hostility, if not a "red badge of courage." With this kind of thinking, the employee is less likely to really try to do any better than just be good enough to avoid further punishment.

The affirmative approach seeks to eliminate these employee reactions by eliminating punishment or, more correctly, the sense of punishment. This is accomplished, as indicated earlier, through a series of reaffirmations of commitment. The steps in the traditional approach are replaced by the following "events."

Initial Hire

At the time an individual is employed and oriented he or she is given a complete set of company policies, including rules of conduct. Time is spent with the employee making sure that everything is properly understood. The new employee then signs, not only a receipt for the documents, but a statement of assent and commitment to the rules of conduct. The employee is given a copy of the assent and commitment statement. A copy is retained in the employee's permanent personnel file, and another copy is given to the immediate supervisor for his or her file.

By going through this rather formal and solemn exercise, several objectives are achieved. First, the employee receives an impression that somehow this employment is different from others and that mutual commitments are taken more seriously. Second, the employee receives general notice of all rules and specific notice of many. Third, the employee receives specific notice of the employer's expectations beyond those mentioned in the individual rules. Finally, the entire exercise is documented in a fashion which makes the denial of such notice impossible at some later date.

Completion of Probation

Upon the employee's completion of probation, he or she meets with the immediate supervisor. The supervisor tells the employee that, based on the employee's work record to date, the company has made a decision that it would like to retain him or her as a permanent employee. The supervisor then asks the employee if he or she wishes to become a permanent employee, recognizing that permanent employment includes assent and commitment to the company's policies and rules. The employee is then shown another copy of these policies and rules; is told that a copy is available to him or her in the supervisor's office, in addition to the one the employee was already given; and the employee is asked to sign a second statement of assent and commitment. Again, the employee is given a copy of this document, a copy is sent to the personnel department for the employee's permanent file, and a copy is retained by the supervisor.

This second conference, not only reinforces all of the objectives of the employment conference, but also serves the additional purpose of breaking barriers and building bonds between the supervisor and employee. The special bonus is the effect this conference has on the supervisor. Theoretically, the supervisor will now be more comfortable with confronting the employee about any infractions of his or her commitment. After all, the commitment was made by the employer with the employee through the supervisor. The supervisor now has a personal interest in the employee's success, which allows the supervisor to become more involved with the employee. Finally, the second conference requires the employee to accept the seriousness with which the employer views their mutual commitment.

First Decisional Conference

If the employee violates any of the company's minor policies or rules, the supervisor meets with the employee and refreshes his or her recollection of the rule. (Minor policies or rules are distinguished from major ones in that the violation of a major policy or rule would normally subject an employee to immediate discharge.) At that time, the supervisor asks the employee whether he or she remembers the employment commitment, and the supervisor obtains a vebal assurance from the employee that he or she understands both the rule and the nature of his or her obligation and commitment. The details of this conference is then confirmed to the employee in writing. If the employee violates a major rule, the supervisor may go immediately to a final decisional conference, or in some cases, may summarily discharge the employee.

Decisional conferences go one step further than the verbal warning stage in the progressive system. While advising the employee his or her errant behavior cannot be continued, the conference produces an affirmative act by the employee, *i.e.*, a verbalization of his or her employment commitment and a willingness to live up to that commitment. While this difference appears small, or to be illusory upon first glance, it is of real significance.

Take, for instance, an employee who is excessively absent. Under the progressive system, the employee's supervisor would take the employee aside and warn him or her that any future absences will result in a written warning which will be put in the employee's personnel file. The employee nods his or her understanding of the warning and, so chastised, returns to his or her workstation. Under the affirmative system, the supervisor would tell the employee that as a permanent employee he or she is expected to comply with the company's rules and regulations and that a continued failure to do so would signify that the employee no longer wants to be employed by the company. The supervisor then asks the employee whether he or she understands how he or she has failed in meeting the commitment to the company and extracts from the employee a specific verbal commitment to rectify the situation.

The employee in the progressive system example will leave the conference with a sense of having been punished. The employee in the affirmative system example will leave the conference with a feeling of having failed to live up to a promise he or she had made and of having made a fresh commitment. The first employee believes that it will be necessary to toe the line to avoid more severe punishment. The second employee believes that he or she must now try harder to fulfill a personal promise. This promise is made even more tangible, when the employee receives a note from the immediate supervisor specifically detailing this commitment.

Second Decisional Conference

If an employee violates any of the company's minor policies or rules a second time within an established time period, the employee is again counseled by the supervisor, as in the first decisional conference. The difference is that the employee is now required to reaffirm his or her permanent employment assent and commitment by signing a special reaffirmation statement. This reaffirmation is written into the original documents. Copies are then distributed as before.

The second decisional conference attempts to achieve the same objective as the first, except in a more forceful manner. Not only is the employee required to verbalize a new commitment, but must actually sign a written statement of that commitment. Again, the employee is not left with the feeling of having been punished but of having failed to live up to a personal commitment. The employee is again affirming his or her responsibility.

Final Decisional Conference

If the employee violates a minor rule for the third time within a specified period or a major rule for the first time, the supervisor counsels the employee as before. This time, however, the supervisor asks the employee a very pointed question, "Do you want to continue your employment with this Company?" If the employee answers in the affirmative, the supervisor has him or her sign a statement which contains the following four elements:

1. Recognition of the rule violated and agreement that the employee violated it;
2. Statement of a desire to remain employed by the company;
3. Reaffirmation of assent and commitment;
4. Recognition that another similar violation will constitute a lack of desire to remain employed with the company and a voluntary termination.

A copy of this statement is given to the employee and another is sent to the personnel office.

It is again noteworthy that all elements of punishment are absent. Punishment is replaced by an affirmation of responsibility. The sometimes pompous escapism of the progressive disciplinarian's fiction about employee self-discipline ("I didn't fire him; he fired himself") is translated into an honest reality. Under the affirmative approach, employees specifically state that they want to keep their jobs, that they know that to do so they must keep their promises, and that if they do not they no longer wish to be employed. This is strong and sobering for any employee. At the very least, the employee is not able to rationalize the consequences of his or her actions as punishment for some rule infraction. Significantly, the employee has agreed to leave the job if he or she once again violates the same rule. The employer is responsible for nothing. The employee alone is responsible; the burden is on him or her. The employer does not subject the employee to industrial capital punishment. It simply accepts the employee's resignation.

In the event an employee violates the same rule again, the employee will be given a notice that, in accordance with the agreement, the employee has voluntarily terminated his or her employment by virtue of the violative act. The employee's employment record will be closed as a voluntary quit.

Some employers may wish to insert another stage in the affirmative approach which closely parallels the progressive system's disciplinary suspension without pay. Just as the affirmative approach gives a different perspective to the traditional verbal warning, written warning, final warning progression, it does the same with a disciplinary suspension. Either as a step between the second and the final decisional conference or as a part of the final step, the employee is sent home for one to three days with or without pay, depending on how affirmatively the company wishes to eliminate the punitive elements from the discipline system. The employee is told to consider, during this time off, whether he or she wishes to remain an employee. At the end of the suspension, the employee is required to sign the same type of final statement as detailed above. The suspension is intended to more forcefully drive home to the employee the seriousness of the commitment to conform and to give the employee time to contemplate.

To be sure, the affirmative approach has the appearance of simply transmitting the traditional system into more sophisticated language. However, the differences are substantial. The basis of the affirmative approach is to entice an employee into adherence to standards of conduct, rather than drive the employee into conformity through punishment. Rather than try to avoid transgressions, the employee is asked to live up to a standard, which is subtly made the condition of employment. The burden is thus always placed on the employee.

4

Discipline Systems for Nonunion Employees

Traditionally, one of the more complex problems faced by a company with employees not represented by a union has been to develop a credible discipline system. The system must be credible in the sense that employees must feel secure that discipline will occur only when justified and necessary and that it will be free from personal biases. Employee insecurity increases when there is no effective means of testing the justification and necessity of disciplinary action. In this regard, unions, attempting to organize employees, frequently find that their arguments based upon protection from unfair treatment and advocacy within the discipline system are the most difficult for employers to combat. Loud employer pronouncements of fairness cannot overcome a single instance of discipline which employees perceive as unjust, even though the discipline may, in fact, have been warranted.

The reason for the complexity of this problem lies in the nature of discipline. Discipline systems are the confluence of conflicting rights, and the manner in which the accomodation of these rights is attempted requires substantial concessions from traditional managers, if they are to avoid turbulence at the workplace. In the most simplistic sense, the manager of a company is theoretically concerned first and foremost with the operation of the enterprise in a profitable manner. In this context, labor is nothing more nor less than a tool of production, entitled only to those things necessary to enable it to function. What those necessary things may be are subject to great variance in interpretation. Serious problems develop when an employer, with a limited sense of what employees need, is confronted with a workforce which demands, subtly or not, its desire for rights the employer may not even be prepared to consider. (Several of the rights discussed in Chapter 1 are most certainly among those things which many employers would never concede as necessary for employees.) For these employers, a "living" wage and "reasonable" benefits totally fulfill employer obligations to employees. In return, the employees are expected to work hard in docile submissiveness. Protesters and complainers are viewed as troublemakers with bad attitudes and are eventually discharged. After all, so the reasoning goes, the company does belong to the employer, and its representatives should have the unrestricted right to run it as they see fit. If the employees do not like it, they can quit. Wages and benefits will be kept at those levels absolutely necessary to keep employees with the requisite skills.

Any suggested diminution of the employer's total authority and flexibility is met with great resentment and, often, skepticism.

Fragile Systems

While the consumate industrial capitalist is portrayed here only to make a point, it is remarkable how frequently such employers are encountered, even in today's world. They zealously guard their private domains and resist any change which requires them to consider anything which cannot be immediately quantified. However, either as a means of increasing employee satisfaction for the purpose of enhancing productivity or as a means of avoiding unionization, employers find it necessary to yield some of their absolute authority. It is in the area of discipline that they frequently make their concessions. In doing so, however, these employers resist any material infringement upon their discretion and insist that it is vital to the operation of the plant that they maintain ultimate control. Consequently, discipline systems in unorganized companies frequently do not satisfy all of the employees rights. The result is a system which is very fragile and which will only work as long as there is widespread acceptance of the actions of the employer. Any mistake or unpopular decision may totally fracture the credibility of the system and, with it, the security of the employees. As noted earlier, employee insecurity creates innumerable problems for the employer and, ultimately, produces union activity.

Nevertheless, many employers of unorganized workers appear willing to operate in this uncertain atmosphere. They take their chances on always being right, and they have faith that, even if a mistake is made, their goodwill among the employees will overcome temporary unpleasantness. As evidence of their recognition of the fragility of the employee relations, disciplinary discussions are timid or tentative, and the discipline which results is often too liberal. As a result, employees are not well-controlled and take advantage of the employer's hesitancy. The operation acquires a country club atmosphere, and supervisors are reduced to leadmen and referees.

In this respect, one company with about 250 employees had fought off ten union drives in thirteen years. There had been tie votes, one-

and two-vote margins, and lost elections, which had been subsequently overturned and won. The plant's management and supervisors had become so concerned about the effect of every decision on the employees and whether any degree of constraint or unpopularity would shift the delicate balance of votes that the operation of the plant became extremely difficult, and overall productivity was low. Finally, when the union returned for its nearly annual drive, the supervisors simply refused to campaign, believing that the union would actually make it easier to deal with the employees. The company lost the election. Part of the problem was the employer's discipline system, which depended upon the employer's discretion. The employees had been able to use the employer's fears that its actions would be perceived as unfair to obtain inappropriate liberties.

Certainly, increasing, or maintaining, high productivity levels and avoiding union organization are two principal reasons for any employer of unorganized employees to have a credible discipline system. These reasons are not the only reasons, however, and perhaps, are no longer the most important.

Employment At Will

A strong movement is now developing toward making it a requirement of law that employees can be discharged only for just cause after having been accorded due process. This movement may only be in its gestation stage, but the signs are that it will continue to grow and emerge kicking and screaming into the employment world. Consequently, this movement may be heralding the beginning of the end of "employment at will" as even a general proposition.

Actually, the concept of employment at will has been chipped away at for many years, and, having taken off the easy pieces, the sculptors are turning to the foundation itself. Under the banner of developing laws, the present attack is against what are being called "abusive" discharges. The intent is to have state legislatures and courts declare that no employee can be discharged except for just cause,[1] whatever that may turn out to be. Discharges would then be litigated before an arbitrator or in a court as a matter of law, not as the result of an agreement.[2]

Although first popularly espoused during the Industrial Revolution, the courts in most jurisdictions in the United States to this day have persistently held to the common law view that a written or verbal contract for employment for an indefinite period is terminable at the will of the employer for good, bad, or no cause whatsoever. Indeed, this principle was declared by the Supreme Court in *Adair v. United States* and has been actually codified in two states, Georgia and California.[3]

Over the last forty years, however, various federal and state laws have circumscribed and limited this general rule. The Labor Management Relations Act, or the Taft-Hartley Act, prohibits discharges or discipline for participating in concerted activities. Title VII of the Civil Rights Act of 1964 prohibits discipline or discharges based upon an employee's race, color, religion, sex, or national origin. The Rehabilitation Act of 1973 prohibits discipline or discharges due to non-job related handicaps and disabilities. The Age Discrimination Act of 1967, as amended, prohibits the disciplining or discharge of an employee between the ages of 40 and 70 because of his or her age. In addition, several statutes, *e.g.*, the Fair Labor Standards Act and the Occupational Safety and Health Act, prohibit the discharge or disciplining of an employee for exercising rights given by these laws.

Several states have added to these limitations as well by restricting the employer's right to discipline or discharge employees for conviction of certain crimes or for refusing to submit to polygraph tests. Nevertheless, neither the federal government nor any state has passed any legislation which destroys the basic principle of employment at will. Some state legislatures,[4] however, have just such legislation pending, and it is not beyond belief that someday one of these proposed laws will be enacted, opening a new era in employer/employee relations. In fact, the arguments are being made in a most eloquent and learned fashion, and they are not without substantial popular appeal.[5]

While up to this time legislatures appear reluctant to eliminate the basic principle of employment at will altogether, courts have been presented with an ever-increasing assault. The theories to date have been multiple but have had only limited success.[6] By far the most common attack has been formulated on the basis that a discharge has violated public policy because an employer has retaliated against employees for exercising rights given by various laws or for refusing to perform an illegal act. Often approached as an intentional tort, the causes of action have been referred to as "abusive discharges."[7]

Although dismissing the lawsuit because the allegations were "too general, too conclusory, too vague, and lacking in specifics," the Court of Appeals of Maryland nevertheless held in *Adler v. American Standard Corporation* that an employee does have a cause of action in the state of Maryland for "wrongful discharge."[8] The court held as follows:

> ... When terminated without notice, an employee is suddenly faced with an uncertain job future and the difficult prospect of meeting continuing economic obligations. But this circumstance, of itself, hardly warrants

adoption of a rule that would forbid termination of at will employees whenever the termination appeared "wrongful" to a court or a jury. On the other hand, an at will employee's interest in job security, particularly when continued employment is threatened not by genuine dissatisfaction with job performance but because the employee has refused to act in an unlawful manner or attempted to perform a statutorily prescribed duty, is deserving of recognition. Equally to be considered is that the employer has an important interest in being able to discharge an at will employee whenever it would be beneficial to his business. Finally, society as a whole has an interest in ensuring that its laws and important public policies are not contravened. Any modification of the at will rule must take into account all of these interests.[9]

On the other hand, the U.S. Court of Appeals for the Fifth Circuit, in *Phillips v. Goodyear Tire & Rubber Company*, recently refused to erode the basic concept of employment at will in a case in which the employee asserted that he had been discharged in retaliation for his having given truthful testimony in a federal court trial.[10] The Court of Appeals, in reversing the lower court, stated:

> Like the majority of the states, Georgia and Texas follow the rule that when an employee is hired for an indefinite period, the employment relationship may be terminated at will by either party. Under this "at will" rule, the employer may, without liability, discharge the employee for a good reason, a bad reason, or no reason at all.[11]

The court, however, went on to criticize the rule as unjust and outmoded.

Recently, the Court of Appeals of Kentucky in *Firestone Textile Company Division, Firestone Tire and Rubber Company v. Tom Meadows* sustained a $25,000 jury verdict in favor of a former employee who had sued alleging a wrongful discharge.[12] In that case, the employee had been discharged following the filing of a workers' compensation claim. The court stated:

> . . . we are led to the conclusion that by necessary implication the Workers' Compensation Act manifests a public policy that an employee has a right to be free to assert a lawful claim for benefits without suffering retaliation by his employer in the form of discharge. If it were otherwise, the beneficient purposes of the Act could often be effectively frustrated by merely threatening employees with discharge. . . .

One view of the case is that this necessarily implied policy, along with the other provisions of the Act, became a part of the employment contract between the parties so that, if the primary motivating factor in the appellant's discharge of the appellee were retaliation for asserting a compensation claim, then the contract of employment was breached. Other attacks have been based upon theories of implied contract[13] and bad faith.[14] These last two, however, are very limited, because they turn on whether a court can find an implied agreement that the employer would, in fact, deal with the employee fairly and in good faith.

The frequent focus in abusive discharge cases, which are based upon an implied contract theory, is that the employee handbook or manual constitutes an enforceable commitment of an employer to the employee. It is likely that few, if any, considered handbooks to be contracts when they were written and distributed to the employees, and almost none of them have even considered the question. Generally, these documents are prepared for the purpose of setting out in some palatable fashion the rights and benefits of employees and the expectations of the employer. In this respect, they not only regularize operations, but also serve as an effective means for establishing the good will of the employer and for giving assurances of good faith and fair dealings. In line with this, the manuals almost always declare that the employer is committed to the principle of just cause and progressive discipline.

The legal question now being raised in the context of abusive or unjust dismissal litigation is whether the manual contains contractual commitments, which constitute enforceable rights such that a former employee can claim a breach if he or she believes a dismissal was without just cause or was in some other fashion not according to the procedures contained in the manual. For the most part, actions by former employees grounded on this theory have been unsuccessful,[15] because the manuals fail to satisfy one or more of the essential criteria for the existence of a contract.

Since job applicants commonly do not see an employee manual until after the offer of employment has been accepted, the terms, conditions, and policies contained in the manual could not have formed the consideration upon which the employee's acceptance was based. Accordingly, when a former employee claims that the employer was contractually bound to accord him due process, freedom from dismissal for other than just cause, or anything else contained in the manual, the claim is subject to dismissal as a matter of law, because the employee could not have relied on these alleged rights when he or she accepted the employment. Further, manuals are normally not created following negotiations with the employees but are unilateral actions taken by an employer. In that respect, they can be modified or eliminated by the employer unilaterally as well. The element of mutuality is consequently lacking.

In spite of these and other arguments, however, some courts have enforced manual provisions concerning just cause and progressive discipline as contracts. In *Weiner v. McGraw-Hill, Inc.*[16] for instance, the former employee alleged that, prior to the time he was hired, the job security provisions in the manual, particularly those relating to just cause and remedial counseling, had been shown to him in an effort to induce him to leave his former employer and to join McGraw-Hill. In addition, the manual was specifically referred to on the employment application. Finally, he asserted that he had rejected various job offers while employed by McGraw-Hill, in part, due to the job security provisions in the manual. Based on these allegations, the court of appeals reversed a lower court's dismissal of the complaint and held that there had been sufficient consideration to create a contract. The lower court's dismissal had been based upon its finding that the employment was at will and that the manual was not an enforceable agreement. The appeals court ordered a trial on the issues of whether the employee had been discharged for just cause and whether the employer had violated its own system of remedial counseling.

It is relatively simple to avoid the kind of trap the employer in that case constructed for itself. First, people in charge of hiring must be trained to not commit the company to specific terms, conditions, and policies of employment to applicants. Second, the application form itself can be amended, usually in the area in which the applicant separately states his or her understanding that falsification of any information on the form will be a cause for discharge and which gives permission to contact references. This amendment would state simply that the applicant understands that, if employed, he or she will be an employee-at-will and that there exists no written contract of employment between him or her and the employer. Additions to this representation can also be made to the effect that the applicant, in accepting any offer of employment, does not do so in reliance upon any specific or implied representations related in any way to job security. Third, the manual itself should include some statement reserving to the employer the right to alter or change any element unilaterally and without prior notice. Fourth, the manual should state somewhere that it is not a contract of employment, but only a guide to be used in most cases.

Finally, the just cause principle and grievance procedure may be stated in some fashion which would make it arguably inapplicable to all cases and to all situations. By stating that "the employer believes that employees should not be discharged but for good and sufficient cause and that they should be given an opportunity to correct deficient behavior or work performance through a system of progressive discipline, but that in some situations it may be necessary and in the best interest of the company and other employees to summarily terminate an employee without recourse" would adequately provide the defense necessary in abusive discharge cases. To make such a statement, however, obviously detracts from the effect sought to be achieved by most employers in constructing a manual, and this risk must be carefully weighed against the value of the added protection it may give. If this approach is used, care must be exercised to avoid listing examples of summary offenses. To do so may result in a conclusion that only those offenses of a class consistent with the examples are to be considered as outside the progressive system.

By insuring that the employment documents and the hiring process are free from the kinds of things which produce contracts, employers can protect themselves successfully from litigation based on an implied contract theory. In this fashion, those cases which are based on that theory and which constitute the generally unsuccessful thrust now being made will continue to be unsuccessful in the courts.

The tort-based actions can also be thwarted, but not quite so simply. Since the tort of abusive discharge depends to a large extent upon a denial of due process which shocks the conscience of the court, employers who maintain an effective discipline system, which satisfies all or nearly all of the employee rights explained earlier, will be in a very strong position, once litigation has begun. Indeed, an effective due process discipline system will normally avoid litigation altogether, because employees will be less likely to believe that they have been treated unjustly. Due process discipline systems for unorganized employees will be discussed in detail later in this chapter.

Based upon the current state of the law, at least one advocate has spoken out for legislation as the only reasonable way to give employees a legally enforceable right to due process and just cause in discharge. He concedes that the current theories being used in the courts to achieve these rights are critically infirm and that the protections sought must come from legislatures.[17] While the courts may not be the best places to fashion the proposed protections, however, there is no doubt that the attempts will continue to be made; and, for every plaintiff employee, there must be a defendant employer. Consequently, regardless of the current vitality of the rule of employment at will, prudent employers who do not have union contracts, which require just cause and due process in discipline and discharge, must prepare for the possibility that they may have to litigate one of their actions and argue its fairness and appropriateness to a court of law.

There are, then, three strong reasons for unorganized companies to develop and to maintain discipline systems with credibility: to avoid union organization, to enhance productivity, and to avoid expensive court challenges by disgruntled employees.[18]

In designing a credible discipline system, employers of unorganized employees have seemingly had the most difficulty with two employee rights which have as their basis our society's concept of fairness and justice: the right to be represented and the right to have the decision reviewed by an impartial and disinterested person or body. Neither of these elements are normally found in discipline systems in unorganized companies; both of these elements are present in almost all organized company systems. These are, truly, the two employee rights which most employers find to be the greatest encrouchments on managerial prerogatives and authority.

Moreover, these two rights are the most obvious elements which distinguish unorganized from organized plant disciplinary systems. The reasons are easily explained. First, in unorganized companies there is no person comparable to a union steward to act as a spokesman for the employee, and there is no person or organization to bear the employee's cost of an arbitration. Consequently, unless the employer or some other body supplies these things, they simply do not exist. The result is that an employee is left alone to face all of the employer's representatives and must look to the plant manager, or some other equally suspect person, as his or her court of last resort.

These natural defects have long been recognized and many solutions suggested. On the one end of the spectrum is the suggestion that the employer hire an ombudsman, whose only responsibility is to represent employees in the grievance procedure. In addition, the employer would pay the entire cost of any arbitration an employee demands. While this solution certainly cures the infirmities, it is extremely costly and, at least as concerns the employment of a full-time ombudsman, justifiable only in very large companies where the volume of grievances would create enough work.[19]

At the other end of the spectrum is the employer who simply offers no other solution than a campaign of "trust me." As discussed earlier, this technique is successful only as long as the employer's good faith and decisions are preceived by the employees to be fair and just. The technique places a premium on supervisors and personnel employees, who obtain and present all of the facts in an objective fashion to the ultimate authority. In a perfect world with perfect people, this may be a possibiliy. But then, in such a world there would be no need, because there would exist no cause for discipline. At best, this technique creates a fragile system wholly dependent upon the correctness of decisions on a case-by-case basis.

A workable solution which may be considered is as follows:

An employee charged with the violation of a plant policy or rule would be presented with a written statement of facts, setting forth the precise nature of the alleged violation. This would be done as early as the verbal warning stage and continued through all later stages in the discipline progression. As a result, the employee would always be aware of the precise charge, and the issue would be clearly defined for him or her.

Upon receipt of this bill of particulars, the employee would then be allowed from one to five days, depending on the step in the grievance process, to make a response. Failure to make a response within the time stated in the notice attached to the recital of facts would constitute acceptance of the discipline.

To assist the employee in developing a defense either against the factual basis for the charge or the penalty, the employee would be permitted to select any uninvolved supervisor to assist him or her. Supervisors would be given special training in the preparation and handling of grievances on behalf of an employee. The representation must be taken very seriously by the supervisors, since they should realize that the system depends in great measure on the trust the employees have in the quality of their representation. In addition, it would provide an excellent chance for supervisory growth and consistency through analysis by supervisors of actions taken by others. To avoid the over-use of a few particularly eloquent supervisors, the director of personnel would have the authority to declare, upon documentation given to the employee, a condition of over-use and require the designation of another supervisor. Where the employee desires representation but does not wish to designate any particular supervisor, a supervisor would be provided on a rotating basis.

Supervisory representation would continue through the final step in the process, arbitration. If the employee desires to retain outside counsel, he or she would be permitted to do so for the arbitration only, and the total cost must be paid by the employee. Injection of outside counsel at any earlier stage should not be permitted. An arbitration service, such as the American Arbitration Association, should be used, because it requires the employee to pay a fee to demand arbitration. In addition, the employee should be required to pay one-half the cost of the arbitrator, up to a maximum of $300. This amount, or the one-day charge of the arbitrator, whichever is less, must be deposited by the employee with the arbitration service or the employer at the time the arbitration is demanded.

The costs to the employee would not be so substantial as to effectively prohibit the employee from demanding arbitration but would be high enough to discourage frivolous demands. Significantly, an employee should personally bear his or her own costs, and general collections or contributions from other employees should be prohibited. This latter rule is intended to discourage the development of informal employee organizations with sufficient resources to press unmeritorious grievances to arbitration.

The system just described would achieve the objectives of an unorganized company in constructing a discipline system with credibility. Employees would be accorded due process in that they would be provided with a clear statement of the facts and the alleged violation, an opportunity to present a defense or mitigating circumstances, representation by a trained advocate of their choice, and an opportunity to have the issue finally determined by an independent and disinterested party. The concession from authority and the cost for the employer are not unreasonable and are offset by coincidental benefits of credibility and supervisory involvement. Obviously, much of the success for this type of system would depend on the quality of the training given to supervisors, and an employer who is not committed to the success of this or any other system will quickly discover that it will not work.

An Alternative to Arbitration

As either an additional step prior to arbitration or as a substitute for arbitration, an employer may wish to establish the following procedure:

An employee who continues to disagree with either the fact of discipline or its degree would be allowed to appeal to a committee of employees and supervisors for consideration of his or her grievance. The composition of the committee should be dictated by the employee and the director of personnel, the employee selecting two other nonsupervisory employees and the director selecting two first-line supervisors. The personnel director, plant manager, or some other similarly high-ranking individual should serve as the moderator, who may or may not have a tie-breaking vote depending on whether the committee is intended to serve as a step prior to arbitration or as a final step replacing arbitration.

The committee would examine all of the relevant facts and conduct a hearing at which the involved supervisor and the employee are present to discuss and argue their respective positions. The employee would be represented at the committee hearing by his or her spokesman.

After considering all of the relevant facts, the committee would render its decision. If the committee is deadlocked, the moderator would cast the deciding vote or refrain from voting. If the moderator abstains, the supervisor's discipline would stand. The employee would then be permitted an appeal to arbitration, if the system allows for such appeals. If the moderator were to cast the deciding vote and the vote favors the disciplinary action taken, the employee would, or would not, be allowed an appeal to arbitration, if the system permits. If the moderator votes in favor of the employee's position and either overturns or modifies the disciplinary action, the employer would be bound and could not appeal.

This system, especially when used as a substitute for arbitration, has the advantage of economy. It also offers a measure of due process which is derived from the opportunity of an employee to be heard by a panel at least partially composed of his or her peers. Additionally, it provides for an expanded role for supervisors, which will promote consistency in the supervisory operation of the discipline system.

Regardless of the type of discipline system chosen, it is beyond question that the prudent employer must provide for its employees protection against arbitrary and abusive actions which affect their employment status and which go substantially beyond the more traditional "take-it or leave-it" and "trust me to be fair" system common in unorganized situations.

Notes to Chapter 4

1. *E.g.*, in Pennsylvania, H.B. 1742, Pa. Gen Assembly, 1981 Session, would impose a just cause requirement upon employers seeking to discharge employees, and aggrieved employees could resort to mediation and arbitration.

2. *See* Summers, "Individual Protection Against Unjust Dismissal: Time for a Statute," 62 VA. L. REV. 481 (1976); Stieber, "The Case for Protection of Unorganized Employees Against Unjust Discharge," *Proceedings of the 32nd Annual Meeting*, Industrial Relations Research Association (Madison, Wis.: IRRA, 1980), p. 155; Peck, "Unjust Discharges From Employment: A Necessary Change in the Law," 400 OHIO ST. L.J. 1 (1979); Howlett, "Due Process for Nonunionized Employees: A Practical Proposal," *Proceedings for the 32nd Annual Meeting*, Industrial Relations Research Association (Madison, Wis.: IRRA, 1980), p. 164; Blumrosen, "Strangers No More: All Workers Are Entitled to 'Just Cause' Protection Under Title VII," 2 INDUS. RELS. L.J. 519 (1978); Aaron, "Constitutional Protections Against Unjust Dismissals from Employment: Some Reflections," *New Techniques in Labor Dispute Resolution* (Washington, D.C.: The Bureau of National Affairs, Inc., 1976), p. 13; Blades, "Employment at Will vs. Individual Freedom: Of Limiting the Abusive Exercise of Employer Power," 67 COLUM. L. REV. 1404 (1967); St. Antoine, "Protection Against Unjust Discipline: An Idea Whose Time Has Long Since Come," *Arbitration Issues for the 1980s*, Proceedings of the Thirty-Fourth Annual Meeting of the National Academy of Arbitrators (Washington, D.C.: The Bureau of National Affairs, Inc., 1948–), p. 43.

3. *Adair v. United States*, 208 U.S. 161 (1908); Ga. Code Ann. §§ 66–101; Cal. Lab. Code § 2922 (West), respectively.

4. *See, e.g.*, Pennsylvania H.B. 1742, *supra*, note 1.

5. *See* Summers, *supra*, and other articles listed in note 2.

6. *See generally* Madison, "The Employee's Emerging Right to Sue for Arbitrary or Unfair Discharge," 6 EMPLOYEE RELATIONS L.J. 422 (1980–81).

7. *E.g.*, *O'Sullivan v. Mallon*, 160 N.J. Super. 416, 390 A.2d 149 (1978) (x-ray technician refused to perform operation restricted by labor agreement to licensed nurses or physicians); *Sventko v. Kroger Co.*, 69 Mich. App. 644, 245 N.W.2d 151 (1976) (filing workers' compensation claim); *Harless v. First National Bank in Fairmont*, 246 S.E.2d 270 (W. Va. 1978) (reporting violations of consumer protection laws); *Tameny v. Atlantic Richfield Co.*, 27

Cal.3d 167, 610 P.2d 1330 (1980) (refusing to participate in gasoline price fix scheme); *Nees v. Hocks*, 272 Or. 210, 536 P.2d 512 (1975) (accepting jury duty against employer's instructions).

8. *Adler v. American Standard Corporation*, 290 Md. 615, 432, A.2d Rep. 464 (1981).

9. *Id.*, at 470.

10. *Phillips v. Goodyear Tire & Rubber Company*, 651 F.2d 1051, _____ LRRM _____ (5th Cir., 1981).

11. *Id.*, at 1054.

12. *Firestone Textile Company Division, Firestone Tire and Rubber Company v. Tom Meadows*, _____ S.W.2d _____ (Nov. 12, 1982).

13. *E.g., Grouse v. Group Health Plan, Inc.*, 306 N.W.2d 114 (Minn. 1981) (employment contract implied on basis of employer's detrimental reliance on offer); *Delzell v. Pope*, 200 Tenn. 641, 294 S.W.2d 690 (1956) (one-year contract implied from past employment); *Toussaint v. Blue Cross & Blue Shield of Michigan*, 408 Mich. 579, 292 N.W.2d 880 (1980) (contractual rights implied on basis of employer's detailed personnel manual which included just cause provision); *but, compare Edwards v. Citibank N.A.*, 74 A.D.2d 553, 425 N.Y.S.2d 327 (1980) (court refuses to imply contract from personnel manual); *Weiner v. McGraw-Hill, Inc.*, 457 N.Y.S.2d 193, 443 N.E.2d 441 (1982) (court finds employees' manual to be a contract and orders trial on issues of "just cause").

14. *E.g., Fortune v. National Cash Register Co.*, 373 Mass. 96, 364 N.E.2d 1251 (1977) (written employment contract which was terminable at will held to contain an implied convenant of good faith).

15. *See* the cases cited in note 7.

16. *Weiner v. McGraw-Hill, Inc., supra,* note 13.

17. St. Antoine, *supra,* note 2.

18. The proposed legislation would give binding effect to systems which award due process and end in binding arbitration.

19. With few variations, this is the system used successfully by the Northrop Corporation. *See* Littrell, "Grievance Procedure and Arbitration in a Non-Union Environment: The Northrop Experience," *Arbitration Issues for the 1980s,* Proceedings of the Thirty-Fourth Annual Meeting of the National Academy of Arbitrators (Washington, D.C.: The Bureau of National Affairs, Inc., 1948–).

2

Discipline: Practices

5

Poor Attendance: Absenteeism/ Tardiness

Issue: Whether an employee may be discharged or otherwise disciplined for poor attendance, excessive absenteeism, and/or tardiness.

Principle: An employee may be discharged or otherwise disciplined for poor attendance where the action taken is pursuant to a reasonable rule of which the employee is actually or constructively aware and which has been consistently applied and enforced. The employee must have actual notice of the consequences of poor attendance or continued poor attendence. In addition, there must be an absence of mitigating circumstances which justify either the employee's absences or a reduction in the degree of discipline.

Considerations:

1. Whether the attendance rule is reasonable and consistent with the just cause provision of the labor agreement or general company policy;
2. Whether the rule has been communicated to the employees generally or, at least, in such fashion that the employee has actual or constructive notice of the standard of attendance required;
3. Whether the employee actually knew or had reason to know that the consequence of his or her actions, or continued actions, would be the discipline actually given;
4. Whether the discipline given the employee is consistent in occurrence and

55

degree with the discipline given to other employees in similar situations;

5. Whether the employee's seniority, work history, attitude, type of absences (intermittent or extended), and/or likelihood of improvement would justify a mitigation of the discipline.

Discussion: As a general rule, discipline up to and including discharge for poor attendance will more likely be sustained if effected according to a progressive discipline system following a well-communicated, reasonable attendance rule. When such a system has functioned to counsel and warn the employee of the consequences of poor attendance and has provided the employee with the opportunity to change his or her behavior, arbitrators will find that the discipline was warranted.[1]

When the progressive discipline system has been followed, the arbitrator is more likely to favor the action taken by the employer, and the arbitrator's ability and willingness to impose his or her own punishment will be limited.[2] When the employer has not used progressive discipline or has not applied the system consistently, the arbitrator is more likely to create an *ad hoc* system and reinstate an employee if he or she feels that discharge was too severe in light of the previous discipline or the employee's general work record.[3] In *Niagara Machine and Tool Works,* for instance, the arbitrator reinstated an employee who had been terminated for failure to maintain acceptable attendance levels.[4] The arbitrator felt that the employee's seventeen years of seniority outweighed his excessive absenteeism and that he might have been helped by progressive discipline.

It is clear from a review of arbitrators' opinions that discipline is more readily sustained when it is pursuant to an employer's formal attendance and absenteeism/tardiness policy. Arbitrators have found, however, that even though there may not be formal policy or rule, an employer can discipline an employee for violating some generally accepted attendance standard.[5] That is, an employer has a right to expect regular attendance from its employees: "Regularity of attendance is a basic employee responsibility and an inherent employee obligation."[6] In cases where formal rules exist, however, an employee must be made aware by the employer that his or her absenteeism will result in discipline up to, and including, discharge. Arbitrators have reinstated or reduced discipline when the employer has failed to communicate to the employee the consequences of his or her continued absenteeism.[7]

Commonly, arbitrators employ a fairly systematic process in the review of discipline for poor attendance. At the outset, an arbitrator will make a determination concerning the validity of the employer's attendance rule or absenteeism policy. The review of the rule is for reasonableness and for consistency with the labor agreement. The arbitrator will then determine if the employee was made aware of the rule and whether or not the rule was consistently enforced. Failure to meet these requirements may be sufficient rationale for the lessening or voiding of the discipline imposed on an employee.

Unless restricted or curtailed by the language of the labor agreement, the creation and enforcement of an attendance policy is generally held to be part of the employer's right to manage its enterprise.[8]

An employer's absenteeism policy is considered reasonable if it has been adopted to correct and not to punish absenteeism and tardiness.[9]

Employees must receive notice of the attendance policy and any changes which may be made to it. In *Marley Cooling Tower Co.,* the arbitrator found that any changes the company made in the type of absence that did or did not count in its no-fault absentee program, (*e.g.,* snow days, jury duty, funeral leave) should have been made known to the employees prior to the change and prior to the enforcement.[10] Arbitrators will not enforce a rule or practice of which employees are not informed or are informed of only as a consequence of their behavior.[11]

Similarly, arbitrators will not sustain discipline if the employer fails to uniformly enforce the rule.[12] In *General Mills,* the arbitrator reduced the discipline given to the employee, because the company failed to apply the procedures of its established system of corrective discipline.[13] The arbitrator found that the company had a good discipline system that it should have used; the company had both the means and the method to penalize the employee; and the company failed to do so properly. In *Georgia Pacific Corp.,* considerable confusion existed within the company about the accuracy of the attendance records, so the absentee program was ineffectively maintained and inconsistently applied.[14] There was enough confusion present that the grievant's discharge could not be sustained. In another case reflecting the problems with record keeping and enforcement, *Dunlop Tire and Rubber Corp.,* the arbitrator found that the company could not count absences in its absenteeism program when an employee submitted a doctor's note or excuse, if the company had previously taken an inconsistent position as to whether such a note excused an absence.[15]

If the rule survives the initial level of scrutiny—that is, whether the employer uniformly enforces its attendance rule—then the arbitrator will proceed to examine how the rule was applied to the specific grievant. If the employee was aware of the rule and the discipline was a result of a consistent application and enforcement of the policy, the discipline will almost certainly be sustained.[16]

If the employee was not aware of the rule or the employer did not make the existence of the rule adequately known to the employees, the discipline will be reduced.[17]

In *Werner-Continental, Inc.*, the employer had no policy requiring discharge for absenteeism.[18] The grievant was, without question, excessively absent. However, his absences primarily were due to union business and other responsibilities pursuant to the labor agreement. In addition, the company, until its decision to discharge him, had accepted his excuses without negative comment and had not discharged any other employee for absenteeism. The grievant was reinstated.

Similarly, in *General Electric Co.*, the grievant was placed in a special program due to his excessive absenteeism.[19] The grievant was not informed of his responsibilities to the program, which included his receipt of counseling services and his adherence to certain attendance standards. His discharge for a subsequent absence was not sustained, because the arbitrator found that the grievant had no reason to believe that special rules now applied to his behavior.

✓ In *Wilson Paper Co.*, the arbitrator found that the employee was not aware of any discipline policies regarding attendance and that his attendance was no worse than that of other employees.[20] Accordingly, the discharge was not sustained.

Most arbitrators also impose a requirement that the employer must have notified the employee of the consequences of his or her continued absenteeism. If this notice requirement is satisfied, the discipline, including discharge, normally will be upheld.[21] In *Witco Chemical Co.*, the employee was repeatedly warned and suspended for his absenteeism and, prior to his discharge, the employer sent a letter advising the employee that the next absence would result in discharge.[22] His discharge was sustained. In *Alameda-Contra Costa Transit Dist.*, the arbitrator stated, "The necessity of putting an employee on prior notice as to the probable consequences of his misconduct is one of the hallmarks of industrial discipline; in the absence of any such notice, the grievant's discharge cannot be sustained based on his absence record alone."[23] Applying similar logic, the discharges in *Pickands Mather & Co.* and *Northrop Worldwide Aircraft Services* were not sustained.[24]

Some arbitrators, however, do not require that the employer must have given the employee specific notice of the probable consequences of his or her behavior; rather, they assign to the employee the responsibility of acting in a reasonable and responsible manner. In *City of Detroit*, the employee was required to notify specific persons of an intended absence; the employee failed to do so and was suspended.[25] In *Dravo Doyle Co.*, the employee was not warned that his next absence would result in discharge; however, the arbitrator sustained the discharge, concluding that "any reasonable person could not help but be aware that he was approaching a peril point."[26]

✓ If there is evidence that the attendance rule was not applied consistently or was applied inconsistently toward the grievant, the discipline will be reduced.[27]

✓ In *Carborundum Co.*, the arbitrator found that although the employer's attendance rule on its face was reasonable, its application was unclear and inconsistent.[28] There was evidence of instances when some employees could avoid punishment and others could not. The grievant was reinstated, and the discharge reduced to a suspension.

In *Sun Furniture Co.*, when management punished the employee, it went from the initial action in the progressive discipline system directly to the last step.[29] The arbitrator found this discipline too harsh and reinstated the employee.

The last part of the arbitrator's analysis is an overall review of the facts and the equities of the grievance. A determination is made whether mitigating circumstances exist that may justify either the employee's behavior or a reduction of the discipline.[30] The review of mitigating factors includes an examination of the employee's work history, length of service, absence record (*e.g.*, whether absences were chronic or intermittent), the reason for the absence, and the likelihood of improved attendance.[31]

In *Menasha Corp.*, the arbitrator, finding that the grievant's 27 years of service warranted more than a mechanical application of the employer's policy regarding minor offenses, reinstated the employee.[32] Similar determinations were made in *St. Regis Paper Co.* and *Niagara Machine and Tool Works*.[33] In both cases, the employees' long service records served to mitigate discharges to lesser penalties.

In *Northrop Worldwide Aircraft Services*, two employees were suspended for calling in sick and then playing on the employer's basketball team the same evening.[34] The suspensions were not sustained: The arbitrator, in addition to finding that the employees were not warned of the consequences of playing, found that there was no previous record of this type of absenteeism or misrepresentation by either employee. Arbitrators do not sympathize, however, when the employee's behavior forms a pattern or is part of a continuing theme. The employee in *ITT General Controls*, for instance, was discharged for not notifying the employer during a three-day absence; he had been previously discharged for the same offense.[35]

In deciding whether a penalty should be mitigated, arbitrators may also examine the reason for the grievant's absence and the likelihood of improved attendance. In *Automotive Distributors, Inc.*, the employee was chronically absent due to a sinus condition.[36] However, he had not sought treatment for the condition in the year and a half he had been troubled by it. The arbitrator balanced the employee's health problems against the employer's need to have employees available on some reasonable, regular basis; the arbitrator found the employer's need more important. Of particular importance appeared to be the improbability of improved behavior by an employee who had made no attempt to have the condition corrected.

Moreover, in *Safeway Stores, Inc.*, when an employee's absences were attributable to industrial accidents on several occasions and a motorcycle accident on another, the arbitrator found that the absences were not sufficient justification for a discharge, because they were of such a nature, *i.e.*, extended absences, that the company could plan and cover for the employee's absence.[37]

In *Menasha Corp.*, the employee had been absent due to an illness that doctors suspected was cancer.[38] In refusing to sustain the discharge, the arbitrator reasoned that the employee now knew that he did not have cancer and, therefore, the likelihood that the employee's attendance would improve was good. Consequently, he deserved another opportunity. Similar reasoning was employed in *Warner and Swasey*. The employee's absences were due to alcoholism; the employee was rehabilitated and was held by the arbitrator to be deserving of a second chance.[39] But, the employee in *Champion International* did not fair so well.[40] She admitted that her excessive absenteeism was due to her dislike of her job. The arbitrator refused to reinstate her, because her attendance was not likely to improve at the same job.

Often arbitrators appear to make a determination purely on the basis of some notion of fairness which is neither defined nor capable of definition. In *Morton-Norwich Products, Inc.*, for instance, an employee requested two extra days of funeral leave when his father died.[41] The employer denied the request and suspended the employee when he did not show up for work on those days. The arbitrator found that the employer acted unreasonably. In *Ogden Food Service Corp.*, an employee with a poor performance record was discharged when he left work to attend a family friend who had suffered a heart attack.[42] The arbitrator reinstated the employee, finding the employer's reaction was not fair. The arbitrator found probative that the employee had followed all the notification procedures and that the person was, in fact, a close family friend.

No general rule based upon these examples of arbitral fairness can be stated, however, because arbitrators do not always exhibit the same degree of sympathy. In *FMC Corp.*, the employee did not show up for work because he was too upset by a friend's being found murdered, shot through the head.[43] The arbitrator found that the termination was appropriate: The employee had a generally poor attendance record and, if he had taken his job seriously, he would have called his employer. Similarly, in *Boeing Services International*, an employee was terminated because he had been in jail for 10 days, during which time he failed to notify his employer.[44]

Generally, arbitrators appear to agree that mitigating circumstances, if they are to be considered, must be part of the facts prior to the discharge. In *Western Gear Corp.*, and *Johns-Manville Products Corp.*, the employees involved had problems with alcohol.[45] In *Western Gear*, a drinking problem was discovered to be the cause of the employee's absenteeism only after he had been discharged.[46] The arbitrator found the discharge to be in accordance with the company's progressive discipline system, and the discovery that the employee's absenteeism was due to a drinking problem did not present a sufficiently mitigating circumstance to require reinstatement. In *Johns-Manville*, the employee's successful rehabilitation after he had been discharged was not sufficient grounds to earn him a second chance.[47]

Key Points

1   *The attendance rule must be reasonable.*

Examples:

✓Employee *A* was discharged following an unexcused absence. The policy which he violated provided for discharge if an employee had one unexcused absence at any time within twelve months following a disciplinary suspension for poor attendance. Previously, after six unexcused absences in one month, the employee was warned verbally; after three unexcused absences within the next two months, he was given a written warning; and, after one unexcused absence in the month following his written warning, he was given a three-day disciplinary suspension. When the employee returned to work after the suspension, his supervisor told the employee in a letter that he would be discharged if he was absent one more time in the next twelve months. The employee's next absence occurred ten months later, and he was discharged pursuant to the notice in the supervisor's letter. The employee's defense included the fact that he had called the employer prior to his work shift and said that he would not be in due to a family emergency. The arbitrator, noting that the employee had evidenced true concern for his job by calling in and had substantially improved his record, reinstated the employee with full backpay. The arbitrator felt that the rule was unreasonable as applied to this employee, because it punished an employee who was making a good-faith effort to be a responsible employee and who was succeeding.

Employee *B* was discharged for poor attendance. The policy under which he was disciplined requires discharge if an employee demonstrates a continued pattern of excessive absenteeism at any time within twelve months following a disciplinary suspension for poor attendance. After a three-day suspension, the employee had a perfect attendance record for three months. In the fourth month, he had one unexcused absence. In the fifth month, he had another unexcused absence and is warned about redeveloping a violative pattern. In the sixth month, the employee had two unexcused absences and in the eighth, three more. His discharge followed. The arbitrator sustained the discharge, finding that the employee demonstrated a blatant lack of concern for his job.

✓ Employee C had four unexcused absences and two occurrences of lateness in the month of January. He was given a verbal warning. The following month he had three unexcused absences and one lateness. He was given a written warning. He had three unexcused absences and two latenesses the following month. He was given a three-day suspension with a note stating that if he was either late or absent again in the next twelve months he would be discharged. Three months later, after no intervening absences or latenesses, C called his supervisor prior to the work shift and said he would not be in due to car trouble. C was discharged. At the hearing, the employer established that car trouble had never been accepted by the company as a valid excuse. The arbitrator reinstated the employee on the basis that the twelve-month period was too long, thereby, rendering the rule unreasonable; the employee had demonstrated concern for his job and had made an effort to be dependable.

Guidelines

The attendance policy of the employer must not be too restrictive in either the length of time an employee has to demonstrate good attendance or in its definition of good attendance. The policy must be flexible enough to allow for exigencies resulting in isolated occurrences. The policy must only discipline behavior which truly demonstrates a wanton disregard for employee responsibility.

Relevant Cases

Werner-Continental, Inc. (LeWinter), 72 LA 1;
Wilson Paper Co. (Rose), 73 LA 1167;
Ideal Electric Co. (Martin), 77 LA 123;

Park Poultry, Inc. (Hyman), 71 LA 1;
Le Blond Machine Tool, Inc. (Keenan), 76 LA 827;
In re Bon Secours Hospital, Inc. (Feldsman), 76 LA 705;
Dravo Doyle Co. (Jones), 73 LA 649;
Carborundum Co. (Millious), 71 LA 802.

2 *There must be actual or constructive employee knowledge of the
acceptable standard of conduct.*

Examples:

Employee *A* was discharged for excessive absenteeism after an
absence supported by a doctor's note for illness. The employee
asserted at the arbitration that he believed a doctor's note made
the absence excused and not subject to the discipline policy.
The employer could not demonstrate that doctors' excuses had
been considered unacceptable in the past under the attendance
policy and the policy statement itself was unclear. The arbitrator, noting a lack of notice to the employee regarding acceptable conduct, reinstated the employee with backpay.

Employee *B* was discharged for excessive absenteeism after
her return to work following a disciplinary suspension. She
asserted at the arbitration that she was unaware that she could
not be excessively absent, *i.e.*, more than once a month, for a
full six-month period following a disciplinary suspension for
the same cause. Relying on the clear policy set forth in the
rules distributed to all employees at the time of hire, the arbitrator sustained the discharge.

Employee *C* had a bad attendance record. In accordance with
the terms of the employer's progressive discipline system, he
was discharged after an absence caused by an illness which
was supported by a doctor's note. The employer refused to accept the note as an excuse but did not dispute its legitimacy.
The employer told *C* that the note was satisfactory to allow for
the payment of sick leave benefits but not to excuse the absence
for purposes of the absenteeism control policy. *C* disputed this
reasoning and asserted that an excuse is an excuse for all purposes. The arbitrator sustained the discharge after the employer had demonstrated that one of the absences upon which
previous discipline was based had been of the same kind and
was also supported by a doctor's note. Since *C* had not complained then that the discipline was unfair, he could not com-
plain at the time of his discharge, nor could he state that he
had no knowledge of the employer's policy.

Guidelines

The policy which the employer asserts has been violated must have been actually communicated to the employee in some precise form, so the employee can be found to have had constructive notice of it. The policy communicated must be clear and the knowledge transmitted to the employee must be found to be incapable of confusion.

Relevant Cases

Marley Cooling Tower Co. (Sergent), 71 LA 306;
General Electric Co. (MacDonald), 72 LA 809;
Wilson Paper Co. (Rose), 73 LA 1167;
Northrop Worldwide Aircraft Services (Mewhinney), 75 LA 1059;
Bethlehem Steel Corp. (Fishgold), 74 LA 507;
Lucky Stores, Inc. (Darrow), 78 LA 233;
Ludington News Co. (Platt), 78 LA 233;
Burns International Security Services, Inc. (Kelliher), 78 LA 1163.

3   *The employee must be found to have known of the probable consequences of his or her act prior to its commission.*

Examples:

Employee *A* was discharged for excessive absenteeism after a continued pattern of absences following a disciplinary suspension. The notice of suspension did not contain a statement that the continuation of the violative conduct would result in discharge, although the employer's written policy clearly provided for this penalty. The employee presented evidence that the employer did not always discharge other employees in similar circumstances. The arbitrator, noting the confusion created by the employer's failure to follow its own policy, reinstated the employee without backpay, based upon the employee's otherwise good work record.

Employee *B* was discharged for excessive tardiness. The published policy of the employer is that a continued pattern of excessive tardiness after a disciplinary suspension for the same cause may result in discharge. This policy was quoted in the employee's final warning. There was no evidence of any other employee having gone this far in the discipline system. The arbitrator reinstated the employee without backpay based upon his otherwise good work record. The possibility and the uncertainty of discharge as stated in the policy allowed the arbitrator to substitute his judgment for that of the employer. Had the final warning stated to the employee that he would be discharged, the arbitrator may not have felt so much latitude.

Guidelines

The notice to the employee of the consequences of his or her continued violative behavior must be unequivocal and precise. There can be no possible room for any other result. In the absence of this clarity, arbitrators will feel free to examine other elements of the employee's work history to see if the penalty should be mitigated.

Relevant Cases

General Electric Co. (MacDonald), 72 LA 809;
Wilson Paper Co. (Rose), 73 LA 1167;
Northrop Worldwide Aircraft Services (Mewhinney), 75 LA 1059;
Bethlehem Steel Corp. (Fishgold), 74 LA 507;
Witco Chemical Co. (Light), 71 LA 919;
Alameda-Contra Costa Transit District (Koven), 76 LA 770;
Pickands Mather & Co. (Witt), 76 LA 676;
City of Detroit (Coyle), 75 LA 1045;
Dravo Doyle Co. (Jones), 73 LA 649;
Werner-Continental, Inc. (LeWinter), 72 LA 1;
Lucky Stores, Inc. (Darrow), 78 LA 233;
Burns International Security Services, Inc. (Kelliher), 78 LA 1163;
Ludington News Co. (Platt), 78 LA 1165.

4   *The discipline must be consistent with that given to other employees in similar circumstances.*

Examples:

Employee *A* was discharged for excessive tardiness following one reoccurrence after a disciplinary suspension. At the arbitration, *A* presented evidence of another employee who, after being tardy three weeks after his suspension, was only warned by a supervisor for that behavior and told that a reoccurrence would result in discharge. The arbitrator reinstated *A* without backpay and gave him a final warning.

Employee *B* was suspended for excessive absenteeism. At the arbitration *B* presented evidence of another employee who was only given another written warning after a similar violative act. The employer countered by showing that in all similar cases, except the one cited by *B*, employees were given suspensions and there were mitigating circumstances to explain the difference raised by *B*. The aribtrator sustained the suspension.

Guidelines

Although variations in the treatment of employees will not necessarily result in the nullification of an entire system, they must be truly exceptions to a well-established and -used policy and supported by sound reasoning.

Relevant Cases

General Mills Fun Group (Martin), 72 LA 1285;
Sun Furniture Co. (Szollosi), 71 LA 928;
Carborundum Co. (Millious), 71 LA 802;
Georgia Pacific Corp. (Imudo), 71 LA 195;
Dunlop Tire & Rubber Corp. (Williams), 76 LA 1228;
Monsanto Co. (Thomson), 76 LA 509;
ITT General Controls (Bickner), 76 LA 1258;
Irwin-Willert Home Products Co., Inc. (Maniscalco), 77 LA 146;
Arkansas Glass Container Corp. (Teple), 76 LA 841;
Shepard Niles Crane & Hoist Corp. (Alutto), 71 LA 828;
Burns International Security Services, Inc. (Kelliher), 78 LA 1163;
Ludington News Co. (Platt), 78 LA 1165.

5   *The employee's work history must not create an aura of injustice.*

Examples:

Employee *A* was discharged for excessive absenteeism. Her final warning had stated that continued excessive absenteeism would result in further discipline, up to, and including, discharge. The arbitrator found that neither the history of the employer's absenteeism policy nor the final warning required the employer to discharge the employee. However, because the employee had a history of barely acceptable attendance and demonstrated no significant improvement as a result of progressive discipline, the discharge was sustained.

Employee *B* was discharged for excessive absenteeism; his final warning had indicated that a continued pattern of excessive absenteeism could result in his discharge. The arbitrator examined the employee's work history, because the employer's policy did not mandate discharge. Noting that attendance appeared to be the employee's only problem and that a prior despicable attendance record had been substantially improved as a result of progressive discipline, the arbitrator reinstated the employee without backpay.

✓ Employee *C* had a record of 25 percent absenteeism in six months and 10 tardinesses. *C* was given a written warning. In the next month, his absenteeism dropped to 15 percent, with only one tardiness of five minutes. Still excessive, *C* was given a disciplinary suspension. In the following month, *C* had one occurrence of absenteeism for four days due to a legitimate illness. He had no other one-day absences nor tardinesses. *C* was discharged. The arbitrator reinstated the employee with backpay. Regardless of the fact that the employee technically violated the rule, the record demonstrated the success of the progressive discipline system and a conscientious effort on the part of the employee to be dependable.

Guidelines

Unless precluded from examining the judgment of the employer, arbitrators will look to an employee's work history to determine whether the employee had demonstrated sufficient disregard for his or her obligations over a significant period of time to be considered incorrigible.

Relevant Cases

Irwin-Willert Home Products Co., Inc. (Maniscalco), 77 LA 146;
Safeway Stores, Inc. (Winograd), 75 LA 430;
Menasha Corp. (Roumell), 71 LA 653;
St. Regis Paper Co. (Andersen), 75 LA 737;
Niagara Machine & Tool Works (Grant), 76 LA 160;
Northrop Worldwide Aircraft Services (Mewhinney), 75 LA 1059;
ITT General Controls (Bickner), 76 LA 1258;
Warner and Swasey (Siegel), 71 LA 158;
Morton-Norwich Products, Inc. (Nitka), 74 LA 202;
Ogden Food Service Corp. (Kelman), 75 LA 805;
FMC Corp. (Doering), 74 LA 1185;
Burns International Security Services, Inc. (Kelliher), 78 LA 1163;
Ludington News Co. (Platt), 78 LA 1165;
East Ohio Gas Co. (Michelstetter), 78 LA 71.

Notes to Chapter 5

1. *Sharon Steel Corp.* (Klein), 71 LA 737; *Witco Chem. Corp.* (Light), 71 LA 919; *Armstrong Rubber Co.* (Williams), 74 LA 362.

2. *Hawaii Transfer Co.* (Tsukiyama), 74 LA 531; *Bethlehem Steel Co.* (Fishgold), 74 LA 507; *Champion Int'l* (White), 74 LA 623.

3. *Werner-Continental, Inc.* (LeWinter), 72 LA 1; *Pickands Mather & Co.* (Witt), 76 LA 676.

4. *Niagara Machine & Tool Works* (Grant), 76 LA 160.

5. *Werner-Continental, Inc., supra,* note 3; *Wilson Paper Co.* (Rose), 73 LA 1167.

6. *Ideal Elec. Co.* (Martin), 77 LA 123.

7. *Werner-Continental, Inc., supra,* note 3.

8. *Werner-Continental, Inc., supra,* note 3; *Scott Air Force Base* (Fitzsimmons), 76 LA 46; *Lime Register Co.* (Heinsz), 76 LA 935.

9. *Park Poultry, Inc.* (Hyman), 71 LA 1; *Le Blond Machine Tool, Inc.* (Keenan), 76 LA 827; *In re Bon Secours Hosp., Inc.* (Feldsman), 76 LA 705; *Dravo Doyle Co.* (Jones), 73 LA 649.

10. *Marley Cooling Tower Co.* (Sergent), 71 LA 306.

11. *General Elec. Co.* (MacDonald), 72 LA 809; *Wilson Paper Co.* (Rose), 73 LA 1167; *Northrop Worldwide Aircraft Services* (Mewhinney), 75 LA 1059.

12. *General Mills Fun Group* (Martin), 72 LA 1285; *Sun Furniture Co.* (Szollosi), 71 LA 928; *Carborundum Co.* (Millious), 71 LA 802; *Georgia Pacific Corp.* (Imudo), 71 LA 195; *Dunlop Tire & Rubber Corp.* (Williams), 76 LA 1228.

13. *General Mills, supra,* note 12.

14. *Georgia Pacific Corp., supra,* note 12.

15. *Dunlop Tire & Rubber Corp., supra,* note 12.

16. *Monsanto Co.* (Thomson), 76 LA 509; *ITT General Controls* (Bickner), 76 LA 1258; *Irwin-Willert Home Products Co., Inc.* (Maniscalco), 77 LA 146.

17. *Werner-Continental, Inc., supra,* note 3; *General Elec. Co., supra,* note 11; *Wilson Paper Co., supra,* note 11.

18. *Werner-Continental, Inc., supra,* note 3.

19. *General Elec. Co., supra,* note 11.

20. *Wilson Paper Co., supra,* note 17.

21. *Bethlehem Steel Corp., supra,* note 2.

22. *Witco Chemical Co., supra,* note 1.

23. *Alameda-Contra Costa Transit District* (Koven), 76 LA 770.

24. *Pickands Mather & Co., supra,* note 3; *Northrop Worldwide Aircraft Services, supra,* note 11.

25. *City of Detroit* (Coyle), 75 LA 1045.

26. *Dravo Doyle Co., supra,* note 9.

27. *Arkansas Glass Container Corp.* (Teple), 76 LA 841; *Carborundum Co., supra,* note 12; *Shepard Niles Crane & Hoist Corp.* (Alutto), 71 LA 828;

Sun Furniture Co., *supra*, note 12; *General Mills Fun Group*, *supra*, note 12.

28. *Carborundum Co.*, *supra*, note 12.
29. *Sun Furniture Co.*, *supra*, note 12.
30. *Irwin-Willert Home Products Co., Inc.*, *supra*, note 16.
31. *See Safeway Stores, Inc.* (Winograd), 75 LA 430; *Menasha Corp.* (Roumell), 71 LA 653.
32. *Menasha Corp.*, *supra*, note 31.
33. *St. Regis Paper Co.* (Andersen), 75 LA 737; *Niagara Machine & Tool Works*, *supra*, note 4.
34. *Northrop Worldwide Aircraft Services*, *supra*, note 11.
35. *ITT General Controls*, *supra*, note 16.
36. *Automotive Distributors, Inc.* (Eisler), 76 LA 552.
37. *Safeway Stores, Inc.*, *supra*, note 31.
38. *Menasha Corp.*, *supra*, note 31.
39. *Warner & Swasey* (Siegel), 71 LA 158.
40. *Champion International*, *supra*, note 2.
41. *Morton-Norwich Products, Inc.* (Nitka), 74 LA 202.
42. *Ogden Food Service Corp.* (Kelman), 75 LA 805.
43. *FMC Corp.* (Doering), 74 LA 1185.
44. *Boeing Services International* (Kramer), 75 LA 967.
45. *Western Gear Corp.* (Sabo), 74 LA 641; *Johns-Manville Prod. Corp.*, (Kates), 76 LA 845.
46. *Western Gear Corp.*, *supra*, note 45.
47. *Johns-Manville Prod.*, *supra*, note 46.

6

Abusive, Profane, or Obscene Language

Issue: Whether an employee may be discharged or otherwise disciplined for abusive, profane, or obscene language.

Principle: An employee may be discharged, or otherwise disciplined, for use of abusive, profane, or obscene language where the conduct demonstrates gross disrespect or insubordination to a supervisor, is not provoked, and causes disruption in operations or among other employees. An employee may be discharged, or otherwise disciplined, for similar conduct directed at coemployees where the conduct is unprovoked and causes or is intended to cause a disruption to production or the peaceful atmosphere of the workplace.

Considerations:
1. Whether language is directed at a specific person, rather than generally.
2. Whether the nature of the work environment or the workplace is such that "shop talk" is similar to or the same as the language used;
3. Whether the supervisor uses similar, or the same, language in his or her dealings with employees;
4. The nature of the specific incident, *i.e.,* whether the language used was at a time of high tension, after provocation, or as part of an insubordinate action;
5. Whether the language used was heard by other employees, customers, or the general public and caused a disruption to production or reflected poorly on the reputation of the employer;

6. Whether the employee's work record reveals prior warnings for similar conduct or is otherwise generally unsatisfactory.

Discussion: While it is apparent from the numerous arbitration awards concerning discipline for use of abusive, profane, and obscene language, the threshold of arbitrator sensitivity varies widely. This variance occasionally affects awards; decisions almost always depend upon elements other than the specific words used. In fact, except in extreme cases, the specific words fade into the background as the arbitrators concern themselves with why the employee deported himself or herself in the particular manner, what the employee intended to impart by his or her conduct, and the effect of the conduct on others.[1]

Consequently, in determining the type of discipline to be meted out to an employee for use of abusive, profane, or obscene language, it is suggested that the decision be based primarily on considerations other than the words used.[2] These considerations differ in emphasis depending upon whether the abusive conduct is directed at supervisors or other employees.[3]

Where abusive language is directed at supervisors, arbitrators generally look to see if the abuse is, in reality, just another form of insubordination; if the abuse is witnessed by other employees or persons, thereby, heightening the effect of the disrespect and its effect on an "orderly" shop; and/or if the abusive language is initiated by supervisory provocation.

In *Jones & Laughlin Steel Corp.,* for instance, an employee who was also a shop steward, came to the plant at a time other than his normal working hours to discuss a grievance.[4] While at the plant and on the production floor, he was informed by a supervisor of his next overtime assignment. In contesting his assignment, the employee used abusive and profane language directed toward the supervisor and, presumably, within the hearing of other employees. Finding the employee's conduct to warrant discipline, the arbitrator sustained the company's action on the basis of insubordination. The fact that the conduct occurred while the employee was "off duty" was found irrelevant, and his defense that he was conducting union business was held insufficient to justify the conduct.

In *Borg-Warner Corp.,* the discharge of an employee was sustained where he had called a female supervisor a "faggot" and had made obscene gestures toward her.[5] The arbitrator made special mention of the fact that the abusive language was within the hearing of other employees who laughed, subjecting the supervisor to derision.

In *Dobbs House, Inc.*,[6] the arbitrator reinstated the employee and commuted the discharge to a suspension without pay, when the employee's abusive conduct took place in a supervisor's lunchroom where only the union steward and supervisors were present.[7]

As a general rule, arbitrators distinguish between cases involving abusive language and gestures directed toward supervisors which occur in the presence of other employees and cases where the conduct takes place in the presence only of supervisors. For instance, an employee may be disciplined to a high degree, even discharged, where he or she abuses a supervisor on the shop floor; the employee may not be disciplined, at least to the same degree, where the same abuse occurs in a supervisor's office. The rationale is that the former is a direct assault on the supervisor's position of authority, while the latter is merely a personal attack with implications that do not go beyond their personal relationship.

The derision of a supervisor in such a place and in such a manner that the supervisor's status is damaged in the eyes of others who he or she may supervise is viewed as extremely serious and warrants severe discipline. It is a direct challenge and threat to the order of the operation. On the other hand, these elements are not as important when the confrontation takes place outside the hearing of others.

Where the abuse is directed toward nonsupervisory employees, arbitrators emphasize the issues of whether the abuse causes a subsequent altercation between employees; whether the language may be common "shop talk"; whether the conduct was provoked; and whether the abuse is of a specifically distasteful nature, *e.g.,* racial or ethnic slurs, as well as sexual comments and actions, are treated as the most serious. In *Anaconda Copper Co.*, for instance, the discharge of an employee for "sexual harrassment" was sustained.[8] The employee had used coarse language with sexual overtones and had made obscene finger and pelvic movements toward a female employee. This conduct had continued over a substantial period of time, and the arbitrator concluded that it had created an intimidating atmosphere for the female employee. The grievant complained that he had been denied progressive discipline. The arbitrator held, however, that the verbal warning and two transfers to get him out of certain areas were sufficient notice to him that his conduct was not being condoned. The arbitrator stated that the company had no further obligation to administer any more corrective discipline.[9]

In this context, it may be that the employer has no alternative but to discharge an employee for obscene conduct which creates an atmosphere offensive to female employees. Allowing such a condition to exist has been held to be a violation of Title VII of the Civil Rights Act and the basis for assessment of damages against both the employer and individual employees. In respect to labor arbitrators, therefore, the failure to stop such behavior through discipline may give rise to a grievance by the offended female alleging a violation of the contract's nondiscrimination provision.[10]

Verbal and physical abuse which provokes fighting, of course, clearly justifies discipline, although the abuse most frequently appears in cases only as a side issue to the discipline resulting from the fight. Where arbitrators are given the latitude and have the inclination to differentiate between two combatants in terms of degrees of punishment, however, the abusive conduct will be used as the basis for sustaining a higher level of discipline for one. Racial and ethnic slurs figure prominently in these cases. (For a more extended discussion of these cases, see Part II, Chapter 12.)

"Shop talk" is a frequent defense raised by grievants and presents evidentiary problems for arbitrators. It is difficult in these cases for an arbitrator to discern what is, and what is not, commonplace in the plant. The theory of the defense is simply that an employee cannot be disciplined for using language, or engaging in conduct, which is usual and ordinary in the workplace. As a rule, arbitrators make short work of this defense and appear to pay little attention to the actual words used during the incident in the case presented to them. Their focus, rightfully, is on the manner with which the words are spoken, the intent of the employee in using them, their effect on the persons in the area, and the present and future orderliness of the workplace.

On the simplest level, an employee cannot be appropriately disciplined for using obscene language in a conversation with other employees or even a supervisor. No matter how coarse the language, its use is not with an improper intent or adverse effect. The language may be offensive and may justify some corrective action, but it rarely justifies discipline in that context.

However, where the language is pointed and apparently intended to abuse a supervisor in such a way that it may diminish his or her effectiveness as a supervisor, it can be the basis for discipline, regardless of the general level of profanities or obscenities in the workplace. The only really significant time that a pointed use of profanity or obscene language may be successfully defended under the rubric of "shop talk" is where the supervisor engages in such language or actions. An employee who can prove that a supervisor uses profane or obscene langauge in his or her day-to-day treatment of employees, or in the specific instance being scrutinized, may successfully avoid the discipline. The attitude of arbitrators appears to be that the supervisor cannot be offended by conduct which is similar to or a variation of his or her own. Nor can such conduct be found to be a significant attack on the supervisor's authority.

Where the abuse is directed toward, or in the presence of, a customer or other member of the public, arbitrators examine the nature of the abuse, the precipitating cause of the conduct, and most important, the effect of the conduct upon the business and reputation of the employer.[11]

Arbitrators universally accept the need of an employer to maintain a good public image as something which can be enforced through employee discipline. No defense on the basis of "shop" or "street" talk will be sufficient to void discipline for abusive, profane, or obscene language or conduct directed toward a customer. Even where a customer is abusive and, perhaps, deserves a verbal thrashing, employees are expected to rise above the provocation. Under these circumstances, however, discipline penalties may be mitigated.

Abusive, profane, or obscene language or conduct—not directed at a customer, but within the hearing or presence of a customer—may also be sufficient cause for discipline. Such conduct is viewed as destructive of an atmosphere conducive to the employer's business. Accordingly, some discipline was sustained in *Washington IGA Foodline,* where the employee's profane and abusive language was directed at a store manager within the hearing of customers.[12]

Where some or all of these elements are proven to the disadvantage of the employee, evidence presented on other issues is generally discounted in some fashion. Of course, in all discipline cases the prior record of the employee and the presence, or absence, of corrective discipline is considered to be of great importance.[13]

Key Points:

1   *Whether the abusive language or conduct is aimed at a specific person, particularly a supervisor.*

Examples:

Employee A was told by his supervisor to stop loafing and to get back to work. The employee exclaimed "Oh, f——," and the words rang out through the workplace in which there were both males and females working. The supervisor discharged the employee. The arbitrator, noting that the words were used only as an exclamation and not directed toward the supervisor or any other person, reinstated the employee, commuting the discipline to a warning.

Employee B was told by his supervisor to stop loafing and to get back to work. The employee replied to the supervisor, "f—— you." Two other employees nearby heard the exclamation. The employee was discharged. Finding that the employee had been previously warned for insubordinate conduct toward his supervisor and that his language was directed at the supervisor, the arbitrator denied the grievance and upheld the discharge.

Guidelines

General exclamations may be cause for discipline, depending on the circumstances. However, discipline for such conduct must be modest, or it will be reversed or reduced. Abusive, obscene, or profane conduct or exclamations which are individual-specific will sustain more extreme discipline and, if coupled with other insubordinate conduct or disruption in the plant, discharge.

Relevant Cases

Leaseway of Western N.Y., Inc. (France), 60 LA 1343;
Glass Container Manufacturers Institute (Dworkin), 53 LA 1266;
Tenneco Oil Co. (Marlatt), 71 LA 571;
Cadillac Plastic & Chemical Co. (Kates), 58 LA 812;
New York News, Inc. (Berkowitz), 58 LA 835;
FSC Paper Corp. (Marshall), 65 LA 25;
E. F. Hauserman Co. (Gibson), 64 LA 1065;
Bunker Ramo Corp. (Somers), 62 LA 18;
Dempster Brothers, Inc. (Haemmel), 57 LA 1279;
PPG Industries (Coburn), 57 LA 866;
Eaton, Yale & Towne, Inc. (Kates), 56 LA 1037;
Economy Forms Corp. (Sembower), 55 LA 1039;
Ekstrom, Carlson & Co. (Davis), 55 LA 764;
O'Neal Steel, Inc. (King), 55 LA 402;
G. Heileman Brewing Co. (Solomon), 54 LA 1;
Permatex Co., Inc. (Goetz), 54 LA 546;
Whirlpool Corp. (Williams), 54 LA 576;
Chalfant Manufacturing Co. (Nichols), 52 LA 51;
Canteen Corp. (Keefe), 52 LA 781;
Circus, Circus (Kotin), 52 LA 1071;
Borg-Warner Corp. (Neas), 78 LA 985;
Jones & Laughlin Steel Corp. (Cook), 78 LA 566;
Dobbs House, Inc. (Hilgert), 78 LA 49;
Washington IGA Foodline (O'Reilly), 78 LA 391;
Michigan Bell Telephone Co. (Dyke), 78 LA 896.

2   *Whether the work environment, including supervisory conduct, is such that the language used is not unusual.*

Examples:

Employee *A* was found by his foreman sitting down reading a newspaper. The foreman said to the employee "Get your f—— ass off the chair and go back to work." The employee replied, "f—— you." The foreman discharged the employee for disrespect. The arbitrator reinstated the employee with full backpay, stating that the supervisor's conduct stimulated, and made acceptable, the similar reaction by the employee.

Employee *B* was a clerk in a large direct mail operation and worked in an open office occupied by 50 other male and female clerks. Although talking was not encouraged, the employees generally carried on conversations as they processed orders, and the level of work noise was subdued. Employee *B* was reprimanded by the supervisor for spending too much time away from his work desk. He replied in bold tones, "Get off my back, you s——of-a-b——." *B* was discharged. The arbitrator sustained the discharge on the basis that the employee's response was not only a direct verbal attack on the supervisor but was heightened in effect by its contrast to the work atmosphere. Consequently, the incident constituted a serious and demeaning act against the employer which demanded a strong response.

Guidelines

Although some distinguished arbitrators refuse to accept the "shop talk" principle, most arbitrators consider the general work environment important, especially where a supervisor is responsible for some of the tone setting, and will not sustain extreme discipline in cases involving use of language common in the conversation between employees.

Relevant Cases

Underwood Glass Co. (Hon), 58 LA 1139;
Cadillac Plastic & Chemical Co. (Kates), 58 LA 812;
E. F. Hauserman Co. (Gibson), 64 LA 1065;
Bunker Ramo Corp. (Somers), 62 LA 18;
Economy Forms Corp. (Sembower), 55 LA 1039;

Circus, Circus (Kotin), 52 LA 1071;
General Electric Co. (Bridgewater), 72 LA 654;
Michigan Bell Telephone Co. (Dyke), 78 LA 896.

3   *Whether the precipitating cause for and factual circumstances surrounding the conduct make the employee's action understandable.*

Examples:

Employee *A*, a black, was approached by his supervisor and told that he saw him having a drink with a white woman and that no "black b—— working for him should mess with white women." *A* responded by calling the supervisor a "s——of-a-b——." Thereupon, the supervisor discharged the employee. The arbitrator reinstated the employee without backpay, concluding that the employee's response, while not justified, was provoked by the supervisor.

Employee *B* was reprimanded by a supervisor for poor work performance. An argument ensued, during which the employee uttered obscenities directly to the supervisor. The employee was discharged. The arbitrator sustained the discharge, refusing to find the tension caused by the argument as justification for the outburst without specific proof of serious supervisory provocation.

Guidelines

Where an employee reacts to provocation or a generally tense atmosphere, severe discipline will not be sustained. However, where the conduct of the employee occurs during a tense atmosphere caused by his or her own actions, the tension will not mitigate the conduct.

Relevant Cases

AMF Harley-Davidson Motor Co. (Christenson), 61 LA 162;
Kast Metals Corp. (Moore), 61 LA 87;
Leaseway of Western N.Y., Inc. (France), 60 LA 1343;
University of Chicago (Seitz), 57 LA 539;
New York News, Inc. (Berkowitz), 58 LA 835;
FSC Paper Corp. (Marshall), 65 LA 25;
E. F. Hauserman Co. (Gibson), 64 LA 1065;
PPG Industries (Coburn), 57 LA 866;

Ekstrom, Carlson & Co. (Davis), 55 LA 764;
Chalfant Manufacturing Co. (Nichols), 52 LA 51;
Circus, Circus (Kotin), 52 LA 1071;
Royal Industries Union (Johnson), 51 LA 642;
Tenneco Oil Co. (Marlatt), 71 LA 571.

4   *Whether offending language or conduct occurred in the presence or hearing of other employees, customers, or the general public.*

Examples:

Employee *A* was reprimanded by his supervisor for lack of production. Later, *A* went to the office of the supervisor; and behind closed doors, an argument ensued, during which the employee made obscene remarks about the supervisor's relationship to his mother. The employee was discharged. The arbitrator reinstated the employee with minor discipline, noting that while the act of the employee was disrespectful and reprehensible, it was not so serious an attack on the supervisor's authority, or standing in the eyes of other employees, that it warranted discharge.

Employee *B* was reprimanded by his supervisor for lack of production. *B* argued with the supervisor and, within the hearing of other employees, called the supervisor a g—— d—— s——of-a-b——. The employee was discharged. The arbitrator sustained the discharge, stating that the conduct of the employee was directed toward destroying the supervisor's authority and, therefore, justified the strongest possible discipline for the supervisor to retain his effectiveness with the other employees.

Guidelines

Abusive, obscene, or profane language against a supervisor in private will not support severe discipline, while the same or similar conduct before other employees, customers, or the general public will. Arbitrators reason that public displays of disrespect or objectionable conduct will cause a breakdown in plant order, disruptions, and/or damage to the good will and reputation of the employer.

Relevant Cases

Leaseway of Western N.Y., Inc. (France), 60 LA 1343;
University of Chicago (Seitz), 57 LA 539;

Glass Container Manufacturers Institute (Dworkin), 53 LA 1266;
Tenneco Oil Co. (Marlatt), 71 LA 571;
Underwood Glass Co. (Hon), 58 LA 1139;
Cadillac Plastic & Chemical Co. (Kates), 58 LA 812;
New York News, Inc. (Berkowitz), 58 LA 835;
FSC Paper Corp. (Marshall), 65 LA 25;
City of Los Angeles (Tamoush), 64 LA 751;
Dempster Brothers, Inc. (Haemmel), 57 LA 1279;
PPG Industries (Coburn), 57 LA 866;
Economy Forms Corp. (Sembower), 55 LA 1039;
G. Heileman Brewing Co. (Solomon), 54 LA 1;
Permatex Company, Inc. (Goetz), 54 LA 546;
Circus, Circus (Kotin), 52 LA 1071;
Prophet Foods Co. (Howlett), 55 LA 288;
Washington IGA Foodline (O'Reilly), 78 LA 391.

Notes to Chapter 6

1. *See Glass Container Mfrs. Inst.* (Dworkin), 53 LA 1266; *Circus, Circus* (Kotin), 52 LA 1071; *Cadillac Plastic & Chem. Co.* (Kates), 58 LA 812; *New York News, Inc.* (Berkowitz), 58 LA 835; *Canteen Corp.* (Keefe), 52 LA 781; *Economy Forms Corp.* (Sembower), 55 LA 1039; *Eaton, Yale & Towne, Inc.* (Kates), 56 LA 1037; *Tenneco Oil Co.* (Marlatt), 71 LA 571; *Washington IGA Foodline* (O'Reilly), 78 LA 391; *Jones & Laughlin Steel Corp.* (Cook), 78 LA 566.

2. *See Underwood Glass Co.* (Hon), 58 LA 1139; *E. F. Hauserman Co.* (Gibson), 64 LA 1065; *Bunker Ramo Corp.* (Somers), 62 LA 18; *Economy Forms Corp., supra,* note 1; *Kast Metals Corp.* (Moore), 61 LA 87; *University of Chicago* (Seitz), 57 LA 539; *PPG Indus.* (Coburn), 57 LA 866; *Royal Indust. Union* (Johnson), 51 LA 642.

3. *See Leaseway of Western N.Y., Inc.* (France), 60 LA 1343; *G. Heileman Brewing Co.* (Solomon), 54 LA 1; *Permatex Co., Inc.* (Goetz), 54 LA 546; *Whirlpool Corp.* (Williams), 54 LA 576; *Chalfant Mfg. Co.* (Nichols), 52 LA 51.

4. *Jones & Laughlin Steel Corp., supra,* note 1.

5. *Borg-Warner Corp.* (Neas), 78 LA 985.

6. *Dobbs House, Inc.* (Hilgert), 78 LA 49.

7. *See also Kast Metals Corp., supra,* note 2; *Glass Container Mfrs. Inst., supra,* note 1; *Cadillac Plastic & Chem. Co., supra,* note 1; *Circus, Circus, supra,* note 1; *Economy Forms Corp., supra,* note 1; *Tenneco Oil Co., supra,* note 1; *G. Heileman Brewing Co., supra,* note 3; *Permatex Co., Inc., supra,* note 3; *Michigan Bell Tel. Co.* (Dyke), 78 LA 896.

8. *Anaconda Copper Co.* (Cohen), 78 LA 690.

9. *See also University of Chicago, supra,* note 2; *Leaseway of Western N.Y., Inc., supra,* note 3; *Bunker Ramo Corp., supra,* note 2; *United States Steel Corp.* (McDaniel), 53 LA 1210; *United States Steel Corp.* (McDermott),

55 LA 990; *Underwood Glass Co., supra,* note 2; *General Elec. Co.* (Bridgewater), 72 LA 654.

10. *See* Redeker, "Sexual Harassment: Facing the Problem," Delaware State Chamber of Commerce (1982); Redeker, "Sexual Harassment: Employer's Vigilance Needed," *Apparel World* 4 (January 1983), p. 42.

11. *See G. Heileman Brewing Co., supra,* note 3; *Thiokol Chem. Corp.* (Williams), 52 LA 1254; *Briggs & Stratton Corp.* (Gundermann), 57 LA 441; *Prophet Foods Co.* (Howlett), 55 LA 288; *Washington IGA Foodline, supra,* note 1.

12. *Washington IGA Foodline, supra,* note 1.

13. *See Chalfant Mfg. Co., supra,* note 3; *International Paper Co.* (Jaffe), 56 LA 558; *Anaconda Copper Co., supra,* note 8.

7

Alcohol and Alcohol-Related Conduct

Issue: Whether an employee can be discharged or otherwise disciplined for problems related to alcohol, alcoholism, or the use of alcoholic beverages.

Principle: Alcoholism, itself, is not a cause for discipline. Alcoholism is a defense which may be raised by an employee to avoid discipline. The effectiveness of the alcoholism defense will depend upon when it is raised for the first time, the acts which precipitated the decision to discipline, the willingness of the employee to enter a treatment program, the likelihood of rehabilitation, or the proven success of the program.

The use and/or possession of alcoholic beverages at times proximate to the employee's workday, on the job, on the employer's premises, or throughout the employee's workday are just causes for discipline, and rules prohibiting such conduct will be enforced as written. Such rules may also be enforced in accordance with their intent so long as some legitimate employer interest warrants a broader interpretation of the rule. Where there is no rule, discipline for alcohol-related conduct will be justified when it infringes upon some employer interest or creates a safety risk.

Considerations: Alcoholism

1. Whether the behavior of the alcoholic while intoxicated is bizarre, aberrant, or otherwise disruptive;
2. Whether the alcoholic's condition has an adverse effect on his or her work performance and/or attendance;

81

3. Whether the employee is participating, or is willing to participate, in an alcohol treatment program and the reasonable likelihood of the program's success;
4. Whether the time when the defense of alcoholism is first raised is sufficiently early to give credibility to the employee's expression of intent to solve the problem.

Alcohol-Related Conduct

1. Whether the employee is drinking, or intoxicated, while working or on the premises of the employer;
2. Whether the employee is drinking at a time which is proximate to his or her worktime and appears under the influence of alcohol at the time he or she reports to work;
3. Whether the employer has a clear and communicated rule against drinking during the employee's workday, on the employer's premises, or at a time proximate to the employee's workday;
4. Whether the proof of the employee's intoxication is clear and convincing.

Discussion: There are two distinctly different, but sometimes related, alcohol problems faced by employers. The first involves employees who are *bona fide* alcoholics and provably have that disease. The second involves the discovery of employees who are drinking while on the job, who are intoxicated while on the job, or who are drinking at a time proximate to their worktime. The considerations for an employer encountering these problems are distinctly different from those encountered with alcoholism. Alcoholism is in the nature of a defense and the employer must determine the effect, if any, that should be given to that defense. This determination often requires compassion rather than the strict administration of a discipline system. Other conduct resulting from the use of alcohol requires discipline. Because these two related problems are treated so differently by arbitrators, patterns of decisions can be constructively discussed only when they are taken separately.

Alcoholics and Alcoholism

In recent years, alcoholism has been perceived as a disease and has been treated similarly to other medical disabilities. (See Chapter 11.) Consequently, arbitrators, while recognizing the right of an employer to have a regular and productive workforce, demand a direct effect of the employee's condition on the workplace and a rehabilitative approach by the employer, except in extreme and unusual circumstances. That is, alcoholism, as the sole criterion, will not justify discipline.

Employers usually encounter alcoholism when an employee uses it as a defense, explaining conduct and seeking to avoid discipline. Whether it will be an effective defense, or whether an employer must even consider it, will depend on the severity of the conduct for which discipline is given and the time when the defense is raised. Generally, there are two distinct classes of conduct, or effects on the workplace, which produce different arbitrator responses when an alcoholism defense is considered, *i.e.*, aberrant behavior which would normally result in summary discharge and conduct which is commonly unacceptable, such as poor work performance or absenteeism, which would properly be subject to progressive discipline. In the former, the defense of alcoholism may be allowed to mitigate the discipline. In the latter, the defense generally will not be effective when raised for the first time in the context of a discharge. The differences in arbitral treatment seem to be based on the belief that a summary discharge offense usually involves a single, isolated event; the employee would not have revealed his or her alcoholism prior to the event; and the employee would not have had the chance to seek the employer's tolerance and assistance in obtaining treatment. On the other hand, if the employee has gone through several progressive discipline steps without revealing the nature of the problem and only does so to avoid the immediate discomfort of a summary discharge, arbitrators tend to doubt the employee's sincerity in seeking treatment.

The nature of the aberrant behavior at the workplace, however, may override an arbitrator's willingness to accept an alcoholism defense as mitigation of a summary discharge. For instance, in *Asarco, Inc.*, an employee was discharged for being intoxicated on the job.[1] The employee was a miner, and his condition placed not only himself but others in danger. The arbitrator distinguished cases in which the danger was less severe and found that the alcoholic's participation in an alcohol treatment program would not be sufficient assurance of continuing safe conduct. In *National Gypsum Co.*, the discharge of an employee was sustained, when it appeared that he was prone to seizures as a result of his alcoholism.[2]

Two additional cases demonstrate the parameters of arbitrators' decisions in this area. In *Standard Packaging Corp.*, the discharge of an employee, who had lied about the death of his mother to get time off and who had other previous disciplinary problems, was effectively reduced to a one-year suspension without pay (reinstatement without backpay).[3] Although the situation might otherwise have justified discharge, the arbitrator reduced the discipline because of the employee's alcoholism and placed the employee on six months probation, during which time he was to get control over his problem.

By contrast, in *NCR,* where an alcoholic employee vandalized his supervisor's home, the discharge was upheld, even though, as the arbitrator noted, alcoholism is a disease and the employee was in a treatment program. The conduct was too egregious and reinstatement would have undermined company discipline.[4]

In situations not involving egregious behavior normally subject to summary discharge, however, arbitrators frequently look to the time when the defense of alcoholism was first raised and the likelihood of rehabilitation in determining the appropriateness of the discipline. In *Greenlee Bros. & Co.,* for instance, an employee's discharge for excessive absenteeism was mitigated to a suspension on the basis of the employee's excellent work record prior to the onset of the disease and a determination by the arbitrator that the employee deserved one last chance.[5]

The time when an employee raises the defense of alcoholism is often relevant in progressive discipline situations, because it is viewed as an indication of an employee's sincerity and the likelihood of improvement. In *Armstrong Furnace Co.,* for example, the arbitrator found the defense to be insufficient when raised for the first time only after the discharge.[6] As in *Bethlehem Steel Co.,* the arbitrator restricted his authority to events that occurred before the discharge.[7]

In this respect, the employer's knowledge of the employee's condition is also relevant. Where, for instance, an employer is aware that an employee's absenteeism is a result of his or her alcoholism and the employer does nothing to encourage the employee to enter a treatment program as a condition of further employment, a discharge may be found to be without just cause. Thus, in *St. Joe Minerals Corp.,* the arbitrator voided the discharge to give the employee a chance at rehabilitation.[8] However, where the employee's poor record goes unabated after repeated warnings and the treatment program appears to be ineffective, a discharge will be warranted.[9]

Another major factor in discipline cases where alcoholism appears as a defense is whether the employee submits to, or is willing to submit to, a treatment program. Arbitrators usually will reduce the discipine when the employee is in an alcohol treatment program or where the employee expresses a timely willingness to enroll in such a treatment program.[10]

On the other hand, when the employee refuses treatment, does not comply with the treatment requirements of the program, or the program proves unsuccessful, arbitrators will uphold the discharge.[11]

One arbitrator has set out what appears to be the three generally accepted elements that should be met prior to disciplining an alcoholic: (1) the employee should inform the employer of his or her illness; (2) the employer should direct or encourage the employee to seek treatment; and (3) the employee must refuse, or not abide by, the conditions of the treatment.[12] While other arbitrators may not denote these criteria so clearly, they do, however, seem to apply them with one caveat, *i.e.,* the employee cannot raise the issue of a treatment program for the first time either as a defense or as an alternative to the discipline after he has been disciplined. Rather, alcoholics must have applied for treatment before their condition hampers their work performance to the point where the degree of discipline required by the normal application of the system is discharge.

Key Points

1   *Alcoholism itself does not constitute just cause for discipline.*

Examples:

Employee *A* was disciplined for excessive absenteeism on several occasions. The problem continued unabated and the employee was given a three-day suspension. At the time of this discipline, he admitted to being an alcoholic. The employer warned the employee that he must get the problem under control. After the next absence, the employee was discharged. Noting that in all prior cases of discharges for absenteeism employees had been allowed up to three additional absences after a suspension, the arbitrator reinstated the employee with full backpay, but directed a treatment program. The employer's argument that the employee's alcoholism constituted a sufficient basis for concluding that he would not conquer his attendance problem was dismissed without merit.

Employee *B*, intoxicated, entered the plant after his shift was over and proceeded to batter his machine with a metal pipe. When a supervisor and another employee tried to stop him, he attacked them with the pipe. Only after a struggle, during which *B* injured two other employees, was he subdued. At the discharge hearing, *B* argued for reinstatement, using alcoholism as his defense. The discharge notice showed alcoholism as the cause. The arbitrator, discounting the notice as inartfully drawn, sustained the discharge, basing the decision upon the egregious conduct of the employee.

Guidelines

Alcoholism as a defense may or may not be effective, depending on the circumstances of the case. The conduct or work performance which results from alcoholism is the basis for discipline, not alcoholism itself.

Relevant Cases

St. Joe Minerals Corp. (McDermott), 73 LA 1193;
Greenlee Bros. & Co. (Wolff), 67 LA 847;
Eastern Airlines, Inc. (Turkus), 74 LA 316;
Armstrong Furnace Co. (Stouffer), 63 LA 618;
Bethlehem Steel Co. (Porter), 43 LA 1215.

2 *Where the aberrant behavior is so severe that it would normally justify summary discharge, alcoholism will be an effective defense when raised for the first time at the discharge hearing, unless the conduct was exceptionally damaging to the employer or constituted an extreme risk to the safety of the employee or others.*

Examples:

Employee *A* was discharged following a company picnic; he had became intoxicated and by his generally obnoxious behavior, was disruptive. The employer had intended the picnic to be a family affair, and many children were present. The employee's work record was average. At the discharge hearing, the employee confessed to alcoholism and offered to enter a treatment program to avoid the discharge. The arbitrator reasoning that the conduct, while justifying some discipline, was not so extreme or so directed against the employer that discharge would be appropriate, reinstated the employee without backpay. The arbitrator accepted the employee's defense of chronic alcoholism as complete but ordered treatment as a condition of continued employment.

Employee *B* was discharged after he became intoxicated at a company picnic and boisterously denounced the quality of the employer's product, and the company in general, using a great deal of profanity. The picnic was a family affair at which various customers and their families were also present. At the time of his discharge, the employee pleaded alcoholism, offered to enter a treatment program, and noted that his problem with drinking was generally known in the plant, although he had kept it in sufficient check to avoid any serious work performance problem. The arbitrator sustained the discharge on the basis that the conduct was too extreme to be mitigated by an alcoholism defense first raised seriously in connection with the discharge.

Employee *C* reported to work intoxicated. Rather than punching in, he went to a remote place in a warehouse and fell asleep. When discovered by a supervisor, he was discharged. The employee raised alcoholism as a defense at the time of discharge. The arbitrator, noting that, while *C* had reported for work intoxicated, he neither attempted to punch in nor to work. Accordingly, the arbitration ruled that while some discipline may have been warranted, discharge was too severe. The interest of the employer had not been so abused that the same degree of discipline, *i.e.,* summary discharge, should be given to this employee as to another who had not been drunk.

Employee *D* reported to work intoxicated. He punched in and proceeded to his work station where he immediately began to throw all his tools in the trash. He then went to his supervisor and told him to f—— himself and left the premises. The employee was discharged. In reducing the discharge to a leave of absence, the arbitrator held that the conduct warranted removal from the workplace, but not termination, until the employee had been given a reasonable time to try a rehabilitation program.

Employee *E,* a batch operator in a chemical plant, reported to work intoxicated. His condition was discovered after he had put chemicals in incorrect proportions into the batch mixer. The employee was sent to the locker room to shower and to go home. He showered with his clothes on, put on another employee's trousers, and was discovered in his car trying to start it with the other's keys. The employee revealed his alcoholism at the discharge hearing and offered to enter a treatment program, as a condition of reinstatement. Reasoning that the damage to the company's product was so great and that the danger to other employees, due to a possible reoccurrence and the volatility of the chemicals involved, was so substantial that the employer could not reasonably take a chance, the arbitrator sustained the discharge.

Guidelines

Egregious behavior normally justifying summary discharge may be mitigated by alcoholism, even when raised for the first time in connection with the discharge. Discipline will be sustained, however, if the conduct was so severe that a repetition would create a substantial safety hazard to the employee, or to his or her fellow workers, or if the conduct so shocked the conscience of the arbitrator that the discipline is viewed primarily as a punishment.

Relevant Cases

Standard Packaging Corp. (Fogelberg), 71 LA 445;
NCR (Gundermann), 70 LA 756;
Asarco, Inc. (Grooms), 76 LA 163;
Greenlee Bros. & Co. (Wolff), 67 LA 847.

3 *Where the conduct would normally have justified progressive discipline, alcoholism will constitute an effective defense only if raised prior to the step calling for discharge or if the employer is actually shown to have known of the disease and has not required the employee to enter a treatment program.*

Examples:

Employee *A* was discharged for poor production in accordance with the employer's progressive discipline systems. At the arbitration, the employee raised the defense of alcoholism. The arbitrator found the defense insufficient to avoid the discipline of discharge, noting the numerous warnings the employee had been given and her failure to reveal her illness and seek treatment before her discharge.

Employee *B* was discharged for excessive absenteeism in accordance with the employer's progressive discipline system. The employer maintained an alcohol control program and advertised the availability of treatment to the employees. *B* had not volunteered for the program. At the discharge hearing, however, he sought entry into the program. Concluding that the employee was seeking to avoid the discharge and was not, based upon his prior inaction, sincere in his desire to be treated, the arbitrator sustained the discharge.

Employee *C* was discharged for excessive absenteeism in accordance with the employer's progressive discipline system.

The employer maintained an effective alcohol control program and frequently advertised the availability of treatment. C had not volunteered. However, C's problem with alcohol was known to her supervisor, who on occasion had urged her to enter the treatment program. C denied that she was an alcoholic. At the arbitration, the union raised C's alcoholism as a defense. C, however, continued to deny the condition. The arbitrator, finding fault with the employer's failure to condition C's continued employment upon treatment at an earlier stage in the progressive discipline, ordered the employee into the program and instructed the employer to reinstate C at such time as it may appear that C has her problem under control.

Guidelines

Alcoholism will not be a sufficient defense to discharge following progressive discipline if the condition is revealed for the first time in connection with the discharge. However, if the employer had knowledge of the condition prior to the commission of the dischargeable offense and failed to condition future employment on entry into a treatment program, the defense will be effective; the employee will be given a chance to see if treatment will work.

Relevant Cases

Greenlee Bros. & Co. (Wolff), 67 LA 847;
St. Joe Minerals Corp. (McDermott), 73 LA 1193;
Armstrong Furnace Co. (Stouffer), 63 LA 618;
General Electric Co. (Clark), 72 LA 355;
National Gypsum Co. (Jacobs), 73 LA 228;
Asarco, Inc. (Grooms), 76 LA 163.

4   *The employee must evidence a will and a desire to overcome the problem, and there must be a reasonable possibility of the employee's success in doing so.*

Examples:

Employee *A* was discharged for intoxication on the job. There was no other record of similar conduct, but the employee's attendance and production were only marginal. *A* sought reinstatement and entry into an alcoholism treatment program. The arbitrator reinstated the employee, with the condition that she enter an alcohol rehabilitation program.

Employee *B* was discharged for excessive absenteeism after exhausting all of the steps in the progressive discipline system. During the grievance procedure and at the arbitration, the employee raised his alcoholism as a defense and offered to enter a treatment program as a condition of reinstatement. The discharge was sustained: The employee should not have waited until his discharge to reveal his problem and to offer to enroll in an alcohol program. His delay cast suspicion on the likelihood of the treatment's success.

Employee *C* was suspended for excessive absenteeism. During the disciplinary conference, *C* admitted to alcoholism. The employer recommended that the employee enter an alcohol treatment program. The employee entered a program. But, while his record improved, it was still not good enough to avoid the next step in the absenteeism control program, and he was discharged. The employee was reinstated by the arbitrator without backpay. The arbitrator found that the employee had demonstrated an honest effort to overcome his problem, even though he had not been completely successful at that time.

Employee *D* was suspended for excessive absenteeism. During the disciplinary conference, *D* admitted to alcoholism. The employer recommended an alcohol treatment program and gave *D* time off for therapy. When the absenteeism did not significantly improve, *D* was discharged. The discharge was sustained, with the arbitrator noting the apparent failure of the treatment.

Employee *E* was disciplined for excessive absenteeism. The employer, learning of *E*'s alcoholism, recommended an alcohol treatment program. The employee asked the employer to assume the cost of the program. This request was denied, and the employee did not enter a program. When her excessive absenteeism continued, *E* was discharged. *E* asked for reinstatement on the grounds that the employer would not pay for the treatment program and she was, therefore, not obligated to go. The discharge was sustained.

Guidelines

The efforts of the employee to treat his or her alcoholism must be sincere and must show a reasonable chance of success. Where the employee's dedication or progress is found to be insufficient, the employer will be entitled to terminate the employment.

Relevant Cases

Land O'Lakes (Smythe), 65 LA 803;
St. Joe Minerals Corp. (McDermott), 73 LA 1193;
Greenlee Bros. & Co. (Wolff), 67 LA 847;
Johns-Manville Products Corp. (Kates), 76 LA 845;
United States Military Traffic Management Command (Friedman), 75 LA 968;
Dahlstrom Manufacturing Co., Inc. (Gootnick), 78 LA 302;
Continental Airlines, Inc. (Ross), 75 LA 896;
National Gypsum Co. (Jacobs), 73 LA 228;
Bordo Citrus Products Co. (Naehring), 67 LA 1145;
Sterling Drug, Inc. (Draper), 67 LA 1296;
United States Steel Corp. (Garrett), 63 LA 274;
Eastern Airlines, Inc. (Turkus), 74 LA 316.

Alcohol-Related Conduct

Most cases involving alcohol do not involve or, at least, do not discuss alcoholism. In reviewing these cases, there are several matters which arbitrators seem to find significant.

The most serious violation is when the employee is intoxicated or drinking while on the job or premises. In such cases, the discharge will almost always be upheld.[13]

A corollary of the drinking-on-the-job issue is that, due to the extended time effects of alcohol, drinking during an employee's lunch hour or break may be sufficient to uphold a discharge for drinking "on duty," "during working hours," or "during the workday."[14]

Another matter related to drinking on the job to which arbitrators give consideration is whether the nature of the work or operation the employee is performing is dangerous. Where such danger is substantially increased when the employee drinks, a discharge is more likely to be upheld.[15]

The plant setting may serve to mitigate a drinking-on-the-job infraction when, for example, a "holiday spirit" prevails before a holiday shutdown.[16]

Of prime significance in these cases is the existence of a company rule and its precise wording. For instance, where the company rule prohibited drinking "on-the-job," an employee, who returned to work from lunch intoxicated and was discharged, was reinstated by the arbitrator.[17] On the other hand, some arbitrators have more expansively interpreted contract language, especially where a specific employer interest, such as the safe operation of motor vehicles, is involved.[18] Employers are obliged, therefore, to insure that their rules cover all situations over which they wish to have control. As a general principle, arbitrators are unwilling to consider such issues as the degree of intoxication or impaired ability where the conduct itself is specifically prohibited.[19] A rule which prohibits "being under the influence of alcohol" or "intoxication," therefore, presents a substantially more difficult case, because it requires proof of a condition, rather than the circumstances of an event. Proof of intoxication has presented numerous and special problems for employers and arbitrators. Several cases hold that intoxication can be established through observation of the employee. The signs include the employee's speech, appearance, demeanor, walk, the smell of alcohol, etc.[20] The smell of alcohol alone, however, is insufficient to prove intoxication, especially where the employee defends on the basis that he or she was suffering from a hangover, which would explain the odor.[21]

Blood alcohol content (BAC) tests have figured instrumentally in several cases. Frequently, these cases discuss the necessary BAC level to show intoxication. Often, the level of the state's motor vehicle law will be used—.10 percent in most states.[22] One arbitrator, however, reinstated an employee with backpay where the employer had not established a standard for what BAC level would constitute "under the influence."[23] Also, at least one arbitrator has stated that a blood alcohol test alone is not sufficient, but must be supported by observational evidence of intoxication, like that discussed above, because of the different tolerances people have to alcohol.[24]

In *Blue Diamond Coal Co.*, the arbitrator held that the refusal to submit to a BAC test, without other evidence of intoxication, was insufficient to sustain an intoxication discharge.[25] However, this arbitrator did not raise the question of insubordination that such refusal properly presents. On the other hand, in *Champion Spark Plug Co.*, the arbitrator sustained a 15-day suspension because the employee refused to submit to a search for the bottle he was seen drinking from.[26]

Key Points

1 *An appropriate rule against drinking should anticipate whether drinking during the workday, but during nonworking hours and/or off the premises, should be prohibited. A technically defective rule or too limited a rule may be broadened by an arbitrator where the conduct infringes on the employer's interest and violates the intent of the rule.*

Example:

Employee *A* went off the employer's premises for lunch and was seen by her supervisor drinking a beer. *A* was discharged for drinking during her workday. The employer's rule prohibited the consumption of alcoholic beverages during an employee's workday and stated that a violation of the rule would result in summary discharge. A defended on the basis that one beer would have no effect on her and that the consumption took place off the premises and "on her own time." The arbitrator denied the grievance, holding that the prohibition was against all drinking, and stated that he was without authority to distinguish between amounts consumed.

Employee B went off the employer's premises for lunch and was seen by his supervisor drinking a beer. B was discharged for drinking during his workday. There was no company rule regarding the consumption of alcoholic beverages. B defended on the basis that he was off the premises and on his own time. Further, B said that one beer would have no effect on him. The arbitrator, noting the absence of intoxication or other infringement on the employer's interests, reinstated B with backpay and commuted the discipline to a warning.

Employee C went off the employer's premises for lunch and was witnessed by a supervisor having a beer with her sandwich. C was discharged for drinking during her workday. The company rule prohibited drinking on the job. C defended on the basis that her drinking was off the premises and on her own time. Further, C defended on the basis that one beer would have no effect on her. C was reinstated without backpay: The arbitrator found that the rule had been discriminatorily applied, because supervisors occasionally drank beer at lunch. Consequently, C had been misled into believing that the rule did not reach this type of conduct.

Employee D was discharged for drinking on the job, when it was discovered that during his lunch break he went to his car in the parking lot and drank a beer. D defended on the grounds that the incident occurred on his own time and that one beer had no effect on him. The discharge was sustained. While the violation was not covered by the employer's rule prohibiting the consumption of alcoholic beverages on company premises, the arbitrator construed the discharge as a reasonable extension of the employer's intent.

Employee E was discharged for drinking when he was seen by a supervisor consuming a beer with his lunch at a nearby restaurant. The employer's rule prohibited drinking on company premises or elsewhere while on the job. E was a local delivery truckdriver. The discharge was sustained. The arbitrator reasoned that E was in the course of making a delivery and, hence, was on the job; and because he was responsible for the truck, he was technically on the premises of the employer. The arbitrator added that the employer had an interest in the safe operation of its vehicles and in community relations. Drinking by the employee at any time during the workday placed both of these interests at risk.

Guidelines

Consuming an intoxicating beverage at any time during an employee's workday is acceptable as a cause for discipline, particularly when the prohibition is set forth in a broad rule consistently applied. Neither technically deficient rules nor the absence of rules will necessarily result in the overturning of discipline for an employee's conduct, if a specific interest of the employer is shown to have been violated or put at risk.

Relevant Cases

Shaefer-Alabama Corp. (LaValley), 70 LA 956;
Cal Custom/Hawk (Ross), 65 LA 723;
AMF Lawn & Garden Div. (Wyman), 64 LA 988;
Browning-Ferris Industries of Ohio, Inc. (Shanker), 77 LA 289;
Beatrice Foods (Thornell), 73 LA 191;
City of Milwaukee (Maslanka), 71 LA 329.

2 *Where an employee has been discharged for drinking just prior to his or her workday, there should be some evidence that the drinking had, or could have had, an adverse effect on the employee's work performance or on the safety of the employee or others.*

Examples:

Employee *A*, a third-shift employee, was seen by a supervisor in a local bar drinking beer before the start of his shift, and when he reported to work, he was discharged for having alcohol on his breath. The employee's work and attendance record was good, although he was a known troublemaker. *A* was reinstated without backpay. The arbitrator stated that the employee's lack of responsibility, deserved some discipline, but without more proof of the employee's actual condition, summary discharge was too harsh.

Employee *B*, a third-shift employee, was seen by a supervisor in a local bar drinking beer before the start of his shift, and when he reported to work, *B* was discharged for drinking at a time too close to the start of his workday. Noting that the employee had a bad tardiness record and that the employer lacked a precise discipline system for tardiness, the arbitrator sustained the discharge, reasoning that the employee's lack of concern for his job duties made him an unsatisfactory employee.

Employee *C* was discharged for drinking at a time proximate to his workday when he was seen drinking beer in a bar just prior to the start of his shift. The discharge was sustained, for even though the employee's work record was good, the arbitrator held that the employee was a heavy equipment operator and should have known that any diminution of his capabilities could endanger himself as well as others.

Guidelines

An employee may be disciplined for drinking at a time proximate to his or her worktime, when the consumption of alcoholic beverages can be shown to have had a material effect on his or her work performance, caused intoxication, or created a risk to the safety of others, product, or equipment.

Relevant Cases

Beatrice Foods (Thornell), 73 LA 191;
City of Milwaukee (Maslanka), 71 LA 329;
Jehl Cooperage Co. (Odom), 75 LA 901.

3   *The employer must be able to prove that the employee violated the rule, i.e., intoxication, consumption, etc.*

Examples:

Employee *A* was discharged under a rule which forbade drinking or intoxication on the job. *A* was reinstated with backpay when the only evidence was the smell of alcohol on his breath. The arbitrator noted that there was no evidence of either drinking on the job or intoxication.

Employee *B* was discharged under a rule which forbade drinking during the workday. The only evidence was the smell of alcohol on the employee's breath. Noting that the smell was detected six hours into the shift, the arbitrator sustained the discharge.

Employee *C* was discharged for intoxication on the job when he displayed sleepiness and had the smell of alcohol on his breath. The employee refused to take a breathalyzer test. *C* was reinstated on the grounds that there was inadequate proof of intoxication.

Employee *D* was discharged for intoxication on the job when he had the smell of alcohol on his breath at the start of the shift. When the employee refused to have blood drawn by the company nurse for analysis, insubordination was added as a reason for discharge. The arbitrator, noting a lack of evidence of intoxication, nevertheless sustained the discharge for insubordination.

Employee *E* went off the premises to have lunch. When she returned, her supervisor detected the smell of alcohol on her breath, and *E* was discharged. The employer's rule prohibited drinking, or possessing, alcoholic beverages on the premises. *E* was reinstated with backpay. The arbitrator held that there was no proof *E* had been drinking on the premises and no proof of intoxication.

Guidelines

Drinking during the workday can be proven through such external signs as appearance, odor, eyewitness accounts, or other physical evidence. Proof of intoxication on the job, however, is more difficult because, in addition to the external signs mentioned above, the proof involves the physical condition of the employee and requires evidence of extremely aberrant behavior or the results of scientific tests. The employer has the right to compel the employee to submit to reasonable tests, and an employee's refusal may constitute a separate cause for discipline, *i.e,* insubordination.

Relevant Cases

Tennessee River Pulp & Paper Co. (Simon), 68 LA 421;
Champion Spark Plug Co. (Cassellman), 68 LA 702;
General Felt Industries, Inc. (Carnes), 74 LA 972;
Memphis Light, Gas & Water Div. (Rayson), 66 LA 948;
Hayes-Albion Corp. (Kahn), 76 LA 1005;
Northrop Worldwide Aircraft Services, Inc. (Goodstein), 64 LA 742;
Blue Diamond Coal Co. (Summers), 66 LA 1136.

Notes to Chapter 7

1. *Asarco, Inc.* (Grooms), 76 LA 163.
2. *See also National Gypsum Co.* (Jacobs), 73 LA 228.
3. *Standard Packaging Corp.* (Fogelberg), 71 LA 445.
4. *NCR* (Gundermann), 70 LA 756.
5. *Greenlee Bros. & Co.* (Wolff), 67 LA 847.
6. *Armstrong Furnace Co.* (Stouffer), 63 LA 618.
7. *Bethlehem Steel Co.* (Porter), 43 LA 1215; *see also Dahlstrom Mfg. Co., Inc.* (Gootnick), 78 LA 302.
8. *St. Joe Minerals Corp.* (McDermott), 73 LA 1193.
9. *General Elec. Co.* (Clark), 72 LA 355. *See also Dahlstrom Mfg. Co., Inc., supra,* note 7.
10. *Land O'Lakes* (Smythe), 65 LA 803; *St. Joe Minerals Corp., supra,* note 8; *Greenlee Bros. & Co., supra,* note 5.
11. *Johns-Manville Prod. Corp.* (Kates), 76 LA 845; *U.S. Military Traffic Management Command* (Friedman), 75 LA 968; *Continental Airlines, Inc.* (Ross), 75 LA 896; *National Gypsum Co., supra,* note 2; *Bordo Citrus Prod. Co.* (Naehring), 67 LA 1145; *Sterling Drug, Inc.* (Draper), 67 LA 1296; *U.S. Steel Corp.* (Garrett), 63 LA 274; *Dahlstrom Mfg. Co., Inc., supra,* note 7.
12. *See Eastern Airlines, Inc.* (Turkus), 74 LA 316.
13. *Shaefer-Alabama Corp.* (LaValley), 70 LA 956; *Cal Custom/Hawk* (Ross), 65 LA 723; *AMF Lawn & Garden Div.* (Wyman), 64 LA 988.
14. *Browning-Ferris Indus. of Ohio, Inc.* (Shanker), 77 LA 289; *Beatrice Foods* (Thornell), 73 LA 191; *City of Milwaukee* (Maslanka), 71 LA 329.
15. *Beatrice Foods, supra,* note 14 (forklift operator); *City of Milwaukee, supra,* note 14 (equipment operator); *Jehl Cooperage Co.* (Odom), 75 LA 901 (punch press operator).
16. *Okonite Co.* (Ghiz), 74 LA 664 (insufficient to support discharge but enough to uphold suspension.)
17. *Baumfolder Corp.* (Modjeska), 78 LA 1060.
18. *Browning-Ferris Indus. of Ohio, Inc., supra,* note 14; *City of Milwaukee, supra,* note 14.
19. *City of Milwaukee, supra,* note 14.
20. *Tennessee River Pulp & Paper Co.* (Simon), 68 LA 421 (the discharge was upheld); *Champion Spark Plug Co.* (Cassellman), 68 LA 702 (a 15-day suspension upheld); *General Felt Indus., Inc.* (Carnes), 74 LA 972 (the employee was reinstated with backpay because he was only boisterous and there was no other evidence of intoxication).
21. *Memphis Light, Gas & Water Div.* (Rayson), 66 LA 948 (the employee was reinstated without backpay); *Hayes-Albion Corp.* (Kahn), 76 LA 1005 (the discharge was denied.)
22. *Tennessee River Pulp & Paper Co., supra,* note 20 (the discharge was upheld where .10 percent was used); *General Felt Indus., Inc., supra,* note 20 (reinstatement was ordered where employee's BAC was tested at .05 percent and .08 percent; the state motor vehicle law was .10 percent; *Mem-*

phis Light, Gas & Water Div., supra, note 21 (the employee was reinstated but without backpay where the BAC was only .01 percent, allegedly due to a hangover condition; *Beatrice Foods, supra,* note 14 (the suspension was sustained where BAC was .07 percent two hours after consumption and testimony accepted that BAC falls at a rate of .02 percent/hour after peak occurring about one hour after consumption.

23. *Northrop Worldwide Aircraft Services, Inc.* (Goodstein), 64 LA 742.

24. *Hayes-Albion Corp., supra,* note 21 (the employee's discharge was denied.)

25. *Blue Diamond Coal Co.* (Summers), 66 LA 1136.

26. *Champion Spark Plug Co., supra,* note 20.

8

Poor Attitude or Disloyalty

Issue: Whether an employee may be discharged or otherwise disciplined for either a poor attitude or disloyalty towards the employer.

Principle: An employee may be discharged or otherwise disciplined for a poor attitude or disloyalty where there is a continuing course of conduct which results in damage to workplace morale or efficiency or which creates so serious a breach between the employer and employee that a continuing relationship is impossible. If there was no other independent basis for the discipline (*e.g.*, insubordination, inadequate job performance), the employee must have exhibited the unacceptable conduct repeatedly and failed to respond to warnings and/or counseling.

Considerations:
1. Whether the employee's poor attitude causes, or is combined with, other unacceptable conduct;
2. Whether the employee's attitude affects the morale or performance of other employees;
3. Whether the employee's conduct has an adverse effect on customer relations;
4. Whether there has been progressive discipline.

Discussion: In cases involving discipline for poor attitude, arbitrators appear to be heavily influenced not only by the nature of the final incident resulting in the discipline, but also by the employee's entire record of performance, attitude, and conduct.

In *Uarco Company, Inc.,* for instance, an employee with six and one-half years seniority was discharged for generally unacceptable behavior resulting from a bad attitude.[1] The arbitrator noted that the employee had been counseled on numerous occasions about his attitude and concluded:

> ... In this case, the Grievant, union representatives, everyone affected, all were aware the Grievant had several warnings; that he was on probation; that if his attitude did not improve or if he violated the Company rules again within the six month period, he would be discharged.[2]

Although the employee had a good work record in some respects, the arbitrator sustained the discharge because the employee failed to respond to the progressive discipline.

In *National Council of Jewish Women, Inc.*—perhaps the most extensive and unique case of this kind—the arbitrator sustained the discharge of a high seniority employee where the precipitating incident was a letter which some coemployees wrote regarding the grievant.[3] The text of the letter amply sets forth the parameters of that case.

FROM: All Professional   Feb. 8, 1971
        Staff of Community
        Activities Department
TO: K——
SUBJECT: N——

We feel that N ———'s behavior has reached the point where it cannot be tolerated. Following our meeting with you last Thursday, we are listing the reasons:

N ——— poses a major irritant and distraction, so that she cuts down on the productivity of both professionals and other secretaries, both in our department and in nearby departments.

She poisons the atmosphere by constantly complaining, downgrading professionals and secretaries to other professionals and secretaries.

She constantly complains about being overworked, while spending a good amount of time wandering around the office complaining and generally wasting time.

She talks incessantly and compulsively in an extraordinarily loud voice, making it impossible for anyone not to hear her, and making it extremely difficult to concentrate.

She often leaves at 4:00 P.M. if the Department Head is not in. Sometimes she lays the groundwork by complaining in the morning about being sick, and finally leaving early. At other times she simply leaves, without telling anyone. She has been seen leaving early by the mail-room elevator. Since she has usually been our only full-time secretary, this means that the professional staff then has to answer the phone and take messages, using time better spent in getting their work done.

Her work is not always of good quality. She makes minor errors in all her work, her letters must be read very carefully, as there are frequently errors. Her longer pieces of work contain major errors, such as omitting whole paragraphs, phrases, etc., in short she is very careless. If she makes an error and is asked to correct it, she spends several minutes loudly justifying the error on the basis of overexhaustion due to overwork, or to mistreatment by members of the department.

She terrorizes the secretaries whom she supervises. At least two have been reduced to tears by her browbeating and telling them loudly how stupid and inefficient they are so that no one can escape hearing. Supervision of the Day Care report temporary secretaries was taken away from her for this reason; a professional spends time breaking them in and supervising them in order to protect them from N____, hoping that they will not quit.

She is sometimes insubordinate, either refusing or loudly protesting work a professional has given her, even when the professional has not set a deadline, but in fact has asked her to do it when she has time.

She tries to order the professionals around, has even ordered one professional to retype a draft of a letter before she, N____, would copy it. She tries to summon professionals to her desk by loudly calling them across the room.

Sometimes if she is given material to do at 4:15 or 4:30, she puts it in her folder for the next morning and goes to the ladies' room to get ready to leave. Sometimes when she is given work late in the afternoon she laughs scornfully and recites the list of all the people she works for, before starting to type the work, then complains aloud while she does it.

She rewrites professionals' material according to her own ideas of grammar, punctuation and language. She has been so impolite to some people who have called on the telephone that they have stopped leaving messages with her. At the same time she objects vehemently if anyone calls in and leaves a message at the switchboard rather than with her.

She has called a professional's home to see if she had gone home instead of to the meeting she had told N＿＿＿ she was going to. She wastes a great deal of time by complaining loudly at her desk or by walking around and complaining loudly to anyone who will listen, even, in fact, to people who turn their back and try not to listen. She tells her personal problems loudly to anyone who will listen.

She expresses a resentment at the fact that the Assistant Head has a full-time secretary whom N＿＿＿ does not supervise. She tries to act as the supervisor of the whole department, both secretaries and professionals.

Signed LW ＿＿＿

JR ＿＿＿

NK ＿＿＿

SE ＿＿＿

(Signature on ML's return)

However, in *Woodward's Spring Shop, Inc.,* the arbitrator overturned a discharge, because the employer had based the discharge, not upon a record of poor attitude, but upon a single incident similar to an earlier one which the employer had tolerated.[4]

Even where there is a less grievous but similarly well-established and documented pattern of consistent complaining and minor troublemaking, as in the *National Council of Jewish Women* case, arbitrators are generally willing to sustain fairly severe discipline, particularly where the poor attitude is accompanied by inadequate or borderline job performance. However, for discipline to be sustained, the employer must have adequately documented the employee's conduct and must have properly warned the employee.[5]

The factors of central importance to these types of cases are that (1) the employee's bad attitude continued over a long period of time; (2) the employer made good-faith efforts to improve the situation by less drastic measures, with no corresponding effort on the employee's part; (3) the employee's conduct continued unabated up to the time of discipline; and (4) the employee's attitude had some negative effect on the workplace, such as causing general morale to drop or creating emotional disturbances in other specified employees.[6]

However, there must also be evidence to support the contention that the situation was both extreme and irremediable, that every effort had been made to resolve the problem in other ways, or that the final confrontation, or incident, was severe enough to warrant discharge. Unless there is a very substantial history of an unacceptable attitude or other behavior which would usually support discharge, arbitrators require a showing of progressive discipline before they will sustain a discharge for poor attitude.[7]

Finally, evidence is frequently required showing that the employee's attitude had a demonstrably negative impact on either his own job performance, the job performance of other employees, or on some other aspect of the employer's business. In *Mead Corp.*, for instance, the employee was justifiably discharged when his discourteous conduct with customers resulted in his being barred from making any further deliveries to that location.[8] The employer had previously counseled the employee on numerous occasions about his attitude and behavior. While the terms of the discharge were stated as discourtesy to customers, it was obvious that the employee's troubles stemmed from his poor attitude and the material and adverse effect this attitude had on his job performance.[9]

It is important to note that there are only a limited number of cases on bad attitude, and as a result, arbitrators generally focus on specific testimony to support their awards. It is, therefore, hard to accurately assess how extreme an employee's attitude problems must be before he can be discharged. However, an employee's bad attitude may act effectively as an additional ground for discipline where an employee's inadequate job performance, or other undesirable conduct, alone would not sustain the discipline. Further, in dealing with a persistent attitude problem, the employer's best course would be to thoroughly document incidences where the employee's poor attitude has a demonstrably negative effect on the employer's business, as well as to document the steps taken to help the employee improve. Where a substantial number of such occurrences exist, their cumulative effect will produce a justifiable cause for discipline.

Key Points

1   *The employee's poor attitude should have caused, or have been combined with, other unacceptable conduct.*

Examples:

Employee *A*, a skilled mechanic, made frequent complaints about work assignments, the work environment, etc. He had never actually refused to do a specific project that he was ordered to do. He was discharged, during an argument with the manager, on the basis of his stated intention of refusing to do certain work in the future. The arbitrator reinstated him, but without backpay or seniority credit for the period of discharge.

Employee *B* was a machine operator who complained continually about work assignments, management, etc. He also had an above-average rate of defective output and failed to follow instructions. He was discharged without any progressive discipline or prior warning. Noting the cumulative effect of inadequate job performance and poor attitude over a period of time, the arbitrator sustained the discharge.

Employee *C* was a frequent complainer about work assignments, work environment, etc. Although a constant complainer, however, he never actually refused to do a job. *C*'s production was excellent. On a particular day *C* was directed to operate a second machine along with his original assignment, and he complained. While operating the two machines, he said to his supervisor that the next time he was told to operate two machines at the same time, he would refuse. The supervisor finally had had enough and suspended him. The arbitrator reinstated *C* on the basis that he had never actually refused to do the work and that his production appeared to be unaffected by his complaining.

Guidelines

If an employee's work record is otherwise good and the employee is not causing problems with the other employees, poor attitude alone will not support discharge, although it may justify milder forms of discipline. However, if an employee is not performing well and/or is creating substantial amounts of discontent among the other employees, more severe forms of discipline are likely to be upheld.

Relevant Cases

Woodward's Spring Shop, Inc. (Pinkus), 63 LA 367;
National Council of Jewish Women, Inc. (Scheiber), 57 LA 980;
Tex-A-Panel Mfg. Co. (Ray), 62 LA 272;
Gardner Motors, Inc. (Lightner), 64 LA 428;
Craftool Company, Inc. (Weiss), 63 LA 1031;
Safeway Stores, Inc. (Gould), 64 LA 563;
Apollo Merchandisers Corp. (Roumell), 70 LA 614;
Mead Corp. (Morgan), 75 LA 957.

2 *The employee's attitude must have affected the morale or performance of other employees.*

Examples:

Employee *A* had a long history of continually complaining about her work; downgrading other employees; loud, constant, distracting talk; refusing to do minor tasks or doing them carelessly; being rude to superiors; and generally poisoning the atmosphere of the workplace. In addition, there was substantial testimony that this employee's attitude and conduct had a detrimental effect on the efficiency and morale of all the other employees, and even the employees who testified on her behalf characterized her behavior as abrasive. The employee's discharge for bad attitude and general misconduct was upheld in spite of the fact that she had 21 years of seniority.

Employee B was rude and uncooperative and was discharged on the basis that he had created friction among fellow employees. Although there was evidence of a bad attitude, the testimony of other employees failed to support the charges that B's attitude had seriously affected the morale of the workplace and was the primary cause of other employees leaving, or threatening to leave, their jobs. The arbitrator, therefore, reinstated the employee.

Guidelines

Where the employee's negative attitude and behavior is extreme enough to have a detrimental effect on the work performance or morale of other employees, severe discipline may be justified. However, there must be substantial and well-documented evidence of both the employee's misconduct and its effects on other employees, and the charges must be supported by the testimony of other employees.

Relevant Cases

Ourisman Chevrolet (Robertson), 56 LA 512;
National Council of Jewish Women, Inc. (Scheiber), 57 LA 980;
Tex-A-Panel Mfg. Co. (Ray), 62 LA 272;
Gardner Motors, Inc. (Lightner), 64 LA 428;
Mead Corp. (Morgan), 75 LA 957.

3   *The employee's conduct should have had an effect on customer relations, where relevant.*

Examples:

Employee A, who had a history of complaining, was fired after engaging in a loud and angry argument with the manager in front of a customer. The arbitrator reversed the discharge on the grounds that there was neither evidence of an effect on customer relations nor was there any other independent grounds for supporting the discharge. The employee, upon agreeing not to repeat the conduct in the future, was reinstated without backpay.

Employee *B*, a newspaper reporter, wrote an article for a competing magazine in which he made extensive criticisms and attacks on the newspaper which employed him. Subsequently, he repeated his negative comments about his employer on talk shows and on other public occasions. A discharge on grounds of disloyalty was upheld, because both the public nature of his attacks on the paper and the unnecessarily vindictive tone in which they were delivered made it impossible for the employer to continue in a working relationship with its employee.

Guidelines

Arbitrators consider any conflict, or poor relationship, between an employer and an employee which is made public or which otherwise affects the employer's relationship with its customers or clientele to be more serious a breach than a dispute which is contained within the workplace. Unnecessarily tarnishing the employer's public image may support more severe discipline than mere interoffice griping. The arbitrator may evaluate the employee's attitude and/or disloyalty in determining what discipline would be appropriate for this type of conduct.

Relevant Cases

Woodward's Spring Shop, Inc. (Pinkus), 63 LA 367;
Elizabeth Horton Memorial Hospital (Sandler), 64 LA 96;
Safeway Stores, Inc. (Gould), 64 LA 563;
Corley Distributing Co., Inc. (Ipavec), 68 LA 513;
Triple L. Enterprises (Jeanney),70 LA 97.

4   *Progressive discipline should have been imposed and proven to be unsuccessful.*

Examples:

Employee *A* had received two warning notices over a period of eight months. The first was for a bad attitude, and the second, for a specific job mistake. Her transfer to a less desirable department was not upheld by the arbitrator, because the warnings were too far apart and for two different problems. The arbitrator noted that the employer's attempts to improve her attitude and performance by less drastic measures were insufficient and that the consequences of her behavior were never made clear to her prior to the transfer.

Employee *B* had been put on probation for six months because of a bad attitude and the poor quality of his work. His supervisors attempted to counsel him repeatedly and warned him that failure to improve would result in more severe discipline. He made no effort to improve either his attitude or the quality of his work. The arbitrator sustained the discharge, since *B* had been given every chance to solve his problems, had not filed a grievance over the prior warnings, and had refused to correct his attitude.

Employee *C* was a complainer: His complaints were not focused, but everything having to do with the work, the employer, the work environment, and the other employees was subject to his complaints. Disgusted with the situation, *C*'s supervisor finally called him in and told him that unless he stopped his complaining he would be discharged. *C* pointed to his perfect attendance and to his productivity as the best in the company. He added that his personal opinions were irrelevant and that he could only be disciplined for bad work. The next day he was heard complaining to another employee about the temperature in the plant. The supervisor discharged him. The arbitrator reinstated the employee, but without backpay. Although the employee had been specifically warned about the continuance of his behavior, the arbitrator found that discharge was too severe. There had been too little done by the employer to impress upon the employee the seriousness with which it viewed his conduct.

Guidelines

Arbitrators are much more willing to support the discipline imposed when the employee has been given prior warnings, counseling, and an opportunity to improve. Discharge or severe discipline is not viewed as an appropriate remedy unless there are other, independent grounds to support it; there is a long history of an unacceptable attitude; and there have been repeated attempts to solve the problem with less drastic penalties. Attitude problems must be very extreme before they will suffice to support severe disciplinary

> **Guidelines**—contd.
>
> measures. Even then the offense is not that the employee exhibited a poor attitude, but that the employee obstinately refused to respond to the employer's good-faith effort to correct the situation in an affirmative way.

Relevant Cases

Uarco Company, Inc. (Gibson), 58 LA 1021;
Craftool Company, Inc. (Weiss), 63 LA 1031;
Gardner Motors, Inc. (Lightner), 64 LA 428;
Tex-A-Panel Mfg. Co. (Ray), 62 LA 272;
National Council of Jewish Women, Inc. (Scheiber), 57 LA 980;
Woodward's Spring Shop, Inc. (Pinkus), 63 LA 367;
Ourisman Chevrolet (Robertson), 56 LA 512;
Safeway Stores, Inc. (Gould), 64 LA 563;
Apollo Merchandisers Corp. (Roumell), 70 LA 614.

Notes to Chapter 8

1. *Uarco Company Inc.* (Gibson), 58 LA 1021.
2. *Id.*, at 1022.
3. *Nat'l Council of Jewish Women, Inc.* (Scheiber), 57 LA 980.
4. *Woodward's Spring Shop, Inc.* (Pinkus), 63 LA 367.
5. *See Craftool Company, Inc.* (Weiss), 63 LA 1031 (transfer denied); *Ourisman Chevrolet* (Robertson), 56 LA 512 (discharge denied); *Uarco Co., Inc., supra*, note 1 (discharge denied); *Apollo Merchandisers Corp.* (Roumell), 70 LA 614 (discharge denied).
6. *See Gardner Motors, Inc.* (Lightner), 64 LA 428; *Tex-a-Panel Mfg. Co.* (Ray), 62 LA 272 (discharge sustained); *Nat'l Council of Jewish Women, Inc., supra*, note 3.
7. *See Uarco Company, Inc., supra*, note 1 (discharge sustained); *Nat'l Council of Jewish Women, Inc., supra*, note 3 (discharge sustained); *Mead Corp.* (Morgan), 75 LA 957 (discharge sustained).
8. *Mead Corp., supra*, note 7.
9. *See also Elizabeth Horton Memorial Hospital* (Sandler), 64 LA 96 (discharge sustained); *Safeway Stores, Inc.* (Gould), 64 LA 563 (discharge denied); *Corley Distributing, Inc.* (Ipavec), 68 LA 513 (discharge sustained); *Triple L. Enterprises* (Jeanney), 70 LA 97 (discharge reduced to a suspension); *Nat'l Council of Jewish Women, Inc., supra*, note 3.

9

Carelessness and Negligence

Issue: Whether an employee may be discharged or otherwise disciplined for carelessness and negligence.

Principle: An employee may be discharged, or otherwise disciplined, for carelessness and negligence where an employer can sustain the burden of proving that the employee's actions resulted in job performance well below that of similarly positioned coworkers. An employer does not have to have applied progressive discipline for a discharge to be sustained if the employee's act was very costly to the employer or was extremely hazardous to others.

Considerations

1. Whether the frequency and/or nature of the employee's actions reflect a job performance well below that of coworkers in similar positions;
2. Whether the performance expected of the employee was within his or her experience, training, and physical capabilities;
3. Whether the employee was made aware of his or her responsibilities by the company through prior notifications or warnings;
4. Whether the employee's actions were costly to the company; *i.e.*, the actions resulted in damage to equipment or product, significant lost time, etc.; or the actions created a hazardous condition for coworkers or others;

109

5. Whether the company has handled analogous situations in the same fashion.

Discussion: In general, careless and negligent actions by employees take three forms: negligence or carelessness which results in inefficiency or in the production of an inordinate amount of scrap; negligence or carelessness which causes damage to machinery or product; and negligence or carelessness which constitutes unsafe practices. The different forms of carelessness and negligence encountered by arbitrators have resulted in a varying emphasis placed on the several relevant considerations. In cases of this kind, the employee's prior record with the company appears to be an especially significant factor in the arbitrator's determination.

Where an employee's negligence results in inefficiency, a comparison of the employee's performance with that of others in the same job will weigh heavily in the arbitrator's decision.[1] In such a case, it is unlikely that a discharge will be sustained, however, unless the company has employed a system of progressive discipline.

In *National Gypsum Co.,* for example, an employee was discharged for carelessness and negligence following his ninth accident in two and one-half years.[2] In his defense, the employee claimed that only one of the accidents was his fault. He stated that six of the accidents were clearly due to the generally unsafe working conditions and that only one accident resulted in time lost. The arbitrator found, however, that the other employees in the area had worked without accidents. Consequently, the arbitrator reasoned, the employee had been careless. Moreover, the employee had received counseling, during which he had stated that the work environment made him nervous. In a spirit of humanity, the arbitrator concluded that the discharge was for the good of the employee.

Arbitrators frequently assess the attitude of an employee when determining whether the employee would continue to be careless or negligent on the job and whether any further discipline, less than discharge, would have any beneficial effect. In *Rinker Materials Corp.,* for instance, the discharge of a truck driver was sustained following his third accident.[3] While waiting for a traffic light to change, the employee's foot slipped off the brake because something was on his shoe, and the truck rammed into the rear of a car. At the time, the truck was two feet behind the car, in violation of the company's traffic manual which specified that at least one vehicle space must be maintained between the driver's truck and a vehicle in front. During the arbitration, the employee testified that the manual was unreasonable and that he would continue to abide by its rules only on a selective basis. Further, the driver stated that having foreign substances on his shoes was not uncommon. Nevertheless, he had not checked to see if that was the case in this instance. The arbitrator, obviously alarmed by the employee's attitude, sustained the discharge on the basis that the employee's attitude evidenced a proclivity for future negligence.

In *Vulcan-Hart Corporation,* the employee had a history of many injuries to his hands, eyes, and feet, caused, primarily, by the employee's refusal to use available safety equipment. Although he had been warned that continuing to practice unsafe behavior would result in his discharge, the employee did not alter his work habits. The arbitrator, apparently concluding that the employee's attitude offered little hope for an improved work history, sustained the discharge.[4]

Although progressive discipline is usually a necessary prelude to discharge for negligence or carelessness, a very serious offense committed by an employee may abrogate the need for previous reprimands or suspensions. For example, a discharge may be sustained if the employee's carelessness or negligence seriously endangers the lives of others. Also, a discharge without prior discipline may be upheld, if an adequately trained, experienced employee damages equipment through negligence or carelessness which results in great expense to the company; this is particularly true when the amount of damage is probative of the care taken by the employee.[5]

In *Hess Oil Virgin Islands Corp.,* the arbitrator found that the employer had just cause for discharging an employee for gross negligence, even though there had been no prior discipline.[6] In that case, the employee had failed to shut off a gas valve when the flame in a heater went out, and as a result, an explosion caused substantial damage. Even though the employee had only one week's on-the-job experience, she had been trained, and the arbitrator found that she had failed to follow the prescribed emergency procedures. Her negligence not only resulted in severe property damage, but also created a potential danger to other employees. The seriousness of the gross negligence justified the summary discharge.

Similarly, the summary discharge of an employee was approved in *Rohr Industries, Inc.*[7] In that case, an employee had misdrilled a part through negligence. The part disappeared; and the arbitrator concluded that the employee had sought, through deception, to conceal his act. The arbitrator found that the negligence, combined with the dishonest act of concealment, justified the employee's dismissal without prior, intermediate disciplinary steps.

Key Points

1 *The frequency and/or nature of the employee's carelessness or negligence must be reflected in the employee's job performance and must be more excessive than that of coworkers in similar positions.*

Examples:

Employee *A* failed to immediately push an emergency stop button, when trouble was encountered along a production line. Significant time was lost in rectifying the situation, and the supervisor discharged the employee. The arbitrator, noting that other employees have made similar judgmental errors, reinstated the employee.

Employee *B*, a truck driver, had nearly the worst accident record out of 20 drivers. After his third avoidable accident in the most recent three-month period, he was discharged. The arbitrator sustained the discharge.

Guidelines

To uphold disciplinary action for negligence or carelessness, the employer must show that the employee, relative to others in similar jobs, performed significantly worse than average. Negligence which has recurred frequently within a short time will strengthen the company's position.

Relevant Cases

Wheeling-Pittsburgh Steel Corp. (Chockley), 74 LA 793;
VRN International (Vause), 74 LA 806;
Beatrice Foods Co. (Gradwohl), 74 LA 1008;
S&T Industries, Inc. (Madden), 73 LA 857;
United Parcel Service, Inc. (Das), 73 LA 1308;
Reynolds Metals Co. (Frost), 72 LA 1051;
Associated School Bus Service (Krebs), 72 LA 859.
United Metal Trades Assn. (Stephen), 66 LA 1342;
Shop Rite Foods, Inc. (Weiss), 67 LA 159;
Vulcan-Hart Corp. (Ghiz), 78 LA 59;
Greenlee Bros. & Co. (Rezler), 67 LA 686;
National Gypsum Co. (Klaiber), 78 LA 226.

2 ✗ *The performance expected of the employee must have been within his or her experience, training, and physical capabilities.*

Examples:

Employee *A* neglected to check a valve on a tank, and subsequently the tank collapsed. Although the valve-checking procedure did not appear in the operations manual, the employee was discharged. Finding that the employee had been adequately trained by another employee with respect to checking the valve, the arbitrator sustained the discharge.

Employee *B,* after having been promoted to a more difficult clerical position, was discharged for having a higher error ratio than employees who had previously held the position. The arbitrator reinstated the employee, finding that the company had not given the employee suitable time to adjust to the new job.

Guidelines

To sustain disciplinary action for carelessness or negligence, an employer must show that the employee was properly trained, had the job experience, and had the physical capability to do the job properly. Careless or negligent work is identified by poor job results that could have been avoided by the employee. Therefore if a poor work performance is the result of insufficient training or experience, discipline is inappropriate.

Relevant Cases

Rinker Materials Corp. (Lurie), 78 LA 44;
Vulcan-Hart Corp. (Ghiz), 78 LA 59;
National Gypsum Co. (Klaiber), 78 LA 226;
Universal Camshaft & Heat Treat (Keefe), 76 LA 808;
VRN International (Vause), 74 LA 806;
Neville Chemical Co. (Parkinson), 74 LA 814;
S&T Industries, Inc. (Madden), 73 LA 857;
Hess Oil Virgin Islands Corp. (Berkman), 72 LA 81;
Reynolds Metals (Frost), 72 LA 1051;
Standard Oil of California, Western Operations (Walsh), 65 LA 829;
Gates Chevrolet (Coyle), 63 LA 753;
Whitfield Tank Lines, Inc. (Cohen), 62 LA 934;
Santiam Southern Corp. (Mann), 68 LA 46.

3 *The company must have warned or notified the employee of his or her responsibilities prior to the disciplinary action.*

Examples:

Employee *A*, a welder, produced several bad welds and was discharged. Within the preceding two months the company had issued general warnings twice to all welders that improper welds would be cause for dismissal. The arbitrator commuted the discharge to a suspension, finding that the employee was entitled to specific warnings that his work was unsatisfactory.

Employee *B*, a clerk, made numerous errors and was discharged. Although the employee had received no prior written warnings, she had been counseled by superiors to be more attentive to her work. The arbitrator sustained the discharge.

Guidelines

An arbitrator is more likely to sustain severe discipline for negligence or carelessness if the employee has been warned or reprimanded for negligence in the past. The company's position is enhanced if the employee was found again to be in violation of the employer's standards soon after a warning had been issued.

Relevant Cases

Pet Incorporated (Jason), 76 LA 292;
VRN International (Vause), 74 LA 806;
Neville Chemical Co. (Parkinson), 74 LA 814;
Beatrice Foods Co. (Gradwohl), 74 LA 1008;
FMC Corp. (Marlatt), 73 LA 705;
S&T Industries, Inc. (Madden), 73 LA 857;
United Parcel Service, Inc. (Das), 73 LA 1308;
Reynolds Metals Co. (Frost), 72 LA 1051;
Canron, Inc. (Marcus), 72 LA 1310;
Bonded Scale & Machine Co. (Modjeska), 72 LA 520;
Associated School Bus Service (Krebs), 72 LA 859;
Precision Extrusions, Inc. (Epstein), 61 LA 572;
Tex-A-Panel Mfg. Co. (Ray), 62 LA 272;
Whitfield Tank Lines, Inc. (Cohen), 62 LA 934;
United Metro, Inc. (Schutz), 64 LA 7;
May Dept. Stores Co., Kaufmann Div. (Dean), 64 LA 122;
American Standard Inc. (Biddinger), 64 LA 159;
West Chemical Prod. Inc. (Dykstra), 63 LA 610;

Kelsey-Hayes (Keefe), 64 LA 740;
Transport Body Services (Raffaele), 65 LA 894;
Station WPLG-TV (Serot), 66 LA 805;
Greyhound Lines, Inc. (Larkin), 67 LA 483;
Michel Warehousing Corp. (Mallet-Prevost), 67 LA 565;
S&T Industries, Inc. (Madden), 73 LA 857;
Huntingdon Alloys, Inc. (Shanker), 73 LA 1050;
Neville Chemical Co. (Parkinson), 74 LA 814;
Vulcan-Hart Corporation (Ghiz), 78 LA 59;
National Gypsum Co. (Klaiber), 78 LA 226.

4   *The employee's actions must have been costly to the company, i.e., the actions resulted in damage to equipment or product, significant lost time, etc.*

Examples:

Employee *A* neglected to adjust a valve on a tank. Subsequently, the tank collapsed, resulting in the loss of the tank as well as a large quantity of valuable chemicals. *A*'s carelessness cost the company over $10,000. The employee was discharged, and the discharge was sustained by the arbitrator.

Employee *B*, a truck driver, had two avoidable accidents within a six-month period, resulting in his discharge pursuant to a company policy requiring dismissal for two accidents. The arbitrator, noting that the amount of vehicle damage was minimal and expressing some question about whether the accidents had, in fact, been avoidable, reinstated the employee with backpay.

Employee *C* carelessly drove a forklift into a stack of piled skids and knocked it over. One of the falling skids narrowly missed a coemployee working in the area. *C*'s employment history was average and contained no record of any prior carelessness. Nevertheless *C* was discharged. The arbitrator sustained the discharge, finding *C* to have been wantonly in disregard for the safety of others.

Guidelines

Discharge is more readily upheld when the employee's negligence results in great expense to the company; this is particularly so if the amount of damage is probative of the care exercised by the employee. Expense to the company can take forms other than damaged

> **Guidelines**—*contd.*
>
> equipment or product. Lost time and the inability of other workers to perform their jobs because of the employee's negligence can be costly.

Relevant Cases

Hoerner Waldorf Champion International Corp. (Newmark), 75 LA 416;
Wheeling-Pittsburgh Steel Corp. (Chockley), 74 LA 793;
Neville Chemical Co. (Parkinson), 74 LA 814;
FMC Corp. (Marlatt), 73 LA 705;
Hinckley & Schmitt (Goldberg), 73 LA 654;
Hess Oil Virgin Islands Corp. (Berkman), 72 LA 81;
Reynolds Metals Co. (Frost), 72 LA 1051;
Gates Chevrolet Co. (Coyle), 63 LA 753;
Rohr Industries, Inc. (Lennard), 65 LA 982;
Buegers Mining & Mfg. (Grooms), 61 LA 952;
Gulf Printing Co. (Lilly), 61 LA 1174;
VCA of New Jersey (Aiges), 62 LA 951;
Whitfield Tank Lines, Inc. (Cohen), 62 LA 934;
Corns Truck & Tractor, Inc. (Cowan), 63 LA 828;
United-Metro, Inc. (Schutz), 64 LA 7;
General Services Administration (Lubic), 75 LA 1158.

5   *It must be shown that the employee's actions could have created a hazardous condition for coworkers or others.*

Examples:

Employee *A*, a school bus driver, negligently stopped her bus on a railroad crossing to lecture unruly students. Although she had no prior serious offenses on her record, she was discharged. The arbitrator sustained the discharge.

Employee *B*, a machinist, was found sleeping on the job. The employee was discharged by the company, which claimed that the employee, by falling asleep, had created a hazard to himself and coworkers. The arbitrator commuted the discharge to a suspension, noting that the employee had been on the second leg of a double shift and had not had an opportunity to rest.

Employee *C*'s careless driving of a forklift caused a tire to puncture. The cost to the company was $50 for tire repair and one hour lost time in the use of equipment. *C* was discharged. The arbitrator reinstated *C*, noting the minimal cost created by the employee's carelessness.

Guidelines

Negligence by an employee which endangers the lives of others may be cause for discharge without progressive discipline. However, factors may be present which act to mitigate the offense, and these will be taken into account, even when the employee has created a significant hazard.

Relevant Cases

Hoerner Waldorf Champion International Corp. (Newmark), 75 LA 416;

FMC Corp. (Marlatt), 73 LA 705;

Hess Oil Virgin Islands Corp. (Berkman), 72 LA 81;

Bonded Scale & Machine Co. (Modjeska), 72 LA 520;

Standard Oil of California, Western Operations (Walsh), 65 LA 829;

Associated School Bus Service (Krebs), 72 LA 859;

National Gypsum Co. (Klaiber), 78 LA 226.

6 *The company's prior practice must have been consistent in the handling of analogous situations.*

Examples:

Employee *A*, a school bus driver, received a traffic citation for speeding and was discharged. The arbitrator reinstated the employee, noting that two other drivers had received traffic citations during the preceding two years and had not been disciplined.

Employee *B*, a quality control inspector, carelessly allowed an excessive amount of scrap to be produced. He was discharged, although the company had not discharged two other inspectors who had permitted an excessive amount of scrap to be produced. The arbitrator sustained the discharge, finding that the circumstances surrounding the previous cases differed from the case in question.

Guidelines

Two elements must be analyzed when comparing a company's present actions with its past actions in other cases—the severity of the discipline imposed and the circumstances accompanying the respective cases. In

---

> **Guidelines**—*contd.*
>
> general, if the circumstances are the same, discipline
> which departs from past practice reflects negatively on
> the company's treatment of the employee and on its
> view of the severity of the offense.

Relevant Cases

Wheeling-Pittsburgh Steel Corp. (Chockley), 74 LA 793;
St. John Transportation Co. (Modjeska), 73 LA 1156;
Reynolds Metal Co. (Frost), 72 LA 1051;
Canron, Inc. (Marcus), 72 LA 1310.

Notes to Chapter 9

1. *United Metal Trades Assn.* (Stephen), 66 LA 1342; *Shop Rite Foods, Inc.* (Weiss), 67 LA 159; *Greenlee Bros. & Co.* (Rezler), 67 LA 686.
2. *National Gypsum Co.* (Klaiber), 78 LA 226.
3. *Rinker Materials Corp.* (Lurie), 78 LA 44.
4. *Vulcan-Hart Corporation* (Ghiz), 78 LA 59.
5. *See generally Standard Oil Co. of California, Western Operations* (Walsh), 65 LA 829; *Gates Chevrolet Co.* (Coyle), 63 LA 753; *Rohr Indus., Inc.* (Lennard), 65 LA 982; *Hess Oil Virgin Islands Corp.* (Berkman), 72 LA 81; *Buegers Mining & Mfg. Co.* (Grooms), 61 LA 952; *Gulf Printing Co.* (Lilly), 61 LA 1174; *General Services Admin.* (Lubic), 75 LA 1158.
6. *Hess Oil Virgin Islands Corp., supra,* note 5.
7. *Rohr Indus., Inc., supra,* note 5.

10

Dishonesty or Falsification of Company Records

Issue: Whether an employee may be discharged or otherwise disciplined for dishonesty or falsification of company records.

Principle: An employee may be discharged or otherwise disciplined for dishonesty or falsification of company records where the employer can sustain the burden of proving that the employee acted with knowledge of the wrongfulness of the act and with intent to defraud the company. A prior good work record may be insufficient to mitigate a discharge, because the offense is perceived as too serious.

Considerations:
1. Whether the employee's act was a willful, deliberate attempt to defraud the company;
2. Whether the employee attempts to cover up the conduct, or whether upon discovery the employee denies the act or intent to deceive;
3. Whether the employee knew when committing the offense that, if caught, he or she would be subject to discipline;
4. In cases of employment application falsifications, whether the denial or omission of facts would have prevented the hire of the employee, if the facts had been known, or whether sufficient time had elapsed between the act of falsification and its discovery to allow the employee to develop an acceptable work

119

record, which may serve to lessen the severity of the offense;

5. Whether the dishonest act had a detrimental effect on the employer;
6. Whether the company acted expeditiously upon discovery of the falsification or dishonesty, and/or whether the company evidenced willingness to overlook the conduct under certain conditions;
7. Whether the company's past practice in handling similar cases has been applied;
8. Whether the employee's work record has been taken into consideration.

Discussion: Dishonesty, or the falsification of company records, appears to be one of those causes for discipline which are so serious that arbitrators often do not insist upon progressive discipline. In such situations, the falsification of company records is in the same class as the theft of company property. In fact, when the dishonesty involves falsification of records used in incentive systems, expense accounts, etc., the two offenses are closely related.[1]

Falsification of Company Records

As with cases of theft, the most crucial aspect of these cases is often one of proof. If the company can establish that the employee willfully committed a dishonest act for his or her own benefit and that this act had some significant adverse or detrimental effect upon the employer, the discharge will be sustained, absent a gross procedural error.

In *Pacific Telephone and Telegraph Co.,* for instance, an employee was reinstated with backpay where the employer was unable to prove that the employee acted with the intent to deceive for the purpose of obtaining a benefit to which he would have been otherwise unentitled.[2] In that case, the employee was out of the plant due to a summons for jury duty. The employer's contract required employees to return to work upon conclusion of their jury duty, if it ended at a reasonable time prior to the end of the employees' workday. The employee was dismissed by the court and was told to go home and to remain "on call." When the employee did not report for work, stating that he was on jury duty, and later requested jury duty pay for those days, he was terminated. The arbitrator found "that, rather than trying to deceive the Company, the Grievant simply believed that he had a continuous obligation for jury service during those entire ten days."[3]

Falsification of company records may be cause for discipline, even if it has no economic effect on the employer. In *Dresser Industries, Inc., Galion Manufacturing Division,* for example, four employees were justifiably discharged for falsifying production records, even though they had not been paid for more work than they actually performed.[4] The employees were incentive workers who were required to submit their job tickets at the end of their shift. These tickets were then factored into a formula to establish the actual amount of pay for the week. Unknown to the employer, the employees were withholding job tickets and "banking" them for use at a later time. The time came just before Christmas, when the employees decided to pay themselves a "bonus." When the number of job tickets turned in produced a larger than normal payroll for the week, the employer discovered the scheme. All four employees were discharged for falsifying production records. Even though the employees' scheme had resulted in payment to them for work actually done and no more, the arbitrator sustained the discharges for falsification of records.

Unlike their treatment of theft cases, many arbitrators appear to be less demanding in the quantum of proof required in cases involving misrepresentation. Generally a preponderance of the evidence is acceptable, as opposed to proof beyond a reasonable doubt.[5] However, there is significant support amongst arbitrators for a heightened standard of burden of proof. Arbitrator Kanowitz in *Pacific Telephone and Telegraph Co.* for instance, stated that

> ... the Arbitrator is in accord with the overwhelming view of arbitrators that an employer who discharges an employee for alleged dishonesty must establish the facts of that dishonesty by proof beyond a reasonable doubt or at least by clear and convincing evidence. *See, e.g., Kroger Co.,* 25 LA 906, 908 (Smith, 1955); *George H. Dentler & Sons,* 42 LA 954, 956 (Boles, 1964); *Retail Clerks International Ass'n, Local 782,* 69-ARB Par. 8552 (Brothwell, 1969). The consequences for an employee of being discharged for dishonesty, not only in terms of his immediate loss of employment but also in terms of his future employment prospects, are so severe, that no less stringent standard is reasonable under the circumstances. Moreover, as indicated in the course of the hearing in this case, the Company, in order to prevail, must establish that, pursuant to its heightened burden of proof, it had sufficient information at the time it discharged the Grievant for dishonesty to justify the discharge at that time.[6]

The presence of significant arbitral opinion in favor of a more stringent burden is due, primarily, to the issue's close kinship to an offense which is punishable under the criminal law.

Because arbitrators perceive the offense to be a serious one and are apparently willing to concede that progressive discipline is inappropriate in most cases of serious dishonesty, they are less likely to reinstate the employee—but, if they did, it would be without backpay or any other mitigation of the full penalty. Either the employer's disciplinary action is sustained or it is completely voided and the employee made whole.[7]

Employment Application Falsification

Employment application falsification requires special comment, not only because of its frequency, but also because the dishonesty involved differs somewhat from other types of dishonesty. The most frequent instances of application falsification involve prior records of either criminal activities or medical conditions. Employers do not normally discipline employees for employment application falsification unless the employer-employee relationship is affected or unless the employee's work performance is somehow affected by his or her moral or physical capabilities. On the other hand, it may be that other forms of falsification are simply not discovered or that unions do not contest the disciplinary action taken in other cases. Relevant cases are listed under Key Points 3 and 4.

Considerations: Employment Application Falsification

1. Whether the information concealed was important, *i.e.*, would the employer have hired the applicant had it known the information at the time of application;
2. Whether the applicant knowingly and deliberately sought to conceal the information for the purpose of deceiving the employer;
3. Whether the length of time which passed between the application falsification and its discovery, as well as the record of the employee during the interim period, made the falsification immaterial.

Discussion: A single case provides a rather comprehensive review of situations met with in dealing with falsification of employment applications, and the case deserves special note. In *Dart Industries, Inc.*, arbitrator Greene was presented with four discharges for application falsification.[8] Each of these cases involved the employees' answers, or lack of answers, to a series of questions having to do with an applicant's arrest and conviction record. Setting aside and leaving to the courts the question of whether an employer has the right to ask about arrest records, Arbitrator Greene made the following dispositions:

1. Employee A answered "No" to the question of whether he had ever been arrested. When approached later about a substantial arrest and conviction record, A denied having filled out the application and the accuracy of the record. Finding that A evidenced substantial untrustworthiness, Greene sustained the discharge.
2. Employee B left the questions on the application form which had to do with arrests and convictions blank. When confronted by the employer, B then denied the accuracy of the police record. Finding B's answers and demeanor evasive and unreliable, Greene sustained the discharge.
3. Employee C answered "No" to the arrest and conviction questions. His record, however, revealed a conviction for disorderly conduct. C was of limited intelligence and education and had not received help in filling out the application. The company representative testified that had C revealed the conviction he would have nonetheless been hired. Greene reinstated C with partial backpay.
4. Employee D admitted to one arrest and conviction for nonsupport, but he failed to reveal numerous arrests. Because D evidenced no untrustworthiness at the arbitration and honestly believed his arrests, which ended with dismissals on the basis of mistaken identity, did not have to be revealed, Greene reinstated D with partial backpay.

In cases involving the falsification of time cards or of work unit slips or other kinds of dishonesty in the workplace which closely parallel theft, arbitrators are reluctant to apply any mitigating circumstances and will sustain a discharge upon proof of a willful attempt by the employee to defraud or cheat the company. In cases involving employment application dishonesty, however, arbitrators look to the materiality of the deception and are much more likely to void the discharge. There seems to be at least a tacit understanding that progressive discipline can only play a very limited role. How, for instance, can progressive discipline be justified in the case of falsification of an employment application? The dishonest act was finite and incapable of repetition. Either the misrepresentation was material and the discharge was warranted or it was not.

Key Points:

1   *The employee's act must have been a willful, deliberate attempt to defraud the company, and the employee must have had the knowledge that the deception, if discovered, would result in discipline.*

Examples:

The department supervisor saw employee *A* punch in *B*'s time card. The supervisor then saw *B* come in late, look at his card, and go to his work station. At the end of the payroll period, the supervisor went to *B* and asked him if his time card was accurate. *B* said it was. *A* was discharged for punching in *B*'s card, and *B* was discharged for accepting and participating in *A*'s dishonest act. Both discharges were sustained by the arbitrator.

Employee *C*'s supervisor saw her punch in, return to the locker room, and report to her work station fifteen minutes after her shift had begun. *C* was discharged. The discharge was denied. The arbitrator reinstated *C* without backpay after a three-month suspension, because there was some evidence that the employer had not always required employees to be dressed and ready for work before punching in.

Employee *D* had been convicted as a juvenile of breaking and entering to commit burglary. He had been put on probation and had had no further offenses. At the time, his lawyer informed him that upon a successful completion of his probation and upon reaching the age of 21, his record would be expunged. Five years later, he applied for a job with his current employer. To the question on the application "Have you ever been convicted of a crime?," he responded "No." The company discovered the juvenile conviction in its routine check of employee backgrounds three months after it had hired *D*. *D* was discharged pursuant to a contract clause providing for discharge in the event of employment application falsification. The arbitrator reinstated *D* with backpay, finding that the falsification was unintentional because the employee believed that his record had been expunged.

Employee *E* was arrested and pleaded guilty to a charge of larceny. He received a suspended sentence. Five years later, he concealed the record on an employment application, which asked, "Have you ever been convicted of a crime?." The employer learned of the record two years later when a local college professor asked to interview the employee in connection with a survey of convicted felons who had received suspended sentences. *E* was discharged pursuant to a contract clause authorizing discharge for falsification of the employment application. The arbitrator sustained the discharge, finding that the employee had intended to conceal his criminal record.

Employee *F* had made frequent reports to the Department of Transportation (DOT) about the employer's vehicle safety violations, and DOT had responded by giving the employer numerous citations, but not for all of the violations reported. When the employer discovered *F* to be the source of the reports, *F* was fired for dishonesty. The arbitrator sustained the discharge, finding that, while many reports were valid, some were obviously untrue. The arbitrator reasoned further that there was an element of maliciousness involved, since *F* did not use the contract machinery to report safety violations but had made reports verbally to a friend at DOT instead of through the normal channels.

Guidelines

Of necessity, disciplinary action for dishonesty or falsification requires proof of an intent to deceive. If an employee can provide a reasonable explanation for the misrepresentation, an arbitrator is less likely to sustain the discipline.

Relevant Cases

Seaway Food Town, Inc. (Belkin), 78 LA 208;
McDonnell Douglas Electronics Co. (Fitzsimmons), 78 LA 287;
Alco Gravure, Inc. (Adler), 78 LA 368;
Union Carbide Corp. (Teple), 78 LA 603;
Plantation Patterns, Inc. (Dallas), 78 LA 647;
Dresser Industries, Inc., Galion Mfg. Div. (McIntosh), 75 LA 45;
Pacific Northwest Bell Telephone Co. (Render), 75 LA 40;
Pacific Telephone & Telegraph Co. (Kanowitz), 74 LA 1095;
St. Johnsbury Trucking Co., Inc. (Knowlton), 74 LA 607;
Confer Smith & Co., Inc. (Raymond), 73 LA 1278;
Hygrade Food Products Corp. (Chiesa), 73 LA 755;
General Electric Co. (MacDonald), 72 LA 391;
General Electric Co. (Foreman), 71 LA 142;
United States Postal Service (Krimsly), 71 LA 100;
Texas Refinery (Williams), 70 LA 167;
Hayes-Albion Corp. (Glendon), 70 LA 696;
Bucyrus-Erie Co. (Gundermann), 70 LA 1017;

> *Federal Aviation Administration* (Larkin), 70 LA 1249;
> *Factory Services, Inc.* (Fitch), 70 LA 1088;
> *Robertshaw Controls Co.* (Duff), 69 LA 887;
> *Bi-State Development Agency* (Dugan), 67 LA 231;
> *National Vendors* (Edelman), 67 LA 1042;
> *Hooker Chemical Corp.* (Goodstein), 66 LA 140;
> *Lone Star Beer Co., Inc.* (Cowart), 66 LA 189;
> *Genuine Parts Co.* (O'Neill), 66 LA 1331;
> *Commonwealth of Pennsylvania* (LeWinter), 66 LA 96;
> *Alberto-Culver Co.* (Grant), 66 LA 736;
> *Briggs & Stratton Corp.* (Grant), 66 LA 758;
> *Pennsylvania Power Co.* (Altrock), 65 LA 623;
> *Cudahy Foods Co.* (Fox), 64 LA 110;
> *Price Brothers Co.* (High), 62 LA 389;
> *Commercial Warehouse Co.* (Sater), 62 LA 1015;
> *Whitfield Tank Lines* (Cohen), 62 LA 934;
> *Dart Industries* (Greene), 56 LA 799;
> *Blue Chip Stamps Warehouse* (Kenaston), 58 LA 148.

2   *The employee must either continue to deny the dishonest act or attempt to continue the deception upon discovery.*

Examples:

Employee *A* called in sick for a period of three days. In fact, *A* went to a distant city to handle an emergency health and financial problem for his aged parents. Upon discovery of the falsehood, *A* did not deny the truth. The employer discharged *A*. The arbitrator, finding the employee to be contrite and seeing the value of progressive discipline in this case, commuted the discharge to a suspension.

Employee *B* was on an incentive job. The counting device is activated pneumatically. *B* placed the device in such a way as to continue the airflow through the counter while he moved another bin of incomplete work into position. Upon discovery by the foreman, *B* was discharged. The employee protested that his placement of the device was accidental. Finding that the device could only be placed in an "on" position intentionally, the arbitrator sustained the discharge.

Employee *C* had been on a light duty schedule for two years because he had a history of physical problems. The employer conducted a general layoff, and *C* was laid off despite his seniority because of his light duty status and the elimination of all light duty work. When *C* protested that he could do the available work, the employer had the company doctor examine him. The doctor gave C a release for full duty. C then asserted that the release was based upon an examination for only one problem and that the doctor had ignored a second malady. C further stated that if the doctor had examined him for the second problem, then his work would have been restricted to a lighter duty job which was still available. When the company doctor refused to reconsider his initial findings, C went to his own doctor for a modified light duty slip. The second doctor also refused. The employer, finally, discharged C for falsifying his medical conditions. The arbitrator sustained the discharge and stated that C had failed in his obligation to give an honest day's work for his pay.

Employee D witnessed and acted to break up a fight between X and Y. The employer saw D's actions but was unable to determine the cause of the fight. All the employer knew was that D was present at the fight from start to finish and that he was not involved, except as a peacemaker. The employer sought to take disciplinary action against either X or Y, or both, depending upon the facts. When asked what happened, D denied all knowledge. D was given a ten day suspension for failing to cooperate. The suspension was sustained on the basis that D had been dishonest in his denial and had interfered with the company's efforts to investigate the occurrence.

Guidelines

The attitude of the employee at the time the dishonest act is discovered may be relevant in cases which do not have serious economic effect on the employer. However, in most cases the discharge or discipline will be sustained where the dishonesty involved an expense account, sick leave, or a compensation system, such as an incentive pay program.

Relevant Cases

Seaway Food Town, Inc. (Belkin), 78 LA 208;

Dayton Pepsi Cola Bottling Co. a/k/a Holiday General Corp. (Keenan), 75 LA 154;

Dresser Industries, Inc., Galion Mfg. Div. (McIntosh), 75 LA 45;

Super-Valu Stores, Inc. (Evenson), 74 LA 939;

Morrel, John & Co., Partridge Meats, Inc. Div. (Stokes), 74 LA 756;

Warner Robins Air Logistics Center (Dallas), 74 LA 710;

> *General Electric Co.* (MacDonald), 72 LA 391;
> *Hayes-Albion Corp.* (Glendon), 70 LA 696;
> *Bucyrus-Erie Co.* (Gundermann), 70 LA 1017;
> *Federal Aviation Administration* (Larkin), 70 LA 1249;
> *Golden Pride, Inc.* (Jaffee), 68 LA 1232;
> *Hooker Chemical Corp.* (Goodstein), 66 LA 140;
> *Lone Star Beer Co., Inc.* (Cowart), 66 LA 189;
> *Genuine Parts Co.* (O'Neill), 66 LA 1331;
> *Whitfield Tank Lines, Inc.* (Cohen), 62 LA 934;
> *Dart Industries, Inc.* (Greene), 56 LA 799;
> *Air Canada* (O'Shea), 66 LA 1295;
> *Duval Corp.* (Block), 55 LA 1089;
> *International Harvester Co.* (Seinsheimer), 53 LA 1197;
> *Shop Rite Food, Inc.* (Hayes), 55 LA 281;
> *Laughlin, Homer China Co.* (Seinsheimer), 55 LA 360.

3   *In cases of falsification of employment applications, the infor-*
mation concealed must have been of such character that, if known,
it would have prevented the hire of the applicant.

Examples:

Employee *A* answered "No" to an application question concerning the conviction for any crime committed by the applicant. In fact, the employee had been convicted of possessing
hashish two years earlier. Upon discovery of the falsehood, *A*
was discharged. During the hearing, the employer admitted
that had the employee answered the question honestly, he still
would have been hired. The arbitrator denied the discharge
and ordered reinstatement with full backpay.

Employee *B*, when asked on the application form whether he
had any physical condition which might limit or otherwise
affect his ability to do the work, replied in the negative. Six
months later, the employee injured his back lifting a trash
barrel. A check of his medical records revealed a history of
lower back trouble. *B* was discharged. At the arbitration hearing, the employer testified that had it known of the employee's
back trouble, the employee would not have been hired because
the job required some heavy lifting. The arbitrator sustained
the discharge.

Guidelines

Where the concealment on an employment application form is of a material fact which would have prevented employment, the discharge is generally upheld.

Guidelines—contd.

Where the employer testifies, however, that the employee would have been hired even if the information had been given, falsification by itself is generally not sufficient to justify discharge.

Relevant Cases

United States Steel Corp., Fairless Works (Simpkings), 74 LA 354;

Indianapolis Power and Light Co. (Kossoff), 73 LA 512;

Eaton Corp., Cutler-Hammer Group, Bowling Green Plant (Atwood), 73 LA 367;

I. E. Products, Inc., Illinois Envelope Div. (Brooks), 72 LA 35;

Price Brothers Co. (High), 62 LA 389;

Dart Industries, Inc. (Greene), 56 LA 799;

Fruehauf Trailer Co. (Belkin), 58 LA 1169;

Dan-Van Rubber Co. (Rothschild), 68 LA 217;

Air Canada (O'Shea), 66 LA 1295.

4   *In employment application cases, the employee's work record during the time between the act of falsification and discovery and the nature of information concealed may make the falsification lose its materiality.*

Examples:

Employee *A* failed to disclose on his application that he had been convicted of larceny, had served time, and had been on parole for less than a week. Ten years later, the employer learned of the conviction. During the intervening years, the employee had a good employment record and had received promotions up to the top grade in his classification. The employer discharged *A* for falsification of his employment application. The arbitrator reinstated the employee with full backpay, finding that the employee's work record was proof of his rehabilitation and that his discharge would serve no useful purpose, either as a protection to the employer or as a necessary measure for the maintenance of the integrity of the employment process.

Employee *B* failed to disclose on his application that he had been convicted of larceny and had received a suspended sentence less than a week before. Two years later, the employer learned of the conviction. During the intervening years, the employee had established a good work record and was promoted to the top grade in his classification. The employer discharged *B* for falsification of his application. The arbitrator sustained the discharge.

Employee *C* failed to disclose on his application that he had been convicted for possession of hashish. Five years later, this conviction was discovered by the employer. During this time, the employee established a good work record as a tool and dye maker. The employer discharged *C*. The arbitrator reinstated *C* with backpay, finding that the information concealed was not relevant to the employment and that the work record of the employee demonstrated that the use of the drug, if continued, had had no adverse effect on work performance.

Employee *D* failed to disclose on his application that he had been convicted for possession of hashish. Three months later the employer learned of the conviction and discharged *D*. *D*'s work record had been good. The arbitrator sustained the discharge, finding that not enough time had elapsed for the employee to have established ground for mitigation.

Employee *E* tried to conceal a medical problem by answering in the negative the relevant questions on the employment application and post-employment physical form. When the falsification was discovered, the employer told *E* to get a medical certificate stating he could to the job. *E* could not produce a satisfactory certificate, and he was discharged for falsifying the application. The arbitrator held that the employer waived its right to discharge *E* for falsification of the employment application forms by giving *E* an opportunity to produce a medical certificate of fitness. The employer had to prove at the arbitration that *E* was not physically fit to do the job.

Guidelines

Arbitrators often base their decisions on application falsification discharges after balancing numerous factors, including length of time between the date of falsification and date of discovery, the nature of information concealed, and the work record of the employee. Employers must present evidence regarding the specifics of the employee's work record, the materiality of the information concealed to employment (security, etc.), and the importance to the employer of maintaining its unabridged right to discharge an employee for falsifying an employment application.

Relevant Cases

Dan-Van Rubber Co. (Rothschild), 68 LA 217;
Commonwealth of Pennsylvania (LeWinter), 66 LA 96;

Blue Chip Stamps Warehouse (Kenaston), 58 LA 148;
Freuhauf Trailer Co. (Belkin), 58 LA 1169;
Texas Refinery (Williams), 70 LA 167;
Price Brothers Co. (High), 62 LA 389;
Horizon Mining Co., Robin No. 2 Mine (LeWinter), 72 LA 117.

Notes to Chapter 10

1. *See International Harvester Co.* (Seinsheimer), 53 LA 1197; *Shop Rite Foods, Inc.* (Hayes), 55 LA 281 (*contra*); *Laughlin, Homer China Co.* (Block), 55 LA 1089; *Central Motor Lines* (Carson), 56 LA 824; *Belle Cheese Co.* (Torosian), 59 LA 609; *Aristocrat Travel Prods., Inc.* (Koven), 52 LA 314; *Active Indus., Inc.* (Ellmann), 62 LA 985; *Cudahy Foods Corp.* (Fox), 64 LA 110; *Olin Corp.* (Martin), 63 LA 952; *Air Canada* (O'Shea), 66 LA 1295; *City Prods. Corp.* (Goetz), 67 LA 27; *Bucyrus-Erie Co.* (Gundermann), 70 LA 1017.

2. *Pacific Tel. & Tel. Co.* (Kanowitz), 74 LA 1095.

3. *Pacific Tel. & Tel. Co., supra,* note 2, at 1100. *See also Mallinckrodt Chemical Works* (Allen), 57 LA 709 (*contra*); *Whitfield Tank Lines, Inc.* (Cohen), 62 LA 934; *Commercial Warehouse Co.* (Sater), 62 LA 1015; *United Parcel Service* (Nicholas), 63 LA 849; *Dunlop Tire & Rubber Corp.* (Mills), 64 LA 1099.

4. *Dresser Indus., Inc., Galion Mfg. Div.* (McIntosh), 75 LA 45.

5. *See Justrite Super Markets* (Bothwell), 56 LA 152; *Active Indus. Inc., supra,* note 1.

6. *Pacific Tel. & Tel. Co., supra,* note 2, at 1098–99.

7. *But see Kentile Floors, Inc.* (Block), 57 LA 919; *Pacific Northwest Bell Tel. Co.* (Render), 75 LA 40.

8. *Dart Indus., Inc.* (Greene), 56 LA 799.

11

Dress or Grooming

Issue: Whether an employee can be discharged or otherwise disciplined for poor dress or grooming.

Principle: An employee can be discharged or otherwise disciplined for poor dress or grooming where the employer's dress and grooming code is relevant to the legitimate interests of the employer, is communicated to the employees, is not in conflict with the labor agreement, and is consistently enforced.

Considerations:

1. Whether the dress and grooming code is reasonable and related to the workplace or other legitimate interests of the employer;
2. Whether the code has been communicated to the employees so that they have actual or constructive notice of the rule;
3. Whether the rule is consistent with the labor agreement;
4. Whether the rule has been consistently enforced or applied.

Discussion: Arbitrators have recognized that an employer's restrictions on its employees' dress or grooming may restrict the individual employee's right to freedom of expression through his or her appearance. For employers' rules or regulations to be considered reasonable, therefore, they must be related to either the employee's health and safety or to a legitimate business interest or necessity of the employer. An employer cannot impose a dress code which is the result of an arbitrary decision based on personal taste.[1] For example, in *Oxford Nursing Home,* the employer had maintained

132

the same dress code for twenty years that required the female employees to wear white dresses, shoes, and stockings.[2] The female employees filed a grievance requesting that they be allowed to wear white pant suits. The arbitrator sustained the grievance stating that the employer's dress code was an unreasonable exercise of management rights. He also noted that pant suits are acceptable in many medical facilities and that the employer should keep up with the times.

In reviewing discipline cases involving violations of a dress or grooming code, arbitrators look first to see if the rule is reasonably related to the employer's articulated purpose and then to see if it is consistently applied.[3] If the rule is reasonable, arbitrators still appear willing to disallow discipline if the employee later conformed to the standard, or if the employee had a legitimate reason for refusing to conform, or if the employee's years of service or work history entitle him or her to another opportunity to comply with the rule. In *Allied Chemical Corp.*, the employee refused to shave his beard after a company rule was promulgated that all employees using respirators could not have beards.[4] After two suspensions for refusing to shave, he was discharged. The employee then agreed to shave after a test fit. The arbitrator ordered reinstatement based on the employee's fourteen years of service and his present willingness to conform with the rule. Similarly, in *Randall Foods No. 2,* the employer made a no-beard rule and suspended the grievant.[5] The grievant shaved, but filed a grievance to have the suspension removed from his record. The arbitrator sustained the grievance, finding that the employee did conform with the rule and that the employer's motivation, *i.e.,* the desire for a clean-shaven staff, was inappropriate, although the rule itself was reasonable. In *Safeway Stores, Inc.,* an employee, who had worked five years for Safeway and for all of those five years had worn a beard, was discharged when he refused to shave after a no-beard rule was enacted.[6] The employee had a skin condition that prevented him from shaving, and he brought two letters from his physician explaining this to the employer. The arbitrator found that the employer's rule was allowable, because the rule was related to the employer's attempt to present a certain public image and to compete for its market share of the retail food business. The arbitrator also found that the discharge of an employee whose challenge of the rule was not based on vanity or personal preference was too harsh, and he reduced the discharge to a leave of absence.

While the focus in the enforcement of many plant rules is the degree to which the employee conforms with the rule, in the area of dress or grooming codes the primary focus is whether the rule is reasonably related to the employer's articulated purpose. Legitimate employer purposes are limited to health and safety or to company image. Though restrictions on facial hair and on certain types of clothing for health and safety reasons are fairly well accepted, the degree to which an arbitrator will accept limits on the employee's appearance for the sake of company image varies widely.

In the area of health and safety an employer's dress or grooming code must in fact be related to the health and safety reasons given as the employer's rationale. In *Allied Chemical Corp.*, the company made a no-beard rule for all employees.[7] The arbitrator found that the rule was only reasonable when applied to those employees who actually used respirators and then only when it could be shown that the facial hair obstructed the respirator seal. The arbitrator stated that the employees have certain legitimate rights and freedoms regarding their bodies and that if their jobs did not require their use of a respirator, the no-beard rule was unreasonable insofar as it applied to them. It appears a well-established principle that facial hair obstructs a respirator seal, and the arbitrator found that rules restricting facial hair for employees required to wear respirators are reasonable.[8]

Employers may restrict certain types of clothing when employees are required to operate machinery. As in the "respirator, no-beard" cases, the rule must be related to the protection of the employees and not a restriction on their dress for arbitrary reasons alone. In *Babcock & Wilcox*, the arbitrator reviewed the rules the employer had put into effect concerning its employees' dress.[9] The dress code required that the employees wear snug clothing while operating the machinery and that this same clothing be worn from the plant gate to the time clock, *i.e.*, prior to reaching the actual work station. The rules also banned all beads, finger rings, and wigs. The arbitrator sustained only the rule requiring the wearing of snug clothing while operating the machinery and found that without supporting evidence the other rules were unreasonable. As the arbitrator stated, the requirement that an employer's dress or grooming code be reasonable implies that the employees to be protected will be in such geographic proximity to the machinery that their compliance with the rule will contribute to the reduction of risks. The requirement of reasonableness was not met when the employer placed restrictions on employees' clothing while they were not working or when the employer prohibited the wearing of jewelry or wigs without evidence that wearing these items endangered the employees' safety.

Hospitals can require certain dress standards for use in operating rooms for health and safety reasons. But, if an employee has some type of objection to a certain dress or uniform requirement, he or she should be given opportunity to present an alternative that can meet the health and safety standards. In *Hurley Hospital*, the employee was given this opportunity.[10] Her design was unsatisfactory, and the employer found the opportunity to transfer her to another department.

An employer may regulate the dress and appearance of its employees if there is a reasonable relation between its standards for dress and grooming and the public image the company hopes to communicate. It is not clear who has the burden of proof where the reasonableness of the rule is at issue. In *Blue Cross of Northern California*, the arbitrator found that the employer had a right—consistent with the management rights clause in the contract—to enforce its dress code.[11] The arbitrator did not require the employer to prove a relationship existed between its dress standards and the image it wanted to project. Similarly, in *Randall Foods No. 2*, even though the arbitrator felt the employer's motivation for his no-beard rule was inappropriate, he accepted the employer's explanation that it wanted a clean-cut, clean-shaven staff, without any proof that this image made a competitive difference in the company's market share.[12]

The arbitrators in *Big Star No. 35* and *Pacific Southwest Airlines* articulated a requirement that the employer come forward with some showing of reasonable business necessity, or evidence, that the appearance requirement (in both cases, the employer had a no-beard rule) had a rational connection with the operation of the business enterprise.[13] In *Pacific Southwest*, the arbitrator required the employer to meet the burden of proof of the public's real attitudes and reactions, as well as proof of a demonstrable relationship between those attitudes and the rules intended to nurture a positive public image. Without meeting this burden, the employer could not arbitrarily restrict its employees' right to determine their own personal appearance.

Most arbitrators do not require such a strong showing. If the employer can show that its standard applies to those employees who have public contact and that it is trying to project a particular image for competitive business reasons, an arbitrator will uphold the rule, or discipline, if the employee fails to comply.

In *Aslesen Co.*, the company had a clean-shaven rule for its drivers, who were also required to wear uniforms.[14] The grievant, a driver, had been told to shave, and he had refused. The arbitrator sustained the employee's suspension, stating that due to the driver's customer contact and the company's concern about its public image, the company had acted within its right. Similarly, in *Arden-Mayfair, Inc.*, the company had a no-beard rule that applied to employees who worked with customers.[15] The arbitrator recognized the employer's prerogative to project to the public a "clean-shaven, well-attired, clean, appealing type individual" as legitimate. The rules were reasonable and easily understood; the employees who were suspended had been given the opportunity to shave, and they had refused. In *Southern Bell Telephone & Telegraph*, the arbitrator recognized that dress and appearance regulations are not valid unless they are reasonably necessary to serve some legitimate business interest of the employer.[16] In this case, the employer's refusal to allow an employee to wear shorts when he was collecting money from pay phones was found to be an extension of the employer's legitimate desire to project an attractive public image.

In professions that have traditionally required employees to wear a uniform or to project a particular image, arbitrators uphold the rule, as well as any discipline meted out for failure to comply. In *City of Erie*, a seasoned police officer was suspended for not wearing the proper uniform.[17] In *Alameda-Contra Costa Transit District*, the arbitrator sustained the rule that bus drivers wear a particular hat, or no hat at all, and concluded that the uniform requirement established an air of authority for the bus driver.[18] The grievant had been suspended for wearing a turban, and the suspension was upheld.

Similar reasoning has been applied in cases where nurses or nurses' aides have been required to wear certain uniforms. In *Greater Harlem Nursing Home*, there were different colored uniforms for the men and women aides.[19] One of the male attendants requested permission to wear the female uniform, in psychological preparation prior to transexual surgery. The employer allowed him to do so for three years and, then, requested him to dress in the male uniform until his surgery. The employee filed a grievance over this request. The arbitrator accepted the employer's rationale that the employee's dressing as a woman confused the patients. Because the proper care of patients, with due regard for their preferences and rights, is the sole purpose of a nursing home, the arbitrator found the employer's request that the grievant dress as a male in his role as a nurses' aide, as long as he was anatomically male, to be reasonable.

Key Points:

1   *The dress and grooming code must be reasonably related to the workplace or to some legitimate business of the employer.*

Examples:

Employee *A* grieved his forced transfer out of a chemical-mixing department. The employer had established a rule that all employees would be required to wear respirators when working with loose chemicals in the mixing department. After tests, it was determined that facial hair broke the seal of the respirators, and beards were then prohibited. The employee refused to shave his beard, asserting a skin condition which prevented him from shaving. The employer transferred the employee. The arbitrator upheld the transfer.

Employee *B*, a female, was given a three-day suspension for refusing to wear a bra under her T-shirt. The employer asserted that such dress was inappropriate, unduly provocative to other employees, and affected their production. The arbitrator sustained the grievance, noting that the employee's attire was not shown to be reasonably related to levels of production or to the safety of other employees.

Guidelines

Dress or grooming rules must be clearly and demonstrably related to the legitimate interests of the employer. Where the dress or grooming of the employee cannot be shown to have a direct effect upon production, safety, sales, or relationships with public consumers, such limitations on dress or grooming will not be sustained by an arbitrator.

Relevant Cases

Big Star No. 35 (Murphy), 73 LA 850;
Oxford Nursing Home (Wolff), 75 LA 1300;
Pacific Southwest Airlines (Christopher), 73 LA 1209;
Allied Chemical Corp. (Harkless), 76 LA 923;
Randall Foods No. 2 (Sembower), 74 LA 729;
Safeway Stores, Inc. (Madden), 75 LA 798;
City of Erie (Kreimer), 73 LA 605;
Allied Chemical Corp. (Eischen), 74 LA 412;
Allied Chemical Corp. (Harkless), 76 LA 925;
Pacific Southwest Airlines (Jones), 77 LA 320;
Babcock & Wilcox (Strashofer), 73 LA 443;
Hurley Hospital (Roumell), 71 LA 1013;
Blue Cross of Northern California (Barrett), 73 LA 352;
Aslesen Co. (Fogelberg), 74 LA 1017;
Arden-Mayfair, Inc. (Kaufman), 71 LA 200;
Southern Bell Telephone & Telegraph (Duff), 74 LA 1115;
Alameda-Contra Costra Transit District (Randell), 75 LA 1273;
Greater Harlem Nursing Home (Marx), 76 LA 680;
Hotel Bancroft (Wolff), 78 LA 819;
E. I. du Pont de Nemours & Co. (Light), 78 LA 327;
International Minerals & Chemical Corp. (Jones), 78 LA 682.

2   *The employee must have actual or constructive notice of the dress or grooming code prior to discipline.*

Examples:

Employee *A*, a retail store clerk, was issued a shirt to be worn while working in the store. On occasion, the employee would forget to have his shirt cleaned and would wear another. The store manager reminded him of the requirement to wear the shirt on each of these occasions. One day he again forgot his shirt and wore a simple, white dress shirt. The general manager for the store chain visited the store; noted the employee's violation of the dress code; and, upon being told that the employee had been warned about similar violations in the past, ordered the employee to punch out and lose the balance of the work shift. The employee grieved, and the arbitrator sustained his grievance, noting that while the employee had actual notice of the rule, he was not aware that the next violation of the code would result in a disciplinary suspension.

Employee *B* was a bus driver who was given a copy of the company's dress code at the time of his employment, which required that a uniform hat be worn at all times the drivers were on duty and which proscribed discipline for being "out of uniform." The employee was disciplined when seen driving his bus without his hat on. The employee defended by saying that his hat ruined his hair style and that he always had the hat next to him on a ledge of the bus. The discipline was sustained.

Guidelines

The dress or grooming rule must be specific, and the employee must have actual or constructive knowledge that a violation of the rule will result in discipline.

Relevant Cases

Oxford Nursing Home (Wolff), 75 LA 1300;
Allied Chemical Corp. (Harkless), 76 LA 923;
Safeway Stores, Inc. (Madden), 75 LA 798;
Babcock & Wilcox (Strashofer), 73 LA 443;
Hurley Hospital (Roumell), 71 LA 1013;
City of Erie (Kreimer), 73 LA 605;
Alameda-Contra Costa District (Randall), 75 LA 1273;
Greater Harlem Nursing Home (Marx), 76 LA 680;
New Cumberland Army Depot (Mount), 78 LA 630;
Hotel Bancroft (Wolff), 78 LA 819.

3   *The dress or grooming code must be consistent with the labor agreement.*

Examples:

Employee *A*, a car salesman, was given a disciplinary suspension for repeatedly reporting to work in a sport shirt rather than a coat and tie. The employee grieved on the basis that his appearance was neat and clean and that his refusal to wear a coat and tie was not just cause for discipline. The arbitrator noted the absence of any contractual language other than the "just cause" provision of the contract and found the appearance of the salesman in a coat and tie to be within the interest of the employer in maintaining a "high class" public image. The discipline was, therefore, sustained by the arbitrator.

Employee *B* was suspended for failing to wear the company shirt when making service calls. The employee defended on the basis that the employer had agreed during contract negotiations that it would provide shirts and wanted the employees to wear them, but use of the shirts would not be a condition of employment. The arbitrator sustained the grievance.

Guidelines

Even where the business necessity or legitimacy of the dress or grooming rule can be established, the labor agreement cannot be used to establish the parties' agreement that such a rule would not be created or enforced.

Relevant Cases

Blue Cross of Northern California (Barrett), 73 LA 352;
Aslesen Co. (Fogelberg), 74 LA 1017;
City of Erie (Kreimer), 73 LA 605;
Alameda-Contra Costa District (Randell), 75 LA 1273;
Greater Harlem Nursing Home (Marx), 76 LA 680;
New Cumberland Army Depot (Mount), 78 LA 630;
Hotel Bancroft (Wolff), 78 LA 819.

4   *The dress and grooming rule must be uniformly applied and enforced.*

Examples:

Employee *A*, a female, grieved the disciplinary action taken against her for wearing shorts while working. Noting that male employees frequently wore shorts in hot weather, the arbitrator sustained the grievance.

Employee *B*, a male, was disciplined for having shoulder-length hair and wearing earrings. At the arbitration, *B* presented several other male employees who also had long hair and earrings. Noting that the grievant frequently dealt with the public while the other employees did not, the arbitrator sustained the discipline.

Guidelines

Like all rules, dress and grooming rules must be equally applied and enforced. Comparisons between employees must take into account the differences in the employees' jobs and responsbilities, *viz.*, different rules may exist in the same workplace for different classes or types of employees depending upon the nature of their jobs.

Relevant Cases

Greater Harlem Nursing Home (Marx), 76 LA 680;
Alameda-Contra Costa District (Randell), 75 LA 1273;
Arden-Mayfair, Inc. (Kaufman), 71 LA 200;
City of Erie (Kreimer), 73 LA 605;
Hurley Hospital (Roumell), 71 LA 1013;
Babcock & Wilcox (Strashofer), 73 LA 443;
Allied Chemical Corp. (Eischen), 74 LA 412;
Safeway Stores, Inc. (Madden), 75 LA 798;
Oxford Nursing Home (Wolff), 75 LA 1300;
New Cumberland Army Depot (Mount), 78 LA 630.

Special Note

An ancillary, but frequent, problem encountered in connection with dress codes and grooming is that having to do with the wearing of union insignia, or other union-related messages, on hats or other articles of clothing. This issue is raised most often in the context of union campaigns and is resolved under the Labor Management Relations Act (the Act) by the National Labor Relations Board (the NRLB, the Board). Because this question involves the application of law and is not within the primary jurisdiction of labor arbitrators, it is not precisely within the scope of this book. However, because the subject is so closely related to the issue of dress and grooming as a cause for discipline and is normally raised within the context of some disciplinary action, it deserves special mention here.

Consider, for instance, an employee who reports to work wearing clothes appropriate for his job, and otherwise acceptable, but for a slogan on his T-shirt which says "We Care" over a union insignia. Although the employer permits employees to wear T-shirts with all sorts of sayings, it considers this pro-union message to be an affront. Can the employer require the employee to remove the shirt under threat of discipline? Consider also whether an employer has the right to require an employee to remove a hat containing a union insignia, when other hats have been generally allowed.

An employee's right to wear union insignia includes wearing that insignia on a hat or T-shirt.[20] As in other union insignia cases, an employer cannot restrict or ban the wearing of such insignia, without a showing of special circumstances warranting a ban or restriction.[21] In cases where an employer asserts that the hat or T-shirt is in violation of a dress code, the employer must demonstrate that the dress code is enforced and that the rule serves a legitimate purpose.[22] The wearing of some T-shirts, while not bearing union insignia but some message relating to unions, union activity, or terms and conditions of employment, is considered a protected activity.[23] Unless the employer can demonstrate that the shirt is restricted by a valid, nondiscriminatorily enforced nonsolicitation or company uniform rule, that the message disrupts order and discipline at the plant, or that the message is obscene or offensive, the employer cannot prevent the employee from wearing the shirt.[24]

In *Singer Co. v. NLRB*, the employer maintained that shirts with union insignia had to be banned because of the interfactional hostility which existed between different unions at the factory and because the wearing of the shirts caused disruptions, affected discipline, and caused a drop in production. However, the employer was unable to produce any evidence that the drop in production or other objections raised were caused by the wearing of the shirts.[25] Accordingly, the National Labor Relations Board and the Court held that the restrictions violated § 8 (a)(1) of the Act.[26]

The employer in *Honda of America* did not require its employees to wear a hat as part of the company uniform.[27] The employer did have a rule prohibiting other items from being worn with the uniform, but the rule was found by the Labor Board to have been unevenly enforced in that the employer had permitted other nonuniform items to be worn. When one employee took to wearing a hat bearing a union insignia, he was asked to remove it and was offered a company hat instead. The employee refused. The Board found that the employer's request violated § 8 (a)(1) of the Act: The hat was not offensive, hats were not part of the uniform and were not required, and the employer offered no evidence to show that the wearing of the hat with the union insignia interfered with the employer's team-work concept. Moreover, the Board held that the enforcement of the rule as to this employee was selective, since the rule had not been consistently enforced in the past. Similarly, in *Dixie Machine Rebuilders, Inc.*, the employer asked several employees who were wearing hats bearing union insignia to remove them, because the hats were not part of the company uniform.[28] The Board held that the employee's right to wear union insignia was protected by Section 7 and that the employer's request, without any additional evidence, violated § 8 (a)(1) of the Act.

In *The Nestle Company*, all employees were required to wear a uniform supplied by the company.[29] When there was an insufficient number of uniforms, however, employees were allowed to wear their own clothing. It was common at these times for the male employees to wear their own various colored T-shirts, which often bore slogans or product names. When several employees chose to wear T-shirts with union insignia, however, they were told to remove them. Although the employer's uniform rule was valid, the Board found that the employer could not apply the rule selectively to union insignia and permit breaches of the rule for other nonuniform clothing.[30]

What would seem to be a more troublesome area is whether it is protected activity to wear a T-shirt with a message arguably about union activity or about the terms and conditions of employment. The outer limit of this question seems to have been set by *Southwestern Bell Telephone Company*.[31] In that case, a group of employees arrived at work wearing T-shirts that said "Ma Bell is a Cheap Mother." The employees' stated purpose was to demonstrate support for the union during the pending contract negotiations. The employer requested the employees to either remove the shirts, cover the slogan, or leave. The Board, holding that the employer's actions were lawful, stated:

> . . . In view of the controversial nature of the language used and its admitted susceptibility to derisive and profane construction, Respondent could legitimately ban the use of the provocative slogans as a reasonable precaution against discord and bitterness between employees and management, as well as to assure decorum and discipline in the plant.[32]

In contrast, the Board found in three other cases that the wearing of T-shirts that said "Don't simonize, unionize," "Fight Speed-up," and "I'm tired of busting my ass" to be protected activity.[33]

In *Publishers Printing Co.*, the employer was found by the Board to have violated § 8 (a)(1) of the Act by requesting an employee to remove a T-shirt he was wearing that said "Don't simonize, unionize" (a Mr. Simon was the president of the company).[34] The Board's decision was based on the fact that the company had allowed other commercially printed T-shirts with other sayings or signs to be worn in the plant, including a T-shirt imprinted with a marijuana leaf.

In another case, *American Motors Corp.*, the union had printed and sold T-shirts that said "Fight Speed-up" and had distributed literature about wages, hours, and working conditions as well.[35] The wearing of the shirts was found to be protected activity, and the efforts of the foreman to discourage employees from wearing them were found to have violated § 8 (a)(1) of the Act.

The Board also held in *Borman's, Inc.* that an employee was engaged in protected activity when he wore a T-shirt that had the employer's name above a decal showing a man with a pick standing above the pieces of a donkey or jackass with the inscription "I'm tired of busting my ass."[36] The employer objected to the shirt and testified that it felt that the message on the shirt conveyed a negative impression about the company to outsiders. The administrative law judge found, with the Board's approval, that the slogan on the shirt was not an interference with the company's right to maintain order and discipline at the warehouse. Further, the judge held that the slogan did not vilify any company official and that the language was not so obscene as to be objectionable. The judge also stated that the employee had the right to use the company name on a shirt to identify their employer as the one with which they have a dispute and to advertise a grievance with that employer over working conditions.

It is clear from these cases that an employer will have a very difficult time restricting the employees' right to wear T-shirts or hats bearing union insignia, or union-related or working-condition messages. The only protection an employer may create for itself is to establish a uniform rule which is strictly and evenly enforced. Even then, employees will be permitted to wear union buttons, unless there is a reason clearly related to the employer's business interests, such as the employer's public image and personal or product safety, which would preclude the advantage gained by this form of advertising. In the absence of such a rule, the employer has to establish that the message, as distinguished in most cases from a simple union insignia, created actual, or a demonstrably high risk of, interfactional hostility; fights; loss of, or reduced, production; or that the message was intrinsically obscene or libelous.

Of course, the cases cited above in this Note only refer to issues raised when the clothing, which the employer seeks to prohibit, contains messages related to unions, unionization, grievances, terms or conditions of employment, or anything else arguably protected by § 7 of the Labor Act. All other types of messages would be subject to the grievance and arbitration procedure.

Notes to Chapter 11

1. *Big Star No. 35* (Murphy), 73 LA 850.
2. *Oxford Nursing Home* (Wolff), 75 LA 1300.
3. *Pacific Southwest Airlines* (Christopher), 73 LA 1209.
4. *Allied Chem. Corp.* (Harkless), 76 LA 923.
5. *Randall Foods No. 2* (Sembower), 74 LA 729.
6. *Safeway Stores, Inc.* (Madden), 75 LA 798.
7. *Allied Chem. Corp.* (Eischen), 74 LA 412.
8. *Allied Chem. Corp., supra,* note 7; *Allied Chem. Corp., supra,* note 4; *Pacific Southwest Airlines* (Jones), 77 LA 320; *E. I. du Pont de Nemours & Co.,* (Light), 78 LA 327; *but see International Minerals & Chem. Corp.* (Jones), 78 LA 682.
9. *Babcock & Wilcox* (Strashofer), 73 LA 443.
10. *Hurley Hosp.* (Roumell), 71 LA 1013.
11. *Blue Cross of N. California* (Barrett), 73 LA 352.
12. *Randall Foods No. 2, supra,* note 5.
13. *Big Star No. 35, supra,* note 1; *Pacific Southwest Airlines, supra,* note 3.
14. *Aslesen Co.* (Fogelberg), 74 LA 1017.
15. *Arden-Mayfair, Inc.* (Kaufman), 71 LA 200.
16. *Southern Bell Tel. & Tel.* (Duff), 74 LA 1115.
17. *City of Erie* (Kreimer), 73 LA 605.
18. *Alameda-Contra Costa Transit Dist.* (Randell), 75 LA 1273.
19. *Greater Harlem Nursing Home* (Marx), 76 LA 680.
20. *Overnite Transp. Co.,* 254 NLRB No. 11, 107 LRRM 1130 (1981); *Dixie Mach. Rebuilders, Inc.,* 248 NLRB 881, 104 LRRM 1094 (1980).
21. *Honda of Am. Mfg.,* 260 NLRB No. 97, 109 LRRM 1267 (1982); *Singer Co. v. NLRB,* 480 F.2d 269, 83 LRRM 2655 (10th Cir., 1973).
22. *The Nestle Co.,* 248 NLRB 732, 103 LRRM 1567 (1980); *Honda of Am. Mfg., supra,* note 21.
23. *American Motors Corp.,* 214 NLRB 455, 87 LRRM 1393; *Borman's, Inc.,* 254 NLRB No. 130, 106 LRRM 1310 (1981).
24. *Borman's, Inc., supra,* note 23; *Southwestern Bell Tel. Co.,* 200 NLRB 667, 82 LRRM 1247 (1972); *Publishers Printing Co., Inc.,* 246 NLRB 206, 102 LRRM 1628 (1979).
25. *Singer Co. v. NLRB, supra,* note 21.
26. *See also Overnite Transp. Co., supra,* note 20 (wearing of Teamster T-shirt protected activity).
27. *Honda of Am. Mfg., supra,* note 21.
28. *Dixie Mach. Rebuilders, Inc., supra,* note 20.
29. *The Nestle Co., supra,* note 22.
30. *See also Publishers Printing Co., supra,* note 24 (employer, which allowed employees to wear commercially printed T-shirts bearing various legends in the plant, could not restrict union-related materials).
31. *Southwestern Bell Tel. Co., supra,* note 24.

32. *Id.*, at 1248.

33. *Publishers Printing Co., supra,* note 30; *American Motors Corp., supra,* note 28; *Borman's, Inc., supra,* note 23.

34. *Publishers Printing Co., supra,* note 30.

35. *American Motors Corp., supra,* note 23.

36. *Borman's, Inc., supra,* note 23.

12

Drugs: Use and/or Possession

Issue: Whether an employee can be discharged
                     or otherwise disciplined for use and/or pos-
                     session of drugs.

Principle: An employee may be discharged or oth-
                     erwise disciplined for use and/or posses-
                     sion of drugs while on duty, regardless of
whether the employee is on or off the premises of the employer. An
employee may also be discharged or otherwise disciplined for possession of drugs with an intent to sell or for the actual sale of drugs
at any time, regardless of whether the employee's conduct was detected within employment hours or whether his or her actions were
connected in any way with his or her employment. As used in this
chapter, the term "drugs" is intended to mean all controlled substances which, when ingested by an individual, will cause some
behavioral or physical change which will affect the individual's ability to work, exercise reasoned judgment, and/or get along with peers,
subordinates, or others with whom he or she comes in contact during
the workday. Consequently, a "drug" may be a legally prescribed
substance being taken by an employee with a legitimate physical
difficulty and under a doctor's care, as well as an illegal chemical
or organic product. For the purposes of this discussion, the drugs
referred to, except where noted, are those generally referred to as
illegal or street drugs, such as marijuana, heroin, morphine, cocaine,
codiene or opium additives, LSD, DMT, STP, amphetamines, meth-
amphetamines, and barbiturates. The term "hard" drug when used
here is intended to mean all of the drugs listed above except marijuana.

Considerations: 1. Whether the use or possession of drugs
                        takes place while the employee is on
                        the premises of the employer or within
                        his or her workday;
                     2. Whether the employee is under the in-
                        fluence of drugs on the employer's

premises or during the employee's
workday;
3. Whether the employee sells or sold drugs
or whether the employee has possession of drugs with an intent to sell;
4. Whether the employer maintains and
has communicated its rule against use
and/or possession of drugs on the work
premises or during the workday;
5. Whether the drug is within the category of "hard drugs";
6. Whether a "drug problem" exists within
the workplace;
7. Whether the employee's use or possession of drugs affected the orderly operation of the employer's business;
8. Whether the employee's use or possession of drugs had an adverse affect on
the reputation of the employer.

Discussion: The most common circumstances presented to arbitrators involves the discharge of an employee for possession of a
drug, usually marijuana, on company premises and/or while on duty.
In a few of these cases, the arbitrators have reinstated employees,
although without backpay, on the theory that the "mere possession"
of drugs is less serious than its use[1] or on the basis that the plant
rule only prohibited employers from being "under the influence."[2]
However, it is more frequently the case that an arbitrator will uphold the discharge of an employee who possesses a controlled and
unprescribed drug on company premises or while on duty, especially
where the conduct is against a company or labor contract rule.[3]

The second largest group of cases in this area deals with employees
disciplined for the use of or for being under the influence of drugs
on company premises and/or while on duty. Generally, arbitrators
have upheld discharges for the use of controlled and unprescribed
drugs, including marijuana, while on the premises of the employer,
even in cases where it has been a first offense.[4] Remarkably, however, one arbitrator, noting the increasingly liberal legal treatment
of marijuana, ordered an employee who smoked marijuana on the
employer's premises to be reinstated without backpay.[5]

Discipline may also be warranted when the employee is under the
influence of a prescribed rather than illegal drug where there is
some threat to the safety and efficiency of the employee's performance.[6]

While arbitrators generally will uphold discharges of employees
who possess or use drugs on company premises and/or during their

workday, an employee will likely be reinstated when he or she has been discharged for use or possession off the premises. These off-the-premises use or possession cases usually arise when the employee has been arrested, and the employer then invokes discipline. The prevailing view among arbitrators appears to be that an employee's conduct in his private life is not the employer's concern, and an arrest for drug use or possession off the employer's premises, therefore, will not justify discharge, as long as the arrest does not damage the employer's public image or reduce the ability of co-workers to deal with the employee or as long as the employee's work performance is unaffected by drugs.[7]

In contrast to the other cases, in *Arco-Polymers, Inc.*, the arbitrator held that the employee's arrest for possession of heroin with intent to sell did raise a legitimate fear that he would sell to co-workers, and the discharge was therefore upheld.[8] Also, in *Michigan Power Co.*, the arbitrator found that the employer properly suspended an employee whose arrest for the distribution of a controlled substance adversely affected the company's reputation.[9] However, the arbitrator also held that the employee should have been reinstated after the charges were dismissed.

Cases involving the sale of drugs, either on or off the employer's premises, are handled considerably differently from use and possession cases. It does not appear to matter whether the sale is on or off the premises; the offense always appears to be considered a proper subject for summary discharge. In *Eastern Airlines, Inc.* and *Cerro Corp.*, where the employees were selling marijuana to their co-workers, for instance, both arbitrators upheld the discharges.[10] Also, in *State University of New York*, the arbitrator upheld the discharge of a bartender, who had sold "black mollies" to student customers of the campus bar.[11]

Where the employee was selling drugs off the premises, arbitrators still have been willing to uphold the discharge, noting the employer's concern that the employee would sell to other employees.[12] However, in one case, the arbitrator reinstated with backpay an employee who had been discharged when he pleaded guilty to a sale of methamphetamine which had occurred before his employment. The arbitrator noted that there was no evidence that either the employee's work performance or the company's reputation was affected or that there was a drug problem among the other employees; such factors have been considered in the other cases as well.[13]

The existence or the lack of a clear rule prohibiting the use or possession of drugs also appears to have been significant in several arbitrations. On at least two occasions arbitrators have refused to permit the discharge of employees for first offenses for possession of marijuana, because there was no rule allowing for such serious disciplinary action. In making this conclusion, the arbitrators noted the increasingly relaxed legal treatment of marijuana and felt that, without prior notice by the employer, the mere possession of that substance on the company's property should not be cause for summary discharge.[14] However, others have found that employees need no special notice, or that they have constructive notice when the offense involves criminal conduct or something as serious as the use and possession of marijuana.[15]

Arbitrators also give some consideration to the type of drug involved. Generally, arbitrators will permit more severe measures to be taken in cases involving "hard drugs." Thus, in *Wheaton Industries*, the arbitrator upheld the summary discharge of an employee arrested for possession with intent to sell heroin, even though he had not yet been convicted.[16] The arbitrator specifically noted that this case involved a "hard" drug.[17]

Another factor sometimes considered to be relevant is whether a general drug problem exists at the plant. Arbitrators will endorse more severe measures taken against drug offenders when there is evidence of a more widespread drug problem at the plant. For example, in *Arco-Polymers, Inc.*, the discharge of an employee who had been arrested for possession of heroin with intent to sell was upheld; in *Pepsi Cola Bottlers* and in *S. F. Kennedy-New Products, Inc.*, the summary discharges of employees for the possession and sale of marijuana and mescaline on the premises was upheld, and the drug problem within the companies was held to justify the lack of progressive discipline.[18]

Of special note in this regard is the case of *Watauga Industries, Inc.*, in which the discharges of four employees for smoking marijuana on the premises during their lunch break were reduced to suspensions.[19] There was no problem of proof; the employees were caught in the act. While recognizing that smoking marijuana on the plant premises during the workday was a legitimate cause for discharge, the arbitrator nevertheless reduced the penalty to a suspension. Apparently, reasoned the arbitrator, smoking marijuana on the premises had been a common practice for up to five months prior to this incident. Although just prior to the incident the company president had told his supervisors that this practice would no longer be condoned and that the supervisors were to enforce the rule against smoking marijuana, this enforcement policy had not been communicated to the employees. Consequently, the discharge penalty was found to be inappropriate, because the general drug problem in the plant made a clear rule unenforceable on its face and the employees had not been given adequate notice.

Although not within the subject matter of this book, the importance and complexity of the problem of proof of the charges of drug use and/or possession must be noted. The problem includes the burden of proof, the type of proof, and the closely related charges of insubordination, which may result from a demand upon the employee that he or she produce the suspicious material, bag, or the like.

There are two burdens of proof which have been applied to the employers' cases. The first is that the employer must prove its case beyond a reasonable doubt. This criminal standard is used, because the charge is one of a criminal nature.[20] The second standard of proof used frequently in drug cases is that of "clear and convincing" proof.[21] The significance of this difference in the two standards of the burden of proof is not clear. Some arbitrators have suggested that there is little difference, if any.[22]

There is also discrepancy among arbitrators over the sort of proof or evidence that can be offered to support the discipline. One problem area is the weight to be given to the testimony and accusations of the employee's coworkers. In *Structurlite Plastics Corp.*, for instance, the arbitrator upheld the discharge of an employee for using drugs on the job upon the testimony of employees that the grievant looked like he was on drugs.[23] By contrast, in *Casting Engineers*, a suspension was not upheld, because there was no corroborating evidence of the coworker's accusation of use of marijuana.[24] However, in *St. Joe Minerals Corp.*, the arbitrator, in upholding the discharge, gave substantial weight to the conclusion of the company doctor, who had examined the grievant and determined that he was under the influence of marijuana based on the inflammation of the grievant's eyes and his affected reactions.[25]

Another problem confronting arbitrators is that of culpability when more than one person is in an area in which marijuana has been used or found. In *Whirlpool Corp.*, the arbitrator reinstated with backpay two employees who had been merely riders in a truck in which marijuana was later found.[26] However, in *General Foods Corp.*, the arbitrator upheld the 30-day suspension of all four employees, who had been found in a company car which smelled of marijuana.[27] The arbitrator rejected the argument that to uphold the suspensions he had to find which of the four actually possessed and smoked the marijuana.

A final problem area related to proof occurs when an employer demands that the employee produce the suspicious material or container which has been seen, the employee refuses, and the employee is then discharged for insubordination. The employer has the right to make such a demand, and there is no constitutional protection involved in the case of a private employer. The refusal to comply with such a request will sustain a discharge for insubordination.[28]

It is apparent, therefore, that there are many factors which can affect a drug-related discharge or discipline, in addition to those generally considered by arbitrators, such as the reasonableness of the rule against use and/or possession and the employee's length and quality of past service. One arbitrator set out a list of factors for drug-related cases, which can serve as a useful summary:

(1) Whether possession or sale is involved,
(2) The type of drug (marijuana vs. hard drugs),
(3) Whether the transaction was a casual sale,
(4) Whether the conduct occurred on the premises of the employer,
(5) The presence or absence of a drug problem at the workplace,
(6) Impact on the reputation of the employer, and
(7) Effect on the orderly operation of the employer's business.[29]

Key Points:

1 *Where an employee possesses drugs while at the workplace or on duty, some discipline will be sustained. The severity of the discipline will depend upon the nature of the drug, the presence of a general drug problem in the workplace, the existence of a clear rule, and/or the work history of the employee.*

Examples:

Employee A was discharged following a routine locker check which revealed a quantity of marijuana in A's possession. The employer's work rules stipulated that possession of narcotics in the workplace would be cause for summary discharge. The discharge was sustained.

Employee B was discovered in the plant with a user's quantity of cocaine in his possession. The employer had no rule against drug possession, and the employee had an excellent work record. B was discharged, and the discharge was sustained.

Employee C was discharged following the discovery of a user's quantity of marijuana in his lunchbox. The employer had no rule regarding the possession of drugs, and the search was conducted in connection with a company program to prevent theft of product. The employee was only marginal and was also one of those suspected of theft. The discharge was reduced to suspension.

Employee D was discharged following the discovery of a user's quantity of marijuana in his lunchbox as a result of the employer's crackdown against drug use in the workplace. The employee's work record was without blemish. The arbitrator, recognizing the need of the employer to control drug usage in the plant, sustained the discharge.

Employee *E* was discharged for possession of marijuana in the plant. Company policy prohibited employees from working while under the influence of drugs or alcohol. The arbitrator reduced the discharge to a warning, noting that the employer could not rely on the rule in this case because the rule did not cover mere possession.

Guidelines

In the absence of a specific rule which makes the mere possession of drugs on the employer's premises an offense likely to result in discipline, an employee may nevertheless be disciplined for possession of drugs in the workplace, where it can be shown that a general drug problem exists in the plant, the use of drugs would present an immediate and severe safety risk to other employees, or the nature and quantity of the drugs suggests a dealer.

Where prohibited by a clear and communicated rule, the mere possession of drugs in the workplace will be sufficient cause for discipline.

Relevant Cases

B. Green & Co., Inc. (Cushman), 71 LA 685;
Joseph G. Tropiano, Inc. (Belsky), 69 LA 1243;
Detroit Stoker Co. (Daniel), 75 LA 816;
Brooks Foundry, Inc. (Daniel), 75 LA 642;
Georgia Pacific Corp. (Vadakin), 72 LA 784;
Stansteel Corp. (Kaufman), 69 LA 776;
Jeep Corp. (Keefe), 67 LA 828;
Swift & Co. (Rentfro), 72 LA 513;
Abex Corp. (Rybolt), 64 LA 721;
St. Joe Minerals Corp. (Roberts), 70 LA 1110;
Wheaton Industries (Kerrison), 64 LA 826;
Arco-Polymers, Inc. (Milentz), 69 LA 379;
Watauga Industries, Inc. (Galambos), 78 LA 697.

2 *Where an employee uses drugs or is under their influence at the workplace or while on duty, summary discharge normally will be sustained.*

Examples:

Employee *A* was discovered smoking marijuana during his lunch break. The employer has no rule against drugs. Nevertheless, *A* was discharged. The arbitrator sustained the discharge.

Employee *B* was discovered smoking marijuana during her lunch break and was discharged. The employer has no rule against drugs. The employee defended on the basis of her good work record and high productivity. The arbitrator reduced the discharge to a suspension.

Employee *C* was discharged following an accident in a forklift, which resulted in minor injuries to himself and another employee. During the investigation of the incident, the employer discovered that the employee was under medication, which had been prescribed by his doctor and which affected the employee's ability to react and to make judgments. The bottle containing the medication clearly stated that, after taking, the user should not operate machinery or drive. The employee was discharged and the arbitrator sustained the discharge, noting the employer's rule requiring summary discharge for the use of drugs in the plant.

Guidelines

Should any employee be found to be under the influence of drugs while on duty, such conduct will justify summary discharge, regardless of whether there is a rule prohibiting the use of drugs in the workplace, while on duty, or at a time proximate to the employee's worktime.

The use of any controlled drug which affects behavior, or the ability of an employee to work in a safe manner, regardless of whether the drug is a narcotic or "illegal" in the common sense may be cause for discipline where the employee knew or should have known that the drug would materially diminish his or her capabilities.

Relevant Cases

Combustion Engineering, Inc. (Jewett), 70 LA 318;
St. Joe Minerals Corp. (Roberts), 70 LA 1110;
Mississippi River Grain Elevator (Marcus), 62 LA 200;
Monfort Packing Co. (Goodman), 66 LA 286;
Arco-Polymers, Inc. (Milentz), 69 LA 379;
Pepsi Cola Bottlers of Youngstown, Inc. (Klein), 68 LA 792;
S. F. Kennedy-New Products, Inc. (Traynor), 64 LA 880;
Wheaton Industries (Kerrison), 64 LA 826.

3   *Where an employee uses or possesses drugs while off the employer's premises and while not on duty, neither discipline nor discharge will normally be sustained without the presence of some fact which directly impacts on the legitimate business interest of the employer, e.g., the employer's reputation, or without some other element which will justify the discipline.*

Examples:

Following a minor automobile accident, employee A was charged with being under the influence of a controlled substance, marijuana. Upon reading an account of the occurrence in a local newspaper, the employer discharged A. Noting A's acceptable work record, the arbitrator reinstated him with backpay.

Employee B was suspended after his arrest for possession and for being under the influence of cocaine. Following B's admission into an alcohol and drug rehabilitation program, which required as a condition of entry an admission of guilt, B was discharged. Noting that the employer had a restaurant which catered to teenagers, the arbitrator sustained the discharge.

Employee C was discharged following his arrest and conviction for using illegal drugs, marijuana. The employer argued at the arbitration that it had a problem of drug use in the plant which it had been unsuccessful in solving. The arbitrator, stating that the employer's need to rout out drug users in the plant created a special circumstance, sustained the discharge.

Guidelines

The possession or use of drugs while off the employer's premises and while not on duty may be cause for discipline, up to and including discharge, where such conduct can be shown to have a direct and material adverse effect on the employer's business interests, including public image.

Relevant Cases

City of Wilkes-Barre (Dunn), 74 LA 33;
Indian Head, Inc. (Rimer), 71 LA 82;
Nugent Sand Co. (Kanner), 71 LA 585;
Metropolitan Atlanta Transit Authority (Anderson), 70 LA 1022;
Gamble Brothers (Krislov), 68 LA 72;
Emhart Manufacturing Co. (McKone), 63 LA 1265;
General Portland Cement Co. (Davidson), 62 LA 377.

4   *Where an employee is found to be selling drugs or in possession of drugs with the intent to sell, discharge normally will be sustained, regardless of whether or not the discovery is made on the company's premises.*

Examples:

Employee *A* was discharged for possession of marijuana when a locker search turned up a quantity of the drug in excess of the normal user's amount in his locker. The employer had no rule regarding drugs. The arbitrator sustained the discharge on the grounds that the quantity discovered indicated that the employee had an obvious intent to sell.

Employee *B* was arrested and convicted of selling heroin. The sale and subsequent arrest took place away from the employer's workplace, and there was no evidence of any connection between *B*'s activity and his employer. *B* was discharged. The arbitrator, recognizing the employer's legitimate concern over the possibility of *B* making sales to other employees, sustained the discharge.

Guidelines

Regardless of the absence of a rule prohibiting the sale of drugs or possession with intent to sell drugs at any time or any place, such conduct will be cause for summary discharge, since it is perceived as a serious and immediate threat to the employer's business interest in that such an employee will be found to constitute a probable source for the acquisition of drugs by other employees.

Relevant Cases

Arco-Polymers, Inc. (Milentz), 69 LA 379;
Michigan Power Co. (Rayl), 68 LA 183;
Eastern Airlines, Inc. (Turkus), 76 LA 961;
Cerro Corp. (Griffin), 69 LA 965;
State University of New York (Babishkin), 74 LA 299;
New York City Health & Hospitals Corp. (Simons), 76 LA 387;
Joy Manufacturing Co. (Freeman), 68 LA 697;
Missouri Public Service Co. (Yarowski), 70 LA 1208.

Notes to Chapter 12

1. *B. Green & Co., Inc.* (Cushman), 71 LA 685.

2. *Joseph G. Tropiano, Inc.* (Belsky), 69 LA 1243.

3. *Detroit Stoker Co.* (Daniel), 75 LA 816; *Brooks Foundry, Inc.* (Daniel), 75 LA 642; *Georgia Pac. Corp.* (Vadakin), 72 LA 784; *Stansteel Corp.* (Kaufman), 69 LA 776; *Jeep Corp.* (Keefe), 67 LA 828.

4. *Combustion Eng'g, Inc.* (Jewett), 70 LA 318; *St. Joe Minerals Corp.* (Roberts), 70 LA 1110; *Mississippi River Grain Elevator* (Marcus), 62 LA 200.

4. *Monfort Packing Co.* (Goodman), 66 LA 286.

6. *Porcelain Metals Corp.* (Roberts), 73 LA 1133 (3-day suspension upheld).

7. *City of Wilkes-Barre* (Dunn), 74 LA 33 (the employee was reinstated with backpay); *Indian Head, Inc.* (Rimer), 71 LA 82 (employee was reinstated without backpay); *Nugent Sand Co.* (Kanner), 71 LA 585 (the employee was reinstated without backpay); *Metropolitan Atlanta Transit Auth.* (Anderson), 70 LA 1022 (the employee was reinstated with backpay); *Gamble Bros.* (Krislov), 68 LA 72 (the employee was reinstated without backpay); *Emhart Mfg. Co.* (McKone), 63 LA 1265 (a 6-month suspension was denied); *General Portland Cement Co.* (Davidson), 62 LA 377 (a 2-month suspension for a heroin arrest was denied). *But see National Floor Prods. Co.* (Eyrand), 58 LA 1015 (discharge sustained).

8. *Arco-Polymers, Inc.* (Milentz), 69 LA 379.

9. *Michigan Power Co.* (Rayl), 68 LA 183.

10. *Eastern Airlines, Inc.* (Turkus), 76 LA 961; *Cerro Corp.* (Griffin), 69 LA 965.

11. *State Univ. of New York* (Babiskin), 74 LA 299.

12. *New York City Health & Hosps. Corp.* (Simons), 76 LA 387 (the discharge was upheld where the employee had sold cocaine); *Joy Mfg. Co.* (Freeman), 68 LA 697 (the discharge was upheld where the employee had sold marijuana).

13. *See Missouri Pub. Serv. Co.* (Yarowski), 70 LA 1208.

14. *Swift & Co.* (Rentfro), 72 LA 513 (the employee was reinstated without backpay); *Abex Corp.* (Rybolt), 64 LA 721 (the employee's discharge was reduced to a 3-day suspension as with first alcohol offenses).

15. *B. Green & Co., Inc.* (Cushman), 65 LA 1233; *St. Joe Minerals Corp., supra,* note 4.

16. *Wheaton Indus.* (Kerrison), 64 LA 826.

17. *See also Arco-Polymers, Inc., supra,* note 8.

18. *Arco-Polymers, Inc., supra,* note 8; *Pepsi Cola Bottlers of Youngstown, Inc.* (Klein), 68 LA 792; *S. F. Kennedy-New Prods., Inc.* (Traynor), 64 LA 880. *See also Wheaton Indus., supra,* note 16.

19. *Watauga Indus. Inc.* (Galambos), 78 LA 697.

20. *Braniff Airways, Inc.* (Ray), 73 LA 304; *Todd Pac. Shipyards Corp.* (Brisco), 72 LA 1022; *Pepsi Cola Bottlers, supra,* note 18; *Whirlpool Corp.* (Gruenberg), 65 LA 386.

21. *General Tel. Co. of Calif.* (Richman), 73 LA 531; *Keystone Steel & Wire Co.* (Elson), 72 LA 780; *St. Joe Minerals Corp.*, *supra*, note 4; *Day & Zimmerman, Inc.* (Stratton), 63 LA 1289.

22. *St. Joe Minerals Corp.*, *supra*, note 4; *Day & Zimmerman, Inc.*, *supra*, note 21.

23. *Structurlite Plastics Corp.* (Leach), 73 LA 691.

24. *Casting Eng'rs* (Petersen), 71 LA 949.

25. *St. Joe Minerals Corp.*, *supra*, note 4.

26. *Whirlpool Corp.*, *supra*, note 20.

27. *General Foods Corp.* (Maslanka), 65 LA 1271.

28. *Prestige Stamping Co.* (Keefe), 74 LA 163; *Issaacson Structural Co.* (Peck), 72 LA 1075.

29. *State Univ. of New York* (Babiskin), 74 LA 299, at 301.

13

Gambling

Issue: Whether an employee can be discharged or otherwise disciplined for gambling.

Principle: An employee may be discharged or otherwise disciplined for gambling where it is shown that the activity was on the employer's premises; that it was part of a well-established pattern which either pervaded the company or had a deleterious effect on other employees or on production; or that the employee has shown by work and/or discipline record that he or she is unlikely to reform. Discipline is more readily accepted if the activity is in violation of a company rule which is equally enforced.

Considerations:
1. Whether a company rule exists prohibiting gambling and whether the employee had actual or constructive notice;
2. Whether the activity actually constituted gambling;
3. Whether gambling is a general problem in the company;
4. Whether the gambling was on company premises;
5. Whether the gambling had a detrimental effect on the productivity of the company and/or on the morale of the employees;
6. Whether the reinstatement of the employee will have a detrimental effect on the other employees;
7. Whether the employee's work record and prior history of discipline indicate a likelihood of reform;

158

8. Whether the rule against gambling was evenly enforced.

Discussion: There appear to be no settled rules among arbitrators with respect to discharges and discipline for gambling activities. Certainly, where an employee is the principal in an organized and pervasive gambling operation—numbers writing, bookmaking, or floating crap games—and the activity has had a demonstrable effect on employee production and morale, arbitrators normally sustain the discharge of the employee as for just cause. This will occur even where the employer has no established rule against gambling, as such. However, the exceptions to this general rule are too numerous to permit an all-inclusive generalization upon which employers and employees can rely with certainty. It is in this area that the personal backgrounds and predispositions of arbitrators seem most apparent.

Nevertheless, arbitrators do recognize the severity of the problems created for a company by the gambling of employees within the plant, and clearly, gambling can constitute just cause for discharge. These problems were delineated best by Arbitrator Turkus as follows:

> In-plant gambling poses a grave problem to both industry and labor. The direct and indirect deleterious effects thereof have impelled responsible Unions on a high level to institute educational programs for employees as far back as 1953 in an effort to curb and/or eliminate inplant gambling, its concomitant demoralization of plant morale and discipline, the disruption and impairment of plant productivity and enmeshment of workers in hopeless financial difficulty—the natural and inevitable corollaries of such illicit activity.
>
> The magnitude and gravity of the misconduct of operating as a policy collector within the Company plant, taking numbers bets from employees during working hours, is of itself just and sufficient cause for his discharge. The Company had the right, indeed it would seem, the obligation to effectively and irrevocably terminate the employment status of any worker who utilized the Company's premises as a base for the operation of a policy or numbers racket.[1]

Indeed, some arbitrators view gambling on the premises of the employer as so serious that they will find just cause to exist where such an employee has been discharged without progressive discipline or where there is no company rule against such activity.

For instance, in *Sun Drug Co., Inc.*, the employee was discharged when it was discovered that he was "writing numbers."[2] The union argued that the company could not discharge the employee, because there was no provision in the "Rules and Regulations" which prohibited gambling. The arbitrator, however, held that the discharge was for just cause despite the absence of an applicable company rule.

> With respect to the Union's final contention that discharge was too severe a penalty, in view of the fact that no notices were posted by the Company, it is the considered opinion of the Arbitrator that very little consideration can be given to this position. It certainly does not seem either reasonable or necessary that the Company post notices to the effect that acts which are in violation of the State Criminal Code cannot be tolerated. The Arbitrator feels certain that [the Union] does certainly not expect the Company to become an accessory, and for the Company to impose any penalty short of outright discharge would in a sense make it an accessory, insofar as it would be condoning the matter of the booking of numbers on its premises.

* * *

> The contract provides that discharge shall be for violation of reasonable Company rules and regulations. To say that the absence of a rule in the Company's RULES AND REGULATIONS, specifying that an act of any employee in violation of the State Criminal Code on Company time and Company property would not be tolerated, would be to imply that in the absence of such a rule, the Company would condone a criminal act on its premises, and thus make itself an accessory to it. To rule that the Company had no right to discharge for a criminal offense, because it was not spelled out in the Company's RULES AND REGULATIONS, would be writing something into the contract that neither the Company nor the Union had intended to put into it.[3]

Surprisingly, arbitrators have treated the issue of whether the employee was gambling on his or her own time or during working time with some concern. In *Bethlehem Steel Co., Sparrows Point Plant*, for instance, an employee was discharged for conducting a numbers operation.[4] The arbitrator held that the employee "was discharged for just cause for participating in unlawful gambling activities within the Plant."[5] There was no mention in the arbitrator's report of the existence or the absence of a company rule prohibiting gambling.

In that case it was argued by the employee that the discharge was unwarranted, because he was conducting the numbers game "on his own time." The arbitrator ruled that this fact did not immunize the employee from discharge, for it "hardly severs the tie between his numbers activity and his employment relationship."[6] The fact that he was conducting gambling activity on company premises was sufficient.

Most commonly, however, arbitrators who sustain discharges for gambling have relied upon either a contract provision or a company rule which specifically prohibits the activity.[7]

The presence of a clear and communicated rule prohibiting gambling is not necessarily a guarantee that a discharge will be sustained or that the offense will be considered summary in nature. In fact, it would appear that most arbitrators believe gambling to be a nonsummary offense and subject to the progressive discipline system. Consequently, unless the labor agreement or company rules make gambling a summary offense, arbitrators will most likely examine the more traditional aspects of due process and employee history.

In *Black Diamond Enterprises, Inc.*, for example, there was a company rule which prohibited gambling on company premises.[8] An employee was discharged for engaging in a "check pool" and for playing poker. The arbitrator noted that the purpose of the company rule was "to insure good conduct." The arbitrator believed that the employee's conduct in participating in the check pool did not warrant discharge, because this activity was not "detrimental to the conduct of the workforce."[9] However, the company had merely issued reprimands for first violations of other rules, and the arbitrator found that this practice made it inequitable to discharge the employee for playing poker in violation of the gambling prohibition. The arbitrator held that the company must itself correct the practice by rigid enforcement of its rules, and the discharge could not stand. All violations should be treated equally, unless "of such severity as to warrant instant discharge."[10]

In *Radio Corp. of America*, an employee, who was caught gambling on employer premises and who had pleaded guilty to a criminal charge of bookmaking, was also discharged by the employer.[11] There was a company rule prohibiting gambling, which was known to the employee. Nevertheless, the arbitrator held that the discharge was not justified:

> However, gambling violations, per se, are not just cause for discharge regardless of circumstances. Gambling involves a continuum in which the seriousness of the offense and the man's record with the Company constitute important variables which must be considered in determining just cause and appropriateness of penalty.[12]

The arbitrator went on to consider the fact that the employee had a good work record. Such consideration led the arbitrator to reinstate the employee.

> On the other hand, Mr. X____ has an unblemished 35-year record with the Company. Mr. X____ is entitled to have this record weighed in the determination of appropriateness of penalty. . . . Under these circumstances, it is appropriate to give the individual an opportunity to reform. Clearly however, Mr. X____ is to be penalized by denial of back pay. . . . His conduct must be above reproach in the future.[13]

It should be noted, however, that other arbitrators have sustained employee discharges for gambling, even in the face of a long and favorable employee work record.[14] In *Jenkins Bros.,* the arbitrator concluded:

> In view of the seriousness of the gambling problem in this plant and X's obvious involvement in it, [there is] no reason to mitigate the penalty imposed by the Company because of X's good work record.[15]

Thus, as appears to be the case generally in this area, arbitrators disagree as to the weight which should be given to an employee's good work record. It is unclear, therefore, whether an employee discharged for "writing numbers," or engaging in other gambling activities on company premises, would be discharged for "just cause" without a showing of other factors supporting the discharge. If there is no company rule in force, most arbitrators would probably hold that a discharge for gambling activities is unjustified. However, another arbitrator, when faced with the seriousness of a gambling charge, may feel disinclined to overturn management's decision. The result may simply depend on which particular arbitrator is hearing the case. Indeed, gambling offenses have been treated with such variety that it may serve an employer well not to rely on the offense alone as its only justification for the discipline.

In *Advertising Publishing Co., Ltd.,* the employee had been ordered by the employer to cease and desist from his gambling activities, and when he failed to do so, the employee was discharged.[16] The arbitrator held that the employee's actions constituted insubordination and that the employer was justified in concluding that the employee would not reform. The arbitrator stated:

> It is clearly his duty and a part of his employment to be governed by the instructions given him by his supervisor to refrain from gambling.[17]

Accordingly, at least one employer overcame arbitral uncertainty on the issue by ordering the employee to stop all gambling activity, and when he did not, the employer was able to discharge him for insubordination.

Key Points:

1 *There should be a communicated company rule which makes engaging in gambling activity a summary offense.*

Examples:

Employee *A* was discovered operating a numbers writing pool within the company and was discharged pursuant to a rule prohibiting gambling on the premises. The arbitrator, noting the employee's good work record of ten years, reinstated the employee with full backpay. The arbitrator declared that the employee should have been accorded progressive discipline, beginning with a verbal warning.

Employee *B* was discovered operating a numbers writing pool within the company and was discharged pursuant to a contract provision, which made gambling on the premises a cause for immediate discharge. The arbitrator, while noting the unfairness in light of the employee's otherwise unblemished work history of over twenty years, sustained the discharge.

Guidelines

The rule against gambling must be clear, incapable of misunderstanding, and sufficiently broad to cover all conduct the employer seeks to prohibit. The penalty should also be specific to limit the arbitrator's authority and to avoid a requirement of progressive disciplinary action.

Relevant Cases

Metro Contract Services, Inc. (Moore), 68 LA 1048;
Sun Drug Co. (Marcus), 31 LA 192;
Black Diamond Enterprises, Inc. (Nicholas), 52 LA 945;
Radio Corp. of America (Gershenfeld), 49 LA 1262;
City of Flint, Mich. (Stieber), 59 LA 370.

2 *The activity must constitute actual gambling.*

Examples:

Employee *A* was discharged for playing poker with three co-workers during their lunch hour. The players had been making small stake bets. The arbitrator, drawing a distinction between a friendly game of cards and gambling, reinstated the employee under a simple just cause standard and reduced the discharge to a verbal warning.

Employee *B* was discharged for conducting a craps game during his lunch break. The stakes were modest. The arbitrator sustained the discharge, refusing to distinguish between craps and other forms of gambling activity.

Employee *C* was discharged for operating a football pool. The arbitrator sustained the discharge. The arbitrator noted that the organized fashion in which the employee conducted his operation constituted gambling, while occasional pools run by other employees for the World Series and Super Bowl were not.

Guidelines

Even where a company rule is involved, the employer must be able to establish that the activity, in fact, constituted gambling, as the term is normally construed. The operation of a lottery, therefore, is distinguished from a raffle. Card games appear to fall into a grey area, and arbitrators look to the circumstances which surround the games. The difference appears to lie in the scope, intent, and organization of the operation.

Relevant Cases

Bethlehem Steel Co. (Gill), 51 LA 707;
Black Diamond Enterprises, Inc. (Nicholas), 52 LA 945;
Haskell Mfg. Co. (Wood), 33 LA 174.

3   *The gambling activity must be conducted on the company's premises.*

Examples:

Employee *A* was convicted of running a numbers operation and was discharged by the employer. There was no evidence that the employee engaged in any such activity while on the company's property, although some of his coworkers used his service. The arbitrator reinstated the employee, noting that the necessary connection between the employee's activity and the employer's legitimate interest did not exist.

Employee *B* was discharged for running a craps game during his lunch break. *B* defended on the basis that the game took place "on his own time" and did not affect any business interests of the employer. The arbitrator sustained the discharge.

Employee C was discharged for numbers writing. The employee defended on the basis that all of his activities were off the premises and on his own time. The arbitrator found that some of the people using C were employees and that, while collection and payoffs were made off the premises, the receipt of numbers did occur on the premises, although during the employee's breaks and lunch periods. The discharge was sustained.

Guidelines

Nearly all arbitrators require the employer to prove that the gambling took place on company premises in order to justify a discharge. Evidence of gambling, which is conducted by an employee while off company premises, generally cannot be used as a basis for discharge, unless a close connection is established between the gambling activity and the employer's workplace. Whether the activity took place during working time or in work areas is generally perceived to be irrelevant.

Relevant Cases

City of Flint, Mich. (Stieber), 59 LA 370;
Bethlehem Steel Co., Sparrow Point Plant (Porter), 45 LA 646;
Bethlehem Steel Co. (Gill), 51 LA 707;
Radio Corp. of America (Scheiber), 39 LA 621;
General Electric Company (Seitz), 41 LA 823;
Bethlehem Steel Co. (Porter), 45 LA 1007.

4 *Discharge or disciplinary action is clearly warranted where the gambling activity is not an incidental occurrence, but part of a well-established pattern of gambling, especially if it is pervasive within the company.*

Examples:

Employee A was discharged along with three others for playing pinochle for stakes. The evidence indicated that this game was the first time the employees had played at work, although they played regularly in off hours. In the absence of clear contract language to the contrary, the arbitrator reinstated all of the employees and reduced the discharge to a verbal warning.

Employee *B* was discharged for participating in a craps game. The evidence indicated that this was the first time *B* had ever engaged in this activity, that he didn't know the rules and that he lost his only bet, $5. Finding that the discharge was part of the employer's announced crackdown on all types of gambling in the plant and that this was the first time the employer had been successful in catching a game in progress, the arbitrator sustained the discharge.

Guidelines

Arbitrators are more sympathetic to discharged employees if they have participated only in isolated, infrequent gambling activities, *e.g.*, sports "pools." If the evidence reveals that an established gambling operation with a substantial volume exists, then the arbitrator will be more likely to deny the grievance. Moreover, arbitrators consider the seriousness of a gambling problem throughout the company, when determining the propriety of an employee discharge. If it is apparent that gambling is currently widespread among the employees, an arbitrator will often realize the importance of eradicating the problem and will sustain the discharge, regardless of other mitigating circumstances which may surround an individual grievant's case.

Relevant Cases

Jenkins Bros. (Stutz), 45 LA 350;
Haskell Mfg. Co. (Wood), 33 LA 174;
Bethlehem Steel Co., Sparrows Point Plant (Porter), 45 LA 646;
Bethlehem Steel Co. (Porter), 45 LA 1007.

5   *The gambling activity must have had a demonstrably adverse effect on the work operations.*

Examples:

Employee *A* was discharged for continuing to conduct weekly football pools after repeated warnings. Noting that every Monday morning as many as thirty employees would crowd around *A*'s work station and that up to ten minutes of worktime would be lost as a result, the arbitrator sustained the discharge.

Employee *B* was discharged for running a numbers operation. At the arbitration hearing, the employee maintained that the only time he transacted business was before and after the workday in the company's parking lot and that his activity had not interfered with his work or that of his customers. The employer established that *B* frequently gave credit and carried on his collection activities during the workday, although on breaktimes. On one occasion an employee had pleaded with his supervisor to allow him more overtime because of his need to pay *B* a gambling debt. The arbitrator sustained the discharge.

Guidelines

Arbitrators have tended to sustain discharges when it is apparent that the gambling activity is harmful to the company's business. Employers have sometimes shown that the gambling activity reduced the productivity of the affected employees. Also, employers often have been able to establish that employee morale was lessened as a result of gambling losses. However, if the employee can establish that his conduct was not detrimental to work operations, an arbitrator might be less inclined to sustain a discharge.

Relevant Cases

Haskell Mfg. Co. (Wood), 33 LA 174;
Sun Drug Co. (Marcus), 31 LA 191;
Advertising Publishing Co., Ltd. (Cobb), 32 LA 26;
City of Flint, Mich. (Stieber), 59 LA 370.

6   *Whether the prior work record of the employee is good and whether there is an indication of possible reform.*

Examples:

Employee *A* was discharged for participation in a craps game. The employee's work record spanned twenty years and was unblemished. The arbitrator nevertheless sustained the discharge.

Employee *B* was discharged for participation in a craps game. The employee's work record spanned twenty years and was unblemished; the arbitrator reinstated the employee.

Guidelines

Some arbitrators will not consider the employee's work record in ruling on a discharge for gambling. Others, however, will consider a long and favorable work record as a factor to be weighed against the employee's gambling activity and often will give the employee an opportunity to reform. However, if the employer can establish that an employee is unlikely to reform and to abandon his gambling activity, a discharge of that employee will probably be justified.

Relevant Cases

Radio Corporation of America (Gershenfeld), 49 LA 1262;
Radio Corporation of America (Scheiber), 39 LA 621;
Advertising Publishing Co., Ltd. (Cobb), 32 LA 26;
Jenkins Bros. (Stutz), 45 LA 350;
Black Diamond Enterprises, Inc. (Nicholas), 52 LA 945.

7   *The gambling rule must be enforced equally.*

Examples:

Employee *A* was discharged for conducting a numbers game. The arbitrator noted that gambling was one of several types of offenses, published in the company's rules, which would subject an employee to discipline. The arbitrator looked to the degree of discipline to be administered for the first violation of other types of prohibited conduct and found that the firm had a progressive discipline system. The arbitrator, therefore, ordered the reinstatement of the employee with the appropriate degree of discipline to be given as for first offenses of other types of prohibited conduct.

Employee *B* was discharged for operating a numbers game. *B* defended by presenting evidence that *M* had been given a lesser penalty when the latter was caught conducting a basketball pool. The arbitrator reinstated the employee and ordered the same discipline as was given *M*.

Employee *C* was discharged for playing poker for stakes during a lunch break. *C* complained that the other players had only been suspended. The arbitrator reinstated *C* without backpay, commuting the discharge to a suspension.

> ## Guidelines
>
> If the employer does not rigidly enforce work rules in other areas, it cannot selectively enforce a gambling rule. Also, if an employer generally does not discharge employees for first violations of other company rules, it cannot choose to discharge employees for first violations of a gambling rule, unless the stated and communicated rule provides for summary discharge. In addition, an employer cannot discharge one employee and take no action against other employees involved in the same gambling operation.

Relevant Cases

Bethlehem Steel Co., Sparrow Point Plant (Porter), 45 LA 646;
Black Diamond Enterprises, Inc. (Nicholas), 52 LA 945;
Haskel Mfg. Co. (Wood), 33 LA 174;
Lockheed Aircraft Corp. (Roberts), 37 LA 188;
Metro Contract Services, Inc. (Moore), 68 LA 1048;
Bethlehem Steel Co. (Porter), 45 LA 1007;
Radio Corp. of America (Gershenfeld), 49 LA 1262.

Notes to Chapter 13

1. *Charm Footwear Co.* (Turkus), 39 LA 154, 156.
2. *Sun Drug Co.* (Marcus), 31 LA 191.
3. *Id.*, at 194, 195.
4. *Bethlehem Steel Co., Sparrows Point Plant* (Porter), 45 LA 646.
5. *Id.*, at 647.
6. *Id.*, at 646.
7. *See Haskell Mfg. Co.* (Wood), 33 LA 174; *Jenkins Bros.* (Stutz), 45 LA 350.
8. *Black Diamond Enter., Inc.,* (Nicholas), 52 LA 945.
9. *Id.*, at 950.
10. *Id.*, at 951.
11. *Radio Corp. of Am.* (Gershenfeld), 49 LA 1262.
12. *Id.*, at 1264.
13. *Id.*
14. *See Advertising Publishing Co.* (Cobb), 32 LA 26.
15. *Jenkins Bros., supra,* note 7.
16. *Advertising Publishing Co., Ltd., supra,* note 14.
17. *Id.*, at 27.

14

Insubordination

Issue: Whether an employee can be discharged or otherwise disciplined for refusing to perform a task or to comply with an order given to him by a supervisor.

Principle: An employee can be discharged or otherwise disciplined for insubordination where the employee not only understands the supervisor's directive, but willfully disobeys or disregards it under circumstances where the employee's behavior is neither provoked nor justified by reasonable concern over safety.

Considerations:
1. Whether the employee understood or evidenced an understanding of the order or directive of the supervisor, and the employee willfully disobeyed or disregarded it;
2. Whether the behavior of the employee was provoked by supervisory misconduct;
3. Whether the refusal to obey or the disregard of the supervisor's directive was justified;
4. Whether the employee was entitled to and received progressive discipline.

Discussion: Arbitrators generally view employee compliance with reasonable management orders as essential to the functioning of the employer's business. Consequently, arbitrators consistently hold the refusal to obey an order or directive of any importance warrants discipline, up to and including discharge. In fact, the generally ac-

170

cepted rule is that, where the employee refuses to obey or willfully disregards a direct order of significant importance, the employee will be subject to summary discharge and will be denied the rights of progressive discipline. Frequently, the gravity of the offense is defined in terms of the impact of the employee's action on the authority of the supervisory personnel and on the safety and property of the employer or others. Indeed, arbitrator response to discipline for alleged insubordination has not been to automatically sustain discharges. In this respect, the review of Arbitrator Michael Jay Jedel is particularly relevant:

Based on an examination of Labor Arbitration Reports, Volumes 1–10 (Bureau of National Affairs, Inc.), Orme W. Phelps concluded his discussion of insubordination in his 1959 pioneering work on *Discipline and Discharge in the Unionized Firm* as follows (pp. 100, 102):

'The statistical evidence, drawn from reported arbitrations, supports the conclusion that managerial treatment of insubordination tends to exceed the bounds of propriety. The standard remedy is discharge, but the arbitrators either reversed or modified almost two-thirds of the company rulings, which meant, at a minimum, reinstatement of the employee. Where the penalty was less severe, a sizable majority of the decisions were in favor of management.'

'What all this means is not that the plant has become a "debating society." It is still the employee's duty to obey. However, the latitude accorded management in its demand for prompt and unquestioning obedience is considerably narrowed from the principal infinity of noncontractual times. . . . Management, as well as the work force, operates under "a higher law," consisting of limits set by the agreement, standardized practice in industry, and the general rules of fair play. . . .There is no blinking the fact that this is markedly different from the exercise of managerial authority in the absence of an agreement. However, the loss in efficiency, if any, may well be counter-balanced to a considerable extent by a better feeling, a higher morale, and eventually increasing cooperation toward common goals.'

It is apparent that, although discharge is still a frequent response by management to instances of what it perceives as insubordination, that is not the only action taken, nor is discharge automatically accepted at arbitration as proper where management

has chosen this action. Instead, arbitrators have looked
at a variety of factors including the nature of the
alleged insubordination in the specific work setting,
the employee's prior record, the company's approach
to discipline, how management has treated similar
infractions, the existence of a specific rule or contractual language threatening discharge for insubordination, etc.[1]

In *Chromalloy Division-Oklahoma*, the arbitrator sustained the
summary discharge of an employee who had refused to comply with
a supervisor's direct command to return to work.[2] Likewise, in *Arcrods Plant*, the arbitrator sustained the discharge of an employee
who had refused to stop burning trash.[3] On the other hand, the
arbitrator in *Ohio Crankshaft Co.* refused to sustain the summary
discharge of an employee, who had refused to remove a painting
from his work area, until after he had been accorded progressive
discipline.[4] And, in *Acme Industrial Co.*, the arbitrator required
progressive discipline for an employee who had refused to stop whis-
tling and denied the employee's discharge.[5]

Frequently, discipline for abusive language is treated as insubordination, because there is an element of attack on supervisory authority. (For a discussion of this subject, see Chapter 2, Part II.)

By definition, the charge of insubordination requires that the element of willfulness be present for an employer to support disciplinary action against the employee. The offense concerns a considered
and rational decision by an employee to disobey, or disregard, his
or her employer's reasonable directive. Where an employee's ability
to exercise self-control is substantially diminished by some outside
force, however, it becomes highly questionable whether his or her
actions can be considered insubordinate. Although perhaps not articulated in quite this way, it appears to be this element which causes
arbitrators to question and to mitigate discipline for insubordination. This can be seen especially in cases where the employee asserts
that a supervisor provoked the conduct which later resulted in the
disciplinary action.[6] Provocation, however, is generally viewed as
an incomplete defense; provocation may serve to mitigate, but cannot completely overcome, discipline for insubordination.[7] Provocation cases, however, refer only to abusive language situations, since
an arbitrator is unlikely to find that any provocation could be sufficient to justify an employee's willful refusal to obey a reasonable
order of management.

Discharges and lesser disciplinary measures for insubordination
frequently involve claims by employees that they refused to perform
directed tasks because it would expose them and/or other to safety

risks or dangerous conditions. When this type of situation arises, there are several factors which may become involved.

First, the employee may file a grievance over discipline resulting from such an incident. At arbitration, there is a recognized justification for insubordination, where the employee refused to perform a task because of a real and reasonable fear for his or her safety. However, when the employer has taken sufficient action to avoid the danger or has made an adequate explanation of the situation to allay the fear, the employee will be subject to discipline if the employee persists in his or her refusal to obey management's instructions. For example, in *Imperial Foods, Inc.* employees, who had refused to operate a saw for which they had no training, were reinstated without backpay, because the company had made no attempt to train them or to otherwise remove their fears.[8] However, in *Dayton Tire & Rubber Co.* the arbitrator upheld the discharge of an employee who had refused to perform a task he alleged was dangerous. There would have been no such danger, the arbitrator found, if the employee had followed the instructions of the supervisor with regard to the manner in which the task was to be performed.[9] In *United Parcel Service, Inc.*, the arbitrator sustained the discipline of an employee, where he found the employee's allegation of an unsafe practice to be unreasonable.[10] In this case, the employee had refused to write receipt slips while in the process of walking back to his truck after making a delivery. Likewise, the arbitrator in *Canton Drop Forging & Mfg. Co.* approved of the discipline given to employees who had refused to cross a picket line because of an alleged fear for their safety.[11] The arbitrator held that their refusal was unprotected activity and was unreasonably based.

Significantly, the right of employees to refuse to do a job because it is unsafe exists independently of labor agreements. There are labor agreements, however, which permit employees to refuse to do unsafe work, where there exists a good-faith belief that a danger is present.[12]

Second, whether there is a contractual provision permitting refusals to do unsafe work or not, the employee's action may be deemed to be concerted, protected activity under the National Labor Relations Act (the Act), thereby making the discharge or discipline an unfair labor practice. The National Labor Relations Board and many courts have found violations of Section 8(a)(1), and occasionally Section 8(a)(3), of the Act where employees were disciplined for good-faith refusals to do unsafe work pursuant to collective bargaining agreement provisions.[13] However, at least one court has held that before there can be a Section 8(a)(1) violation, more than a single employee must refuse to work because the conditions are unsafe, even when the refusal is pursuant to an agreement provision. Criticizing and distinguishing the *Interboro* doctrine[14] in which individual action on a right secured by a labor agreement is considered concerted activity, the court denied enforcement of the Board's Section 8(a)(1) finding, because there was no concerted activity under Section 7.[15]

The Board and the courts have also found employer violations of the Act where employees have refused to perform tasks for safety reasons, even in the absence of a contractual provision securing such a right. The Board found an 8(a)(1) violation in the discharge of three employees who had refused to wear protective suits, because the employees good-faith belief that the suits were unsafe.[16] However, where a single employee refused to drive a truck he believed in good faith to be unsafe, no 8(a)(1) violation had been found, because there had been no concerted activity.[17] Courts of appeal have upheld unfair labor practice charges and the reinstatement of employees with backpay in cases of refusals to work for safety reasons. For example, where the employees were found to have had a good-faith belief that the radioactive material with which they were to work was unsafe and the employer's assurances had been inadequate to allay those fears the employer was found to have violated Section 8(a)(1), when it discharged those employees.[18]

It should also be noted that the Act provides for the quitting of labor in good faith because of abnormally dangerous conditions and provides that such quitting of labor cannot be deemed a strike.[19] Therefore, an employee so quitting his labor cannot be discharged for violation of an agreement's no-strike clause.

Finally, a regulation of the Occupational Safety and Health Administration provides that employees who refuse in good faith to expose themselves to a dangerous condition are protected against subsequent discrimination. Where possible, the employee must have sought to correct the condition by addressing his or her employer.[20] This regulation was upheld by the U.S. Supreme Court in a case where two employees had refused to work on a suspended wire mesh that had been the cause of past accidents.[21]

There are, therefore, several limitations upon an employer's ability to discipline an employee who refuses to perform an assigned task for safety reasons. Under each provision, however, there is the understanding that the employee must have a good-faith belief that the task involves a dangerous condition. Included in the arbitral determination of the employee's good-faith belief is an assessment of the employer's efforts to assure the employee of the safety of the situation and its efforts to make the condition safe.

The final element considered by arbitrators is the need, except in the most severe cases, for employers to demonstrate that progressive discipline had been administered prior to the discharge. In many cases arbitrators have required that employees be reinstated where there has been no prior discipline, particularly where there has been no prior suspension.[22] Conversely, where there had been prior discipline, whether for insubordination or something else, the discharges have been sustained.[23]

The extent to which arbitrators may go to modify or to void discipline for insubordination because of the lack of progressive discipline or a prior discipline record is seen in *Reynolds Metals Co..*[24] In that case an employee, who had suffered an industrial accident, refused to complete the accident reporting forms on the basis that he could neither read nor write. The supervisor knew this was untrue. The employee then said he was sick and was leaving. The supervisor ordered him to see the company nurse. He did not, and he left the plant through the fire exit without punching out. At the arbitration, the employer presented other instances of bad attitude, erratic behavior, poor performance, and insubordination. The arbitrator refused to consider these additional occurrences, because the incidents had never been "written-up" and the employee had never been disciplined for them. Finding, therefore, a good prior work record, the arbitrator held that the employee had not received progressive discipline commensurate with that record and reduced the discharge to a disciplinary suspension.

Key Points:

1   *The employee must have understood the order or directive of a supervisor, and then the employee must have willfully disobeyed or disregarded it.*

Examples:

Employee *A*, while working, was told by a supervisor to stop smoking. When *A* was discovered smoking in another part of the plant while taking a part to another employee, she was disciplined by the supervisor. The supervisor's disciplinary action was revoked by the arbitrator when the employee testified that her only understanding was that she was not to smoke while at her normal work station.

Employee *B* was told by a supervisor not to continue to burn the trash collected in his department in an incinerator at the rear of the plant's property, but to stack it for cartage. The supervisor had told *B* that the scrap from his department if burned, would give off toxic fumes. *B* stacked the trash next to the incinerator where the trash caught fire. The employee was discharged. The arbitrator sustained the discharge, stating that the employee should have known that the scrap, if stacked next to the incinerator, would catch fire and that the burning of the trash could have had serious consequences.

Employee C was discharged for incorrectly mixing a batch of chemicals. At the arbitration, C admitted that he was aware from the operations manual that the chemicals should have been mixed in different amounts and that his supervisor had told him to follow the manual precisely. C stated that he had run short of a particular chemical, had begun the process without checking his supplies, and rather than stopping the operations to get more of the particular chemical, chose to add only what he had. The arbitrator sustained the discharge.

Employee D had been given a package by his supervisor and had been told to deliver it to a particular address. He was not told of the extreme importance of the delivery to the intended recipient. Receiving no answer at the address, the employee left it next door with instructions to have the package taken to the proper recipient the next day. When the package disappeared, D was discharged. The arbitrator mitigated the discharge to a suspension, noting that the employee had only been negligent and did not have the intent necessary to be found insubordinate.

Employee E, a recent transferee to a new department, received instructions from her supervisor in the operation of various pieces of equipment and the action to take to correct errant conditions. E was also given an operations manual and shown by the supervisor several procedures in the manual which were no longer acceptable. The employee made several errors and was given assistance by her coemployees. When she used an obsolete correction procedure out of the manual, however, she was suspended for insubordination. The arbitrator reduced the employee's discipline to a warning, stating that the employee lacked the training necessary to justify a charge of insubordination.

Guidelines

To be able to sustain discipline or discharge for insubordination, the employer must be able to establish that (a) the employee actually knew and understood the directive of his or supervisor, (b) the order was so clear that no reasonable person could have misunderstood it, and/or (c) the employee intentionally disobeyed, or disregarded, the instruction.

Relevant Cases

Arcrods Plant (Bradley), 47 LA 994;
Chromalloy Division-Oklahoma (Moore), 67 LA 1310;
Ohio Crankshaft Co. (Teple), 48 LA 558;
Acme Industrial Co. (Updegraff), 41 LA 1176;
National Gypsum Co. (Ray), 74 LA 7;
American Sugar Co. (Whyte), 52 LA 1228;
Globe Refractories, Inc. (Bolte), 78 LA 320;
Kay-Brunner Steel Products (Gentile), 78 LA 363;
United Parcel Service, Inc. (McAllister), 78 LA 836;
Canton Drop Forging & Mfg. Co. (Teple), 78 LA 1189;
E. I. du Pont de Nemours & Co. (Light), 78 LA 327;
International Minerals & Chemical Corp. (Jones), 78 LA 682.

2   *The behavior of the employee must not have been provoked by any action of the supervisor.*

Examples:

Employee *A* was discovered by his supervisor during work time, not at his work station, but talking with another employee. The supervisor called to him from a distance, "Hey, you lazy, no-good s——of-a-b——, get your bloody a—— back to work." The employee yelled back, "Up your f—— a——," and slowly returned to his work station by way of the men's room. The supervisor went to the employee's work station and discharged him for insubordination. At arbitration, the employer stated that *A* had verbally abused the authority of the supervisor and had not returned to his work station immediately as directed. The arbitrator reinstated the employee without backpay, holding that the employee's response had been provoked by the supervisor's misconduct.

Employee *B* was discovered away from his work station and was seen talking with a coemployee. *B*'s supervisor yelled at him from a distance, "Hey, you lazy, no-good s——of-a-b——, get your bloody a—— back to work." *B* went to the supervisor and demanded an apology. The supervisor refused and again told him to get his f——, no-good a—— back to work. The supervisor discharged the employee. The arbitrator sustained the discharge, noting that the provocation, while severe, could not justify the employee's refusal to return to work.

> ### *Guidelines*
>
> Provocation of an employee by supervisory miscon-
> duct may result in the mitigation of an employee's dis-
> cipline for insubordination. However, such provocation
> normally will neither serve to protect an employee from
> all discipline nor justify an employee's total refusal to
> perform a directive from the employer.

Relevant Cases

Leaseway of Western New York, Inc. (France), 60 LA 1343;
Armco Steel Corp. (Duff), 52 LA 101;
Chalfant Mfg. Co. (Nichols), 52 LA 51;
Westinghouse Electric Corp. (Altrock), 51 LA 1311;
Anaconda Aluminum Co. (Erbs), 59 LA 1147;
Williams, White & Co. (Guenther), 67 LA 1181;
Michigan Bell Telephone Co. (Dyke), 78 LA 896;
Reynolds Metals Co. (Fasser), 78 LA 687.
See also cases in Chapter 2.

3   *The conduct of the employee cannot have been justified.*

Examples:

Employee *A* was instructed to go into a trench, six feet deep,
and repair a broken pipe. *A* refused, asserting that the walls
of the trench had been inadequately shored. The supervisor
went into the trench, inspected the shoring, declared it safe,
and told the employee to do the work. The employee refused
and was discharged. The arbitrator, finding that the employee's
fear was unreasonable, sustained the discharge.

Employee *B* was instructed to perform electrical repair work
on the roof of the employer's building. *B* refused, asserting that
he was not trained in electrical work and feared for his safety.
The supervisor told him that the work only consisted of changing a household-type fuse. The employee still refused and was
discharged. Holding that the work was not unreasonably dangerous, even for a person who had not been trained in electrical
work, the arbitrator sustained the discharge.

Employee *C* was an electrician who had been instructed to
make certain electrical repairs on the roof of the employer's
building. While *C* was engaged in the work, it began to rain.
C refused to complete the work in the rain without certain
protective equipment. The employer told him that it did not

have such equipment available and ordered C to complete the work without it. C refused and was discharged. The discharge was overturned by the arbitrator on the grounds that the refusal was justified.

Guidelines

An employee's refusal to perform a task may be justified, if the refusal is based upon a reasonable fear of personal injury or safety.

Relevant Cases

Imperial Foods, Inc. (Crawford), 69 LA 320;
Dayton Tire & Rubber Co. (Ipavec), 67 LA 78;
United States Steel Corp. (Garrett), 66 LA 489.
See also Labor Board and Court cases cited in Text.

4   *Except in extreme cases, the employee should be accorded progressive discipline.*

Examples:

Employee A was discharged for shouting to other employees stationed on the other side of the production floor. He had been warned previously that continuing the practice would result in his discipline. When he continued, unabated, the supervisor gave him a direct order to stop shouting. Within an hour, A had resumed his shouting and was discharged. The arbitrator, finding that A had not been accorded all of the steps in the progressive discipline system, reinstated the employee and instructed the employer to issue a written warning.

Employee B was found sleeping in a remote part of the plant and was ordered by his supervisor to return to his work station immediately. B started toward his workplace, but then went into the men's room, where he was later discovered sleeping in a toilet stall. B was discharged. Noting the employee's poor work record, which included a suspension for absenteeism, the arbitrator sustained the discharge, even though the employee had not been accorded progressive discipline.

Guidelines

Unless the insubordination involves an employee's complete refusal to do a job, arbitrators generally require that progressive discipline be administered by the employer in insubordination cases.

Relevant Cases

San Francisco Redevelopment Agency (Koven), 57 LA 1149;
Ohio Crankshaft Co. (Teple), 48 LA 558;
Acme Industrial Co. (Updegraff), 41 LA 1176;
National Gypsum (Ray), 74 LA 7;
Bethlehem Steel Corp. (Harkless), 58 LA 363;
Arcrods Plant (Bradley), 47 LA 994;
Globe Refractories, Inc. (Bolte), 78 LA 320;
Kay-Brunner Steel Products (Gentile), 78 LA 363;
Pepsi Cola Bottling Co. of Canton, Ohio (Keenan), 78 LA 516;
Reynolds Metals Co. (Fasser), 78 LA 687;
E. I. du Pont de Nemours & Co. (Light), 78 LA 327;
United Parcel Service, Inc. (McAllister), 78 LA 836.

Notes to Chapter 14

1. *Prismo-William Armstrong Smith Co.* (Jedel), 73 LA 581, at 584–585.
2. *Chromalloy Div.-Okla.* (Moore), 67 LA 1310.
3. *Arcrods Plant* (Bradley), 47 LA 994.
4. *Ohio Crankshaft Co.* (Teple), 48 LA 558.
5. *Acme Indus. Co.* (Updegraff), 41 LA 1176.
6. *See National Gypsum Co.* (Ray), 74 LA 7 (employee was reinstated without backpay); *Ekstrom, Carlson Co.* (Davis), 55 LA 764.
7. *See American Sugar Co.* (Whyte), 52 LA 1228.
8. *Imperial Foods, Inc.* (Crawford), 69 LA 320.
9. *Dayton Tire & Rubber Co.* (Ipavec), 67 LA 78.
10. *United Parcel Serv., Inc.* (McAllister), 78 LA 836.
11. *Canton Drop Forging & Mfg. Co.* (Teple), 78 LA 1189.
12. *United States Steel Corp.* (Garrett), 66 LA 489.
13. *City Disposal Sys., Inc.*, 256 NLRB No. 73, 107 LRRM 1267 (1981) (the employee refused to drive a vehicle; the discipline was found to have violated §8(a)(1) of the Act); *McLean Trucking Co.*, 252 NLRB No. 104, 105 LRRM 1558 (1980) (an employee refused to drive a truck; the discharge violated §8(a)(1) and (3) of the Act); *United Parcel Service*, 241 NLRB No. 166, 101 LRRM 1067 (1979) (an employee refused to drive a truck and a §8(a)(1) violation arose from the discharge); *Wheeling-Pittsburgh Steel Corp.*,

241 NLRB No. 198, 101 LRRM 1070 (1979), *enforced sub nom., Wheeling-Pittsburgh Steel Corp. v. NLRB*, 618 F.2d 1009, 104 LRRM 2054 (3d Cir., 1980) (an employee refused to operate a crane and a violation of §8(a)(1) and (3) of the Act was found to exist when the employee was suspended); *Roadway Express, Inc. v. NLRB*, 532 F.2d 751, 91 LRRM 2239 (4th Cir., 1976), *enforcing*, 217 NLRB No. 49, 88 LRRM 1503 (1975) (an employee refused to drive a truck and a finding of a violation of §8(a)(1) of the Act was upheld and the employee was reinstated with backpay).

14. *Interboro Contractors, Inc.*, 157 NLRB 1295, 61 LRRM 1537 (1966).

15. *Kohls v. NLRB*, 629 F.2d 173, 104 LRRM 3049 (D.C. Cir., 1980).

16. *E. R. Carpenter Co.*, 252 NLRB No. 5, 105 LRRM 1492 (1980).

17. *Washington Cartage, Inc.*, 258 NLRB No. 93, 108 LRRM 1144 (1981).

18. *NLRB v. Modern Carpet Indus.*, 611 F.2d 811, 108 LRRM 2167 (10th Cir., 1979). *See also NLRB v. Service Mach. & Shipbldg. Corp.*, 662 F.2d 1125, 108 LRRM 3235 (5th Cir., 1981) (reinstatement of four welders who refused to operate electrical equipment in the rain.)

19. 29 U.S.C. §143.

20. 29 C.F.R. §1977.12(b)(2).

21. *Whirlpool Corp. v. Marshall*, 445 U.S. 1 (1980).

22. *San Francisco Redev. Agency* (Koven), 57 LA 1149; *Ohio Crankshaft Co., supra,* note 4; *Acme Indus. Co., supra,* note 5 *National Gypsum Co., supra,* note 6.

23. *Bethlehem Steel Corp.* (Harkless), 58 LA 363; *Arcrods Plant, supra,* note 3.

24. *Reynolds Metals Co.* (Fasser), 78 LA 687.

15

Medical Disability

Issue: Whether an employee may be discharged or otherwise disciplined because of a medical disability.

Principle: The existence of a medical disability cannot be a cause for discipline, except in cases of fraud, because the necessary element of employee volition or fault is missing. Employees can be terminated, however, where their medical disabilities prevent them from performing their jobs, or attending work regularly; where the disability places the employees themselves or their coworkers in danger; where reasonable accommodation for the disabilities is not possible; and where there is little, or uncertain, hope for improvement of the medical conditions within a reasonable period of time.

Considerations:

1. Whether the medical condition prevents the employee from performing the tasks of the job;
2. Whether the medical condition causes the employee to be excessively absent;
3. Whether the medical condition presents a danger to the employee or to coworkers;
4. Whether the medical condition prevents the employee from comporting himself or herself with the needs of the workplace;
5. Whether the medical condition is work related;
6. Whether there is a likelihood of improvement within a reasonable period of time;

182

7. Whether there are suitable alternative positions available.

Discussion: Although the flexibility of most employers in dealing with employees suffering from medical disabilities has been substantially limited by the various discrimination statutes, issues concerning employee terminations due to such conditions still frequently reach arbitrators. The issue is normally raised in the context of an employee who has suffered an injury or illness during his or her term of employment and then has sought to return to the workplace in some fashion unsatisfactory to the employer. Apart from the ability of the employer under the law to reinstate the employee (or to terminate, after reinstatement) following a leave of absence, the question addressed by arbitrators is, "Does the condition of the employee constitute just cause for severing the employment relationship?" More appropriate in many cases, the question is, not "Should employment have been terminated?", but "When is the employer justified in terminating what appears to be an almost hopeless situation?" or "At what point is an employer entitled to declare an employee a hopeless situation and terminate the relationship?"

The most common cases of this kind involve heart conditions, back problems, and mental illness. A complete review of these cases, as decided by arbitrators, does permit several dependable generalizations. Where, for instance, an employee is demonstrably no longer able to perform the tasks of his or her job due to some medical disability, arbitrators consistently recognize the right of the employer to discharge that individual. In allowing for the termination of such employees, arbitrators have generally relied on the fact that one of the primary conditions of a person's employment is the ability of the person to do the work.[1]

There are also several cases, however, where arbitrators have considered other factors and have not upheld discharges, because they have not found the appearance of an employee's immediate inability to do the work to be conclusive *per se*. Prior satisfactory service contributed to the reinstatement order for an employee suffering from severe, but not permanent, back pain.[2] Ten years of prior service was also a major factor in an arbitrator's order for a six-month trial return to work for a schizophrenic employee whose illness was in remission.[3] Finally, in *Reynolds Metals-Sherwin Plant*, the arbitrator denied the discharge and ordered a review to determine whether the employee, who had had back surgery, was eligible for a disability pension.[4]

Arbitrators have upheld discharges where an employee failed, or refused, to return to work after his medical disability had ceased to exist. In *National Can Corp.*, the arbitrator upheld the discharge of an employee who had insisted on being given light duty upon his return to work, even though his doctors had placed no such restrictions on his performance.[5] A discharge was also upheld where the employee, after being given a medical release to return to work, did not report to work for some six weeks.

Arbitrators have also recognized the employers' right to expect regular attendance from their employees, regardless of the medical condition of the employees. The attitude appears to be that, while an employee may be entitled to some adjustment to the nature of the work to be performed due to a disability, the employee must be capable of coming to work and being on time. As a result, arbitrators have sustained the discharges of employees whose medical conditions have resulted in excessive absenteeism.[6] For example, in *Automotive Distributors, Inc.*, the absences of the employee were due to a sinus condition about which the employee had done nothing; in *Monsanto Co.*, the absences of the employee were due to a post-Vietnam stress disorder; in *Asarco, Inc.*, the employee had had many absences over several years due to hepatitis; in *Scott & Fetzer Co.*, the employee had missed over 75 percent of his worktime in one year; in *American Broadcasting Companies, Inc.*, the employee had sought a second leave within one year for hypertension; and, in *Kimberly-Clark Corp.*, the employee had missed 60 to 100 percent of his worktime during the previous four years.[7]

In *Newport News Shipbuilding & Dry Dock Co.*, the discharge of an employee for excessive absenteeism was sustained where the employee claimed he was unable to work due to a chronic back problem.[8] The arbitrator found a lack of evidence to substantiate a serious problem and found no evidence to support the employee's claim that he could not do any work. The arbitrator noted that the employee could have done light work, at least, and did not evidence a desire to get better by doing the exercises prescribed by his doctors.

Arbitrators also will sustain the discharges of employees where their disabilities make their continued employment a danger to themselves or to others. However, the danger must be real and not merely hypothesized, and there must be evidence that the danger cannot be avoided or reduced in the future. For example, the discharges of heavy equipment operators suffering from epilepsy—where there was no guarantee of their not having future seizures and the risk posed by their continued employment was great—have been sustained on these grounds.[9] Similarly, where an employee's mental condition presented a danger to other employees, his discharge was sustained because there was no evidence that his antisocial behavior would not recur.[10]

By comparison, employees have been reinstated, although without backpay, where there was no evidence of future danger,[11] or where the employee has been able to compensate for his condition and, thereby, reduce the danger[12] created by his or her continued employment.

Another situation in which an arbitrator may sustain a discharge is where the employee cannot adjust his or her conduct to the needs of the workplace due to some mental disability. An employee, who had used profane language, had shoved a supervisor, and had been otherwise disruptive in his behavior, was properly discharged, since there was no prognosis for improvement of the employee's diagnosed mental illness.[13] An employee who had destroyed company property while suffering from a mental disorder was also found to have been properly discharged.[14] In another case, an arbitrator denied the discharge of a schizophrenic employee, who had made threats and the like, pending the employee's entry into treatment. However, while ordering an indefinite suspension, the arbitrator acknowledged the ultimate right to discharge such an employee if the treatment was unsuccessful.[15]

In contrast to the preceding cases, at least one arbitrator has reduced a discharge to a one-year suspension for a disruptive and insubordinate employee, because the behavior was not willful, but rather the result of a mental disorder.[16] However, this case was also complicated by the company's failure to follow the grievance procedure.

A factor which arbitrators consider, although it is certainly not controlling, is whether the injury giving rise to the disability was work related. There is some indication in the holdings and dicta of arbitration decisions that work-related injuries, and any attendant disabilities, will be dealt with more leniently than those which are not work related. In *Truck Transport, Inc.*, for instance, the discharge of an employee, who would have been required to miss over nine months due to a nonwork injury, was upheld.[17] The arbitrator suggested that the outcome would have been different if the injury had been work related.[18] However, as suggested, this factor is not controlling, or dispositive. For example, in one case the discharge of an employee for absenteeism caused by a work-related injury was upheld, and the fact that the injury resulted from the employee's job made no apparent difference.[19]

Another factor which arbitrators consider relevent in reviewing discharges for medical disabilities is the outlook for improvement in the employee's condition. Where the employee is responding to treatment and has a likelihood of improving, discharges are generally denied.[20] On the other hand, where there is little likelihood of improvement in the employee's condition, the employee's discharge will generally be sustained.[21]

A final factor which arbitrators consider is the availability of alternate jobs with the employer which the disabled employee could perform. Where no such position is available, arbitrators have upheld discharges, even in the face of a contractual obligation to seek an alternative position.[22] An obligation to seek an alternative position has not included, or been found to include, requiring an employer to create a job to fit the employee's condition. In this respect, arbitrators do not appear ready to require job accommodations for these situations, as have equal employment offices. By contrast, in *West Penn Power Co.*, the arbitrator ordered a lineman, who suffered from acrophobia, to be reclassified pursuant to the contract where there were other suitable positions for the employee.[23]

Key Points:

1   *The medical disability must substantially prevent the employee from performing the normal tasks of his or her job or from attending work regularly.*

Examples:

Employee *A* had a coronary bypass operation. His physician certified that he could return to work provided it was light-duty work and did not involve lifting more than 25 pounds at a time or exerting more than 50 pounds of force. The employer had no job within those limitations, and the employee was terminated. The termination was sustained by the arbitrator.

Employee *B* had a back fusion operation and was permitted to return to work by his physician under the condition that he only do light work. The employer asked the physician if the employee could push trucks weighing up to 200 pounds without danger. The physician said that if the employee felt he could do it without hurting himself, he should be allowed to do so. The employer, nevertheless, transferred *B* to a lower-paying, but less strenuous, job. The employee grieved. At the arbitration, the employer asserted that it had forced the transfer to protect itself from a potentially higher workers' compensation rate. The grievance was sustained, and the employee was ordered back into his original job.

Employee *C* suffered from migraine headaches. As a result, her absenteeism became excessive under the company's absenteeism-control policy. *C* was terminated. The arbitrator commuted the termination to a leave of absence for treatment purposes.

Employee *D* suffered from a deep depression which periodically caused her to be absent from work for periods of up to one month. She had had six such bouts and one two-month leave of absence for treatment. Even though under treatment *D* had been told on several occasions that the employer could not continue to put up with her absenteeism and that she must become regular in her attendance. After her second absence of two weeks within the last four months of her employment, *D* was terminated. Noting that even a long-suffering employer has a right to cry, "Enough," the arbitrator sustained the termination.

Employee *E* had an industrial accident and acquired epilepsy. Although assured by *E*'s doctor that the condition would be controllable, the employer terminated *E*, explaining that it could not take a chance that *E* might hurt himself on a machine if he should have a seizure while working. The arbitrator reinstated the employee, finding the employer's fears to be unreasonable.

Guidelines

After taking into consideration all of the capabilities of the employee, an employer may terminate an employee with a medical disability if the disability acts to destroy the ability of the employee to be of any value to the employer.

Relevant Cases

Zellerbach Paper Co. (Stashower), 68 LA 69;
Central Telephone Co. (Mead), 76 LA 1137;
B. F. Goodrich Chemical Co. (Kimsly), 65 LA 1213;
National Steel Corp. (Traynor), 66 LA 533;
Reynolds Metals-Sherwin Plant (Caraway), 65 LA 678;
Newport News Shipbuilding & Dry Dock Co. (Garrett), 78 LA 202.

2 *Termination may be justified where the employee's disability creates an unusual danger to the employee or others.*

Examples:

Employee *A* acquired epilepsy because of a fall. While *A*'s physician stated that the condition would be controllable if the employee took the medicine as prescribed, the physician would not commit himself to an unequivocal assurance. The employer, fearing that the condition might not be totally controllable and that the employee might fail to take his medicine, transferred the employee from his regular job of driving a forklift truck into a lower-rated, general warehouseman classification. The arbitrator sustained the transfer.

For years employee *B* had missed time from work due to a weak back. After a spinal fusion operation, *B* returned to work and sought to resume his former job. The employer sent the job specifications to the employee's physician, who stated that the work was too strenuous. The employee continued to demand the job. When the employer stood firm, *B* grieved the issue, asserting that he should be allowed to assume the risk. The arbitrator sustained the employer's action, stating that while an employee may be unconcerned about his or her own health, the employer has a legitimate business interest to protect, *i.e.*, workers' compensation insurance costs.

Employee *C* suffered from a disease which caused her to suddenly and unpredictably fall asleep for a short period of time. The condition can be controlled by medication, which the employee had. On occasion *C* forgot to take the medication and suffered a sleeping attack. Fortunately, these occurrences took place while *C* had been on breaks. The employer refused her bid upward into the position of machine operator on the grounds that the employee might have an attack while operating a machine and be injured. The arbitrator overruled the employer, finding that the possibility of any danger by the employee's failure to take her medicine was no greater than that presented by any other machine operator who might be negligent and therefore, *C*'s condition did not constitute an unusual danger.

Guidelines

Where an employee's disability or medical condition creates a danger to the employee or to others, the employer may terminate the employee provided the danger is greater than that which normally exists in the workplace.

Relevant Cases

Acme Galvanizing, Inc. (Moberly), 61 LA 1115;
Weber Manufacturing Co., Inc. (Yeager), 63 LA 56;
Appleton Electric Co. (Roomkin), 76 LA 167;
City of Fenton (Roumell), 76 LA 355;
Samuel Bingham Co. (Cohen), 67 LA 706.

3   *Termination generally will not be justified if an employee's condition is likely to improve within a reasonable period.*

Examples:

Employee *A* suffered from phlebitis for many years. Gradually the condition made it impossible for her to continue her regular job, which involved standing for substantial periods of time. *A* took a leave of absence to have an operation. At the conclusion of the three-month leave, *A* was still unable to return to work, and her physician could not give an estimate of when she would be able to return, beyond "within the next year." The employer terminated *C* but told her that, when she was able, she should reapply for a position. The arbitrator sustained the termination.

Employee *B* was an alcoholic. After this condition was discovered because of *B*'s absenteeism record, the employer gave him a leave of absence for treatment. Following his leave, *B* returned to work under the condition that he continue treatment as an outpatient. After a few months, *B* began to drink again and was terminated. The arbitrator found that there was insufficient evidence to support a belief that *B* could get his condition under control within the reasonable future and sustained the discharge.

Employee *C* had a knee condition, which caused him pain when he stood for long periods of time. As a result of *C*'s complaints and other agitation, the employer allowed the employee to construct a seat-like structure near his machine. The employee then requested a two-month leave of absence for corrective surgery. The employer, noting that company policy only permitted medical leaves of up to one month, allowed *C* only one-half the time he requested. After the one month, *C* attempted to return to work, but left after one day due to excessive pain. The employer terminated him. The arbitrator reinstated the employee, stating that the condition would heal in a reasonably short time and that the employer's action had been unreasonable, without other reasons for the termination of substantial weight.

Guidelines

Absent contract language to the contrary, an employer cannot be compelled to keep a job open and available to an employee for an indefinite, or overly long, period of time. What is overly long will depend upon

> **Guidelines**—contd.
>
> what the employer evidences is reasonable by its ex-
> isting leave-of-absence policy and the nature of the job
> itself. The employer's legitimate need to be able to plan
> and to regulate the workplace will normally be ho-
> nored.

Relevant Cases

City of Hartford (Mallon), 69 LA 303;
City of Fenton (Roumell), 76 LA 355;
Scott & Fetger Co. (Chattman), 69 LA 18.

4   *The employer must have made good-faith efforts to find alternative work which the employee could do and to make some
accommodations for the employee's special circumstances. However, the employer is not required to create a new job just to fit
an employee's special condition.*

Examples:

Employee *A* suffered from lower back pain and, as a result,
lost sufficient time from his job to justify discipline under the
employer's absenteeism-control policy. The employee requested
a light-duty job. The request was persistently denied, and the
employee was ultimately discharged for excessive absenteeism.
The arbitrator, finding that the employer had not made a good-
faith effort to find light work for the employee, sustained the
grievance.

Employee *B*, a secretary, suffered a concussion, which resulted
in a substantial hearing loss. As a result, *B* was terminated.
The arbitrator reinstated the employee upon a showing that
the employer had not investigated devices which could be put
on the telephone to enable the hearing-impaired employee to
use it.

Employee *C* lost an arm in an accident. The employee could
still perform all the functions required in his job, except for
the carting of unfinished material to and from his workstation.
The employer determined that *C* could not do his regular job,
and the employee was transferred to a lower-rated position.
The arbitrator ordered *C*'s reinstatement to his former position
and required the employer to accommodate the employee by
having one of the other workers assist *C* with the carts.

Employee *D* suffered a heart attack, and his doctor limited him
to light-duty work. The employer, not having such work avail-

able terminated the employee. The arbitrator sustained the termination.

Guidelines

The employer must make a good-faith effort to accommodate the employee's condition by finding a suitable, alternative job or by making nonessential changes to the employee's regular job. Where such reasonable accommodation is not possible and a wholly new job must be created, a termination will be sustained.

Relevant Cases

Zellerbach Paper Co. (Stashower), 68 LA 69;
Weber Manufacturing Co., Inc. (Yeager), 63 LA 56;
West Penn Power Co. (Blue), 67 LA 1085.

Notes to Chapter 15

1. Zellerbach Paper Co. (Stashower), 68 LA 69; *see also Central Tel. Co.* (Mead), 76 LA 1137.
2. *B.F. Goodrich Chem. Co.* (Kimsly), 65 LA 1213.
3. *National Steel Corp.* (Traynor), 66 LA 533.
4. *Reynolds Metals-Sherwin Plant* (Caraway), 65 LA 678.
5. *National Can Corp.* (Turkus), 68 LA 351.
6. *Los Angeles Die Casting Co.* (Rose), 61 LA 1218.
7. *Automotive Distrib., Inc.* (Eisler), 76 LA 552; *Monsanto Co.* (Thomson), 76 LA 509; *Asarco, Inc.* (Bothwell), 74 LA 1024; *Scott & Fetzer Co.* (Chattman), 69 LA 18; *American Broadcasting Co., Inc.* (Gentile), 63 LA 278; *Kimberly-Clark Corp.* (Shieber), 62 LA 1119.
8. *Newport News Shipbldg. & Dry Dock Co.* (Garrett), 78 LA 202.
9. *Acme Galvanizing, Inc.* (Moberly), 61 LA 1115; *Weber Mfg. Co., Inc.* (Yaeger), 63 LA 56.
10. *Appleton Elec. Co.* (Roomkin), 76 LA 167.
11. *City of Fenton* (Roumell), 76 LA 355 (a police officer had suffered from a mental disorder.)
12. *Samuel Bingham Co.* (Cohen), 67 LA 706 (an epileptic employee was able to avoid tasks that could create a danger, and the potential for danger was further reduced by the fact that seizures came with several minutes' warning).
13. *Babcock & Wilcox Co.* (Duff), 75 LA 12.
14. *Allis-Chalmers Corp.* (Goetz), 73 LA 1230.
15. *Johns-Manville Perlite Corp.* (Traynor), 67 LA 1255.

16. *Marion Power Shovel Co., Inc.* (McDermott), 69 LA 339.

17. *Truck Transp., Inc.* (Seidman), 66 LA 60.

18. *See also Scott & Fetzer Co., supra,* note 7 (dicta indicating that the arbitrator was intentionally more lenient when the injury was job related); *Ryerson & Son, Inc.* (Zack), 61 LA 977 (reinstatement without backpay was ordered in a situation where the employee was discharged for excessive absenteeism resulting in large part from a work-related injury).

19. *Kimberly-Clark Corp.* (Shieber), 62 LA 1119.

20. *City of Hartford* (Mallon), 69 LA 303; *City of Fenton, supra,* note 11.

21. *Scott & Fetzer Co., supra,* note 7.

22. *Zellerbach Paper Co., supra,* note 1; *Weber Mfg. Co., Inc., supra,* note 9.

23. *West Penn Power Co.* (Blue), 67 LA 1085.

16

Misconduct, Horseplay, and Fighting

Issue: Whether an employee can be discharged or otherwise disciplined for misconduct, horseplay, or fighting.

Principle An employee can be discharged or otherwise disciplined for misconduct where the employee has performed an intentional act which caused, or had the potential of causing, physical injury or property damage; the employee can be discharged or otherwise disciplined for misconduct where the employee committed an act which, although unintentional, was in wanton disregard for the safety of others or of property; an employee can be disciplined, but not discharged for horseplay (unless the discharge is a final step in progressive discipline), where the employee has performed a childish act which has unintentionally caused injury or embarrassment to a person or damage to property; and, an employee can be discharged or otherwise disciplined for fighting where it appears that the employee was the aggressor, or a willing participant, in a fight with the apparent intent to injure another employee.

Considerations: Misconduct or Horseplay

1. Whether the actions of the employee were intentional and were committed with the apparent purpose of wrongdoing;
2. Whether the actions of the employee had the potential for physical injury or property damage;
3. Whether the tone of the workplace or the general behavior of employees in the workplace created an atmosphere which condoned such behavior;

193

4. Whether the employee is contrite to such an extent that the employer can expect that the conduct, or similar conduct, will not be repeated in the future.

Fighting

1. Whether the employee was the aggressor or a willing participant in the fight;
2. Whether the employee was provoked;
3. Whether the employee used an instrument in the fight with an apparent intent to do serious bodily harm to the other employee;
4. Whether the work history of the employee indicates a likelihood of peaceful behavior in the future.

Discussion: Arbitrators distinguish between misconduct and horseplay when reviewing cases of discipline for employee misconduct. Misconduct is defined as those incidents which have "the potential for physical injury and property damage," and are the result of "intentional acts of wrongdoing."[1] Horseplay is generally viewed as behavior which is essentially without malice, but childish and infantile behavior, resulting from "uncurbed impulse", "yielding once to such a temptation," or the "fallible nature of the human condition".[2]

An employer can punish employee misconduct by taking severe disciplinary action, even discharging the employee, while horseplay usually does not warrant the same serious punishment.

In discipline cases involving misconduct, it is not uncommon for the grievant to raise a defense that his or her behavior should be classified as horseplay, rather than as misconduct and, thereby, escape a harsher punishment.[3]

This general distinction between misconduct and horseplay is indicative of the two themes to be found in this area. The first is that arbitrators recognize the employer's right to expect reasonable social behavior from its employees in their relationships between each other, toward their supervisors, and if a service enterprise, toward the public.[4] This expectation is coupled with an employer's responsibility to its employees to provide a safe workplace and with its legitimate interest in protecting its property.[5]

The second theme, which adds some balance to the rights and expectations of the employer, is the arbitrator's awareness of the human element in the workplace or the inevitable consequences when any group of people are thrown together. Arbitrators look to any fact that might explain, rationalize, or lend insight to the employee's behavior. Some of these factors have been recognized as "normal human frailty"; reactions to stress, tension, or fatigue; the tone the employer has set for the workplace, which either condones mischievous behavior or refuses to diffuse hostile situations; and, an employee's misunderstanding of the effects of his or her behavior.[6]

An arbitrator will often reduce the punishment meted out to an employee, if the arbitrator makes the determination that the behavior was a result of one or more of these factors and that the employer overreacted in disciplining the employee, *i.e.*, the punishment did not fit the crime.[7] In *Perfection American*, a 58-year-old male employee with fourteen years of service went into the ladies' locker room at the plant.[8] He was seen by a female employee in the locker room at the time. He made no offensive or suggestive moves toward her, but she later testified she heard him say to himself that he had always wanted to see what it looked like in there. The company discharged him for violating a rule prohibiting any conduct which violates common decency or morality. The arbitrator reduced the discharge to a suspension, finding that discharge for this behavior was too severe. Similarly, in *Southeast Container Corp.*, the arbitrator reduced the immediate discharge of an employee, who had smeared red paint on the handle of a press machine, to a suspension.[9] The arbitrator held that horseplay is a fact of industrial life and that this action did not warrant by-passing the progressive discipline system. In *W-L Molding Co.*, an employee had been discharged for yelling at the representative of a vending machine company, after the employee had lost money in the machine.[10] The employee's discharge was for aggressive behavior and abusive language. The arbitrator found that the company failed to show that the employee, who had used words like "punk" and "clown" toward the representative, was more angry or more abusive than any other employee similarly frustrated. The arbitrator stated, "Vending machines being what they are and people being what they are, Grievant's offense cannot be viewed as overly serious." The discharge was reduced to a two-week suspension.

Arbitrators will often specify which of the two types of action—misconduct or horseplay—the employee has been accused of committing. Arbitrators generally refuse to allow an employer to augment the nature of a minor incident by coupling it with a serious incident of misconduct. For instance, in *Chatham Supermarkets, Inc.*, an employee was discharged for waving a five-inch knife that he used in his job and for saying, "Don't say s—— to me, bitch," to a fellow employee.[11] The arbitrator held that the employee's language was not sufficient to warrant discharge and that the employee's action with the knife had not been proven to be an assault with a weapon. Similarly, in *Kroger Co.*, an employee was discharged for urinating, or pretending to urinate, on the shop floor; then, calling out for the U.S. Department of Agriculture inspector; and for throwing a potato at another employee.[12] The arbitrator found that throwing the vegetable was not a dischargeable offense; but, the urinating incident, even if a ruse, did warrant discharge, because the employee created the risk of causing a plant shutdown.

Many misconduct cases result from the use of a racial slur, the use of a racial epithet, or the eruption of racial hostility. Arbitrators are sensitive to the use of racial slurs in the workplace and approve disciplinary action against the use of such language. In *Memorial Hospital*, a white employee received a three-day suspension for failure to show respect for her fellow employees, when she said she was being "worked like a nigger."[13] In *Bowman Transportation*, the arbitrator upheld a fourteen-day suspension for an employee who had said over a radio dispatch, "Get those niggers off the radio."[14] The arbitrator found that "under any circumstances, and most particularly in the present industrial climate, remarks tending toward racial antagonism cannot be tolerated."

Arbitrators attempt to diffuse the tension created by the underlying racial hostilities which are to be found in some cases involving fights and threats by not condoning the language or the violence, by encouraging employers to assume the primary responsibility for monitoring this behavior, and by giving employees a second chance to curb their physical reactions to such language.

In *Union Camp Corp.*, the arbitrator reduced the employee's discharge for fighting with a fellow employee over a racial slur to a suspension and warned the employee that a similar incident in the future would warrant discharge.[15] The employee in *LTV Aerospace Corp.* received a two-week suspension for threatening to cause bodily harm to employees who had used racial slurs.[16] The arbitrator held that threats of physical violence cannot be condoned and warned the employee that it was his responsibility to inform the company of the use of racial slurs, not to take justice into his own hands. In *Kaiser Foundation Health Plan*, the arbitrator held the employer to be responsible, when physical violence erupted between a supervisor and an employee, for failing to respond to employees' complaints about the racially derogatory comments used by a supervisor about the employees under his direction.[17] This may have been part of the arbitrator's reasoning in *Cavalier Corp.*, when he reinstated a young black employee who had been discharged for hitting an older, white female employee on the back of the head after an exchange of expletives.[18] Though the arbitrator clearly warned the employee that he must rework his attitude, the discussion at the hearing of the blatant hostility which existed between the two employees may have been a suggestion to the employer that it has a responsibility to be aware of and diffuse this type of hostility.

Arbitrators appear to minimize the racial overtones when an argument erupts between a white and a black employee. In *Alvey, Inc.* two employees, one white and one black, were discharged for fighting.[19] The employees ran a "jackpot" lottery each week and got into an argument over a procedural aspect of the drawing. During the argument, the white employee called the other a "dumb nigger." The white employee then challenged the other to a fight in the parking lot. The arbitrator found the name calling sufficient provocation for the black employee to agree to fight. He reinstated both employees because the prospects of industrial harmony were good, especially since the employees had a history of friendship. Similarly, in *Tyrone Hydraulics, Inc.*, a white employee, while intoxicated, kicked his black foreman.[20] In reducing the discharge to a suspension, the arbitrator found that the employee had a great deal of respect for his foreman, had gone to his house to apologize, and had not meant to demean the foreman.

Another consequence of combining random groups of people is the conflict, or continuing saga of the relationship, between the sexes. Though some cases involve incidents of attempted rape and sexual harassment, arbitrators are wary of attempts to characterize normal shop behavior as something other than horseplay just because it involves a man and a woman. The arbitrator in *Chatham Supermarkets, Inc.* expressed this concern, finding that the employer had overreacted to a male meat cutter's use of language and his motion with a knife because the other employee involved was new and a woman.[21] Similarly, the arbitrator in *Powermatic/Houdaille, Inc.* refused to sustain a discharge for immoral conduct, where the male employee had attracted the attention of a female employee, had put his finger through or by the fly of his pants, and had said, "Hey, big mama, look what I have for you."[22] The arbitrator found this type of behavior distasteful, but not immoral. Arbitrators appear to be interested in developing an atmosphere of peaceful coexistence, requiring both sexes to make some modification in their expectations of each other at the workplace.

Arbitrators are less tolerant, however, when there is evidence of physical assault and threats of rape. In *St. Regis Paper Co.*, for instance, a male employed for 13 months was discharged for threatening to rape a female employee.[23] On two prior occasions, he physically assaulted her, touched her, tried to kiss her, and picked her up. In *Monsanto Chemical Intermediates Co.*, the arbitrator upheld a 30-day suspension for two male employees, who had locked a female employee in a supply room, wrestled her to the couch, and attempted to take her clothes off.[24] In both of these cases, the male employees had maintained a defense that their behavior was merely horseplay. In neither case did the arbitrators agree. Rather, they determined that the threat posed by the male employees was real and that the company had a responsibility to maintain a workplace free from fears of threats and intimidation.

Arbitrators also appear cautious when the issue is the occurrence or appropriateness of disciplinary action in cases involving sexual harassment. Part of this caution would seem to be a recognition that definitions of sexual harassment and classifications of conduct as sexual harassment are subjective determinations which vary from individual to individual. As stated by the arbitrator in *Godchaux-Henderson Sugar Co., Inc.*, a case involving a charge of immoral behavior, "When the Company brings a young female employee into the plant and allows her unsupervised freedom to invite male employees to her workplace for conversation and play, trouble is inevitable."[25]

In *University of Missouri*, for example, the discharge of a housekeeping supervisor was primarily sustained because his conduct created an atmosphere of stress and anxiety amongst female employees and because there was a fear of the consequences if the behavior continued.[26] The employee had a habit of putting his arms around females, smacking his lips at them, commenting on their attractiveness and the attractiveness of other employees, and looking at them in a way which made them "feel undressed." The employees testified that his conduct affected their mental health and job performance.

As mentioned earlier, arbitrators, in cases which involve misconduct, also look to a variety of facts and circumstances that may serve to mitigate the punishment. Disciplinary action for misconduct or horseplay can be sustained without a specific company rule governing the situation. If the company is enforcing a particular rule, however, the usual rule analysis is utilized. This analysis examines whether it is a reasonable rule, whether it has been communicated to employees, and whether it is consistently enforced.[27]

In *Rochester Methodist Hospital*, the arbitrator revoked the three-day suspension given to an employee and granted her backpay, when he found that the employees had had no advance notice of the rules and found that the employer's disciplinary system did not follow customary standards of just cause and due process.[28] The arbitrator in *Kraft Foods*, when discussing the employer's rule against fighting, noted "the implementation of the rule, however, must meet the accepted test of reasonableness and any abuse of management discretion should be avoided".[29] In *Welch Foods, Inc.*, the arbitrator reduced the discharge of an employer to a suspension, basing his decision in part on his sense that the employer had treated the two employees involved in the incident differently.[30]

Arbitrators also look to determine whether or not the employees had notice of the behavior expected of them, be it a specific rule or an understood policy. In *Mobil Oil*, the arbitrator questioned the publication of the employer's policy that employees are to avoid conflict and walk away from any threat or potential confrontation.[31] Similarly, in *Flat River Glass Co.* the employee testified that he did not know that his horseplay would be cause for discipline and that the behavior he had indulged in was a way of life on his shift.[32] So also, the arbitrator in *New York Air Brake Co.* refused to sustain the employer's discipline of two employees, because their behavior occurred within a context of poor supervision, leadership, and discipline.[33] However, the arbitrator in *Midland Ross Corp.* dismissed the employee's contention that he was unaware of a rule against exploding firecrackers at his work station.[34] The arbitrator found that the employee's knowledge of the rule was irrelevant and that the employee's common sense should have told him that shooting firecrackers was an improper activity.

Arbitrators also look to other factors that may serve to mitigate the punishment, *e.g.*, the employee's length of service, work record, general relationship with other employees, and the likelihood of a reoccurrence of the incident.[35]

In cases of fighting or of threats, however, arbitrators may examine whether any provocation may have caused the fight or whether the employee's actions were in self-defense, but they rarely accept provocation as justification for physical violence.[36] Self-defense is regarded as a valid defense, particularly if the employee did not provoke the initial violence.[37]

The employee's attitude about his or her behavior may be the most important factor in mitigating discipline for misconduct or horseplay. If an employee is contrite and recognizes the negative aspects of his behavior, arbitrators allow for a lesser discipline, and in the case of discharge, reduce it to a suspension. In *General Electric Co.*, the arbitrator commented on the demeanor of the grievant.[38] The arbitrator found the employee to be an unusually candid witness who recognized the unacceptable nature of his actions and exhibited a sincerely contrite manner. The employee in *Ozark Lead Co.* did not try to avoid the responsibility for his wrongful act: the insertion of a waterhose into the vertical exhaust pipe of a tractor.[39] The arbitrator found the employee's admission of responsibility for the act to be a reflection of the employee's sincerity and forthrightness. In contrast, the arbitrator was disappointed with the employees in *Monsanto Chemical Intermediates Co.* who, when contesting their suspension for attempted rape, were evasive and flippant in the manner in which they provided information.[40]

The initial determination the arbitrator makes in these cases is whether or not the employee is guilty of the conduct with which he has been charged. As a result, many of these cases turn on the credibility of the witnesses and on the facts pleaded by both sides. Some arbitrators have suggested the use of a "clear and convincing" standard of proof as to the guilt of the employee; one arbitrator has applied a "high degree of certainty" test.[41]

Arbitrators often base their credibility findings on the choice of the witnesses and their testimony. In *VA Medical Center*, the arbitrator questioned the employer's selection of three mental patients as its key witnesses, when it was clear that the testimony of other staff personnel would deserve more weight.[42] The arbitrator in *Gateway United Methodist Youth Center* made similar remarks, when the employer based its disciplinary decision and its case on the testimony of two female residents who were receiving psychiatric counselling and who had been responsible for the termination of another employee under similar allegations.[43] The employee in this case had a clean work record, and there was no reason not to believe his testimony.

The most common type of employee misconduct is fighting, or the use of physical violence against another employee, and in most cases it warrants severe discipline, especially where a weapon is used. In *General Electric Co.*, the discharge of an employee, who had hit another employee with a machete, was sustained.[44] Arbitrators will also sustain discharges where employees fight without weapons, if there is the risk of severe personal injury. In *General Electric Co.*, for instance, one employee hit another so hard that the force of the blow caused the employee to knock several compressors weighing 80–90 pounds each to the floor.[45] Also, when the fighting presents a grave and serious threat to the safety and security of other company employees, terminations for fighting have been upheld.[46]

Arbitrators will also look to the reason for the altercation. If it is slight or insubstantial when compared to the reaction, the arbitrator will not allow the reasons for the fight to mitigate the discipline, especially in the presence of a plant rule prohibiting fighting. For example, the arbitrator found the company to be within its rights when it strictly enforced the prohibition against fighting and suspended an employee for striking and threatening another in *Mobay Chemical Corp.* In that case the employee thought the other was driving his tow motor too fast, followed him into the break room, grabbed him, hit him, and told him that if he drove that way again he would kill him. The arbitrator concluded that, even if the other's tow motor had been driven too fast, the employee could not be exonerated.[47]

Nevertheless, arbitrators tend to give employees who have engaged in fighting a second chance if the fight caused no lasting injury and if the arbitrator, given the facts of the case, feels discharge is too severe a penalty.[48] In *General Electric Co.*, for instance, an employee had been discharged for striking another employee.[49] The employee, who had struck the first blow, became angered when the other employee started to give him instructions regarding his machine. The arbitrator found that the employee was understandably offended by the supervisory airs of his fellow employee; he was contrite; his attack on the employee was not violent or depraved; and, with respect to his work record, dicharge was too severe. Similarly, in *Alvey, Inc.*, two employees, who were friends, got into a fight over a lottery which they ran at the plant.[50] The arbitrator held that discharge was too severe a penalty for these individuals, noting the past peaceful history between the two men and the favorable outlook for industrial harmony.

Next in frequency of misconduct cases are threats of physical harm, with and without weapons. Threats made with weapons are viewed as more serious infractions than mere threats. The discharge of an employee with 30 years of service was sustained in a case where the employee pulled a knife on a fellow employee, held it to his stomach, and threatened to cut the employee to pieces.[51] Similarly, in *Mobil Oil Corp.* a 10-day suspension for an employee who had pulled a knife on another employee was upheld.[52] The arbitrator found that the employee, by his actions and language, had created a threat of physical harm to the other employee and warranted discipline.

Unlike most cases involving threats with weapons, arbitrators must determine whether a threat has actually been made in cases where a weapon is not present. Calling someone a "dodo" or a "turkey," for example, has not been considered a threat.[53] However, when an employee, soliciting for the union, told another employee "Big Daddy will get you" for refusing to join, the arbitrator held that the employee could have reasonably believed he was threatened and, therefore, discipline was warranted. In *Emery Industries, Inc.*, the arbitrator found that the employee's comment, "I hope your truck blows up," to a subcontractor was intended to be perceived as a legitimate threat, given the circumstances of the case, and warranted discipline.[54] And, in *LTV Aerospace Corp.*, the arbitrator sustained a two-week suspension for an employee's threat of physical harm simply on the basis that threats of physical violence cannot be condoned in a company plant.[55]

Misconduct which involves the use of fire normally warrants discharge, apparently because of the high risk of personal injury and property damage. For example, in *Abbott & Co.* the discharge of an employee for starting a fire in the ladies' room to set off the smoke alarm was sustained. The arbitrator reasoned that, even if the employee's behavior was intended as a prank or could be categorized as horseplay, such conduct cannot be condoned.[56] Similarly, the discharge of the employee in *Kroger Co.* was sustained.[57] He was discharged for sprinkling lighter fluid on another employee's apron and setting it on fire. The arbitrator found no corroboration of the employee's contention that setting fire to aprons was a common act of horseplay. Also, in *Russer Foods* the discharge of an employee was sustained where the employee had placed lighted cigarettes in the pockets of another employee and, then, had started a fire under the employee's chair.[58]

Other types of conduct which arbitrators have found to be so outrageous as to warrant severe discipline include calling a bomb threat to the plant, making an obscene phone call to a company official's wife, and creating an incident that could have caused the shutdown of the employee's facility.[59] In *Union Commerce Bank* the arbitrator upheld the discharge of an employee for his steadfast refusal to cooperate and work with his coworkers. The company made several attempts to get the employees to work together harmoniously, and in spite of all such attempts, negative forms of behavior continued. In sustaining the discharge, the arbitrator noted that an employee must act in the best interests of the employer and that those interests included employees who can work in harmony with others.[60]

Horseplay, as discussed previously, is usually the result of unbridled enthusiasm and is characterized as conduct that causes no harm and is undertaken without malice. The arbitrator in *Clay Equipment* used this concept in the plant when he held that the presence of horseplay indicated that there was room for a little fun and found that this prevailing attitude was the reason for the excellent relationship between employees and management. "A good healthy laugh between friends and among acquaintances may some day prove to be one of the best indicators of good health in a management/union relationship."[61] In this case, the employee had been discharged for throwing a pie at a management consultant. The arbitrator reinstated him, without backpay and without seniority.

In reviewing cases where employees have been disciplined for horseplay, arbitrators look to the severity of the incident, whether anyone was injured, whether or not the potential for serious injury was present, whether the employee's attitude throughout the incident indicated that the employee had acted without malice, and whether the employee was contrite after the incident. Accordingly, in *Ozark Lead Co.* the discharge of an employee, who had placed a hose in the exhaust pipe of a tractor, was not sustained.[62] At the hearing, the employee confessed to being responsible for the incident, maintained that he did not know the water would damage the machine, and apologized for his behavior. In *Flat River Glass Co.*, an employee was discharged for sliding a hot bottle down the floor to the cold end of the plant. The arbitrator revoked the discharge, reasoning that no one had been seriously hurt, the employee had confessed he had not been aware that such behavior was susceptible to discipline, and that the employee's "insane, stupid bit of senseless horseplay" could not be compared to other intentional acts of wrongdoing which had been the basis of the company's discipline policy.[63]

Similarly, the disciplinary actions taken in *Bechtel Corp.*, where an employee had driven a truck too fast to an intersection, slammed on the brakes, and left a skid mark and in *Southeast Container Corp.*, where an employee had put red paint on the handle of a press, were reduced.[64]

In *Kroger Co.* the arbitrator found that "mooning"—in arbitrator Sabella's words, "an exposure of one's 'butt' to another person"— was not a matter for summary discharge.[65] Reducing the discharge to a suspension, the arbitrator held that, although an employee has an obligation to conduct himself with respect to fellow employees, the employee in this case had accidently been seen by a female employee, and no harm had been done. Similarly, in *United States Internal Revenue Service* the arbitrator refused to uphold the one-day suspension given to two revenue agents for "mooning" a group of women who had been joking with them while off duty.[66] One of the women had seen their car and had reported the license number. The arbitrator found that although "it was a foolish and totally sophomoric display," he did not see how the agency's reputation had been jeopardized by the fact that two agents "with some degree of at least imagined goading decided as a practical joke to bare their bottoms to a lady in the isolation of a garage passageway, without more."

Misconduct or Horseplay

Key Points:

1. *The conduct of the employee must have been intentional and must have had the apparent purpose of causing injury to a person or damage to property.*

   Examples:

   Employee *A* was discharged for misconduct; he had been caught putting water into spare gasoline containers, which were kept in a garage by the employer for the use of the groundskeepers. *A* defended his action by stating that he had only been retaliating against one of the groundskeepers who had struck *A*'s parked car with a lawnmower. The arbitrator sustained the discharge and noted that, no matter how good *A*'s work record may have been, his record could not serve to mitigate his action.

   Employee *B* was discharged for jamming a potato into the exhaust pipe of a jeep used by another employee to carry small parcels between plant buildings. As a result of *B*'s action, the muffler on the tailpipe exploded. At the hearing, the employer argued that the act was obviously intentional and, as any reasonable person would have known, could have caused much more damage than it did. The arbitrator, however, held that discharge was too severe a penalty for such childishness and reinstated *B* without backpay, while ordering him to pay the employer for the damage.

Employee *C* was discharged for throwing a smoke bomb into the window of the ladies' room, which set off the fire alarm and brought the local fire department out to the company. The arbitrator reinstated the employee without backpay.

Employee *D* was discharged for spreading a thin coat of grease on the floor around another employee's machine. Finding that someone could have been reasonably expected to suffer serious injury had they slipped on the grease, the arbitrator sustained the discharge.

Employee *E* was discharged for throwing a whipped cream pie into the face of an outside efficiency expert while the expert was touring the plant. The arbitrator reinstated the employee with backpay for all but one day of the time lost and noted that the incident, while reprehensible, was not without humor.

Employee *F* was discharged following an incident with a female employee in which he grabbed her, pulled her to a couch, and attempted to kiss her. Categorizing the act as an indecent assault, the arbitrator sustained the discharge.

Employee *G* was discharged following an incident in which he exposed himself to two female employees in the lunchroom. The arbitrator, finding the act to be repugnant and deserving of punishment, nevertheless held that discharge was too severe.

Guidelines

a. Where an employee's conduct demonstrates a wanton disregard for the safety of others or of property, misconduct will be sufficient to warrant discharge, even though the harm caused thereby may have been unintentional.

b. Where an employee's conduct has a racial or sexual tone and is directed toward someone of that race or sex, the conduct will deserve a more severe penalty than if it had not.

Relevant Cases

Ozark Lead Co. (Belcher), 69 LA 1227;
Flat River Glass Co. (Newmark), 76 LA 946;

Clay Equipment (Carter), 73 LA 817;
Bechtel Corp. (Raffaele), 71 LA 1049;
United States Internal Revenue Service (Edes), 77 LA 19;
Hilo Coast Processing Co. (Tanaka), 74 LA 236;
Kroger Co. (Berns), 75 LA 290;
Southeast Container Corp. (Seidenberg), 69 LA 884;
Perfection American Co. (Flannagan), 73 LA 520;
W-L Molding Co. (Howlett), 72 LA 1065;
Memorial Hospital (Sinicropi), 71 LA 1252;
Bowman Transportation (Goodman), 71 LA 342;
Union Camp Corp. (Hardy), 71 LA 886;
LTV Aerospace Corp. (Moore), 65 LA 195;
Powermatic/Houdaille, Inc. (Cocalis), 71 LA 54;
St. Regis Paper Co. (Kaufman), 74 LA 1281;
Monsanto Chemical Intermediates Co. (Penfield), 75 LA 592;
Godchaux-Henderson Sugar Co., Inc. (Barnhart), 75 LA 377;
Abbott & Co. (Dworkin), 76 LA 339;
Russer Foods (Grant), 75 LA 305;
Ralston Purina Co. (Brown), 75 LA 313;
Pioneer Transit Mix Co. (Darrow), 72 LA 206;
Kroger Co. (Doering), 74 LA 785;
Union Commerce Bank (Ipavec), 75 LA 1246;
Kroger Co. (Sabella), 72 LA 540;
University of Missouri (Yarowsky), 78 LA 417.

2   *The atmosphere of the workplace must not be such that the activity appears to be condoned or tolerated.*

Examples:

Employee *A* was discharged for fighting, after he had knocked an employee into a machine which caused severe lacerations in the employee's arm. *A* claimed that the accident took place during the course of a friendly wrestling match with another employee. The other employee testified that *A* had assaulted him during the course of an argument about a local sports team. Other evidence was presented showing that arguments, bantering, and playful pushing were common occurrences in the workplace. The arbitrator reinstated the employee and remarked that, as the employer had tolerated similar activity in the past, it could not base its disciplinary action solely upon the outcome of one incident.

Employee *B* was given a three-day suspension for making obscene gestures and comments to a female employee. Noting that the employer apparently condoned such conduct in the plant because it allowed the employees to post lewd pictures and cartoons in their work areas, the arbitrator ordered the reduction of the penalty to a warning.

Employee *C* was discharged for placing a dead rat in the ladies' restroom. Finding that practical jokes were common in the workplace, the arbitrator ordered reinstatement with backpay.

Guidelines

The employer has an obligation to control employee conduct within the workplace. When its failure to exercise adequate control results in behavior which it considers to be reprehensible only in degree and not in kind, the employee cannot be severely disciplined.

Relevant Cases

Viewpoint Nursing Home (Bard), 72 LA 1240;
Mead Packaging Co. (Ziskind), 74 LA 881;
Godchaux-Henderson Sugar Co., Inc. (Barnhart), 75 LA 377;
New York Air Brake Co. (McDonnell), 75 LA 875;
Kaiser Foundation Health Plan (Herring), 73 LA 1057;
Alvey, Inc. (Roberts), 74 LA 835;
Cavalier Corp. (Haemmel), 75 LA 253;
University of Missouri (Yarowsky), 78 LA 417.

3   *The demeanor of an employee, following the misconduct and his or her apparent contrition, may indicate the appropriateness of the degree of discipline.*

Examples:

Employee *A* was discharged for setting the apron ties of another employee on fire, which resulted in the employee's clothes becoming inflamed; the employee suffered severe burns and had to be hospitalized. Although concluding that *A*'s act was a wanton disregard for the other employee's safety, the arbitrator ordered reinstatement without backpay, upon *A*'s expression of deep regret and his assurance that such acts would not be committed in the future and that the result in this case was unintended.

Employee *B* was discharged, after he had put sugar in the gas tank of another employee's car which resulted in $750 in damages to the car. Although *B* admitted to his act and agreed to pay the damage, the arbitrator sustained the discharge on the grounds that the conduct was so completely calculated to cause damage that it indicated an unstable and undependable personality.

Guidelines

Where the arbitrator believes the conduct to have been isolated and there is a strong probability that it will not be repeated in the future, the arbitrator will not accept discharge as an appropriate form of disciplinary action.

Relevant Cases

Alvey, Inc. (Roberts), 74 LA 835;
Tyrone Hydraulics, Inc. (Murphy), 75 LA 672;
Perfection American Co. (Flannagan), 73 LA 520;
Union Camp Corp. (Hardy), 71 LA 886;
General Electric Co. (Foreman), 72 LA 441;
Monsanto Chemical Intermediates Co. (Penfield), 75 LA 592;
Ozark Lead Co. (Belcher), 69 LA 1227;
Flat River Glass Co. (Newmark), 76 LA 946;
Bechtel Corp. (Raffaele), 71 LA 1049;
Southeast Container Corp. (Seidenberg), 69 LA 884.

Fighting

Key Points:

1   *Where there is no rule against fighting or where the rule does not mandate discharge in all cases, discipline will depend upon whether the employee is the aggressor or a willing participant in the fight.*

Examples:

Employees *A* and *B* were discharged for fighting where, following a quarrel about the nonpayment of a debt to *A* by *B*, *A* struck *B* with his fist. *B* retaliated and, when the fight was over, was the clear victor. Although *A* was the aggressor, the arbitrator sustained the discharge of both.

Employees *C* and *D* were discharged for fighting where, following a quarrel about the nonpayment of a debt to *C* by *D*, *C* struck *D* with his fist. *D* grabbed *C* in defense and wrestled him to the ground. When the two combatants were separated, C went after D as he fled. Finding that D had acted in self-defense and had only repelled C's attack, the arbitrator sustained the discharge of C but reinstated D.

Employees E and F were discharged for fighting where, following a quarrel, E struck F with his fist. F grabbed E and wrestled him to the ground, where they both struck each other until separated by other employees. The arbitrator found that, while E was the aggressor, F did not try to escape when the chance was presented. The arbitrator sustained the discharge of E and reinstated F without backpay, which was effectively a three-month suspension for F.

Guidelines

The employee who was struck first must act only in self-defense and only with enough force to repel the aggressor, if the employee is to avoid all discipline.

Relevant Cases

Kraft Foods, Inc. (Rose), 73 LA 493;
Welch Foods, Inc. (Gootnick), 73 LA 908;
Mobil Oil Corp. (Fox), 73 LA 993;
General Electric Co. (Foreman), 72 LA 441;
Nitec Paper Co. (Goodman), 75 LA 1;
General Electric Co. (King), 73 LA 1248.

2   *Fighting is not justified by provocation, but provocation may serve to reduce the degree of disciplinary action.*

Examples:

Employee A was discharged for striking another employee. The employee had made a remark about a birthmark to be found on A's wife and indicated a knowledge of A's wife which exceeded normal expectations. The arbitrator, finding that A had been provoked, reduced the discharge to a suspension.

Employee B, a black, was discharged for striking another employee who had called him a "dumb nigger." The arbitrator elicited facts which indicated that the other employee had harrassed B on other occasions as well. Concluding that B had been provoked, the arbitrator reduced the discharge to a suspension.

Employee *C* was discharged for striking an employee who had called him a "turkey." Finding that *C* had not been sufficiently provoked to justify his action, the arbitrator sustained the discharge.

Guidelines

The provocation must be great enough to result in a finding that the employee may have been momentarily driven to irrational action. Slight provocation will normally not be sufficient to mitigate the employer's disciplinary action.

Relevant Cases

General Electric Co. (King), 73 LA 1248;
Mobay Chemical Corp. (Weitzman), 74 LA 1113;
General Electric Co. (Foreman), 72 LA 441;
Nitec Paper Co. (Goodman), 75 LA 1.

3   *Where an employee uses, or threatens to use, a weapon in a fight with or an assault upon another employee, discharge is almost always warranted.*

Examples:

Employee *A* was discharged, following a quarrel with another employee in which *A* had brandished a wrench and swore he would bash the other's head in. The arbitrator, finding the threat with a lethal weapon to be extreme as well as dangerous, sustained the discharge.

Employee *B*, a black, was discharged after he had thrown a tire iron at another employee who had called him a "half-civilized ape man." Even though *B* may have missed the other employee and even though he may have been greatly provoked, the arbitrator held that *B*'s action had been so life threatening that discharge was warranted.

Employee *C* was discharged following an argument with another employee during which *C* had waved a wrench. The wrench was a tool used by *C* in his work. The arbitrator, noting that there was no proof that *C* had been threatening the other employee with the wrench, reinstated *C*.

> ### *Guidelines*
> The use or threatened use of a weapon reveals an aspect of the character of the assailant which is so severe and unpredictable that an employer has the right, if not the duty, to terminate the employee summarily for the protection of all employees.

Relevant Cases

General Electric Co. (Abrams), 71 LA 884;
Nitec Paper Corp. (Goodman), 75 LA 1;
Emery Industries, Inc. (Gentile), 72 LA 110;
Chatham Supermarket, Inc. (Roumell), 71 LA 1084.

4   *Good work histories or other outside factors may mitigate severe discipline.*

Examples:

Employees *A* and *B* were discharged for fighting after a quarrel about a debt. Neither could be found to have been the aggressor and both had been willing participants. It appeared, however, that both *A* and *B* had good work histories and, in fact, were friends. The arbitrator, noting that the two did not present a future threat to the peace of the workplace, reduced the discharges to suspensions.

Employees *C* and *D* became intoxicated at an impromptu party at the workplace on Christmas Eve. They began to argue and, then, to fight. Both were discharged. Noting the special circumstances created by the party, the arbitrator reduced the discharges to suspensions.

Employees *E* and *F* were both maintenance men, who had been called in by the employer to shore up an area along a stream in advance of an anticipated flood. They had worked twelve hours in the rain without a significant break. A quarrel broke out and ended in a fight; *E* and *F* were both discharged. The arbitrator found that the irrational behavior was caused by fatigue and the unusual working conditions and mitigated the discharges to suspensions.

Guidelines

Special circumstances, which involve unusual tension or fatigue, may serve to mitigate the discipline. It must appear that lessening the discipline will not cause, or stimulate, additional breaches of the peace at the workplace. In this respect, the totality of the situation must be examined.

Relevant Cases

Clay Equipment (Carter), 73 LA 817;
Chatham Supermarkets, Inc. (Roumell), 71 LA 1084;
Cavalier Corp. (Haemmel), 75 LA 253;
Alvey, Inc. (Roberts), 74 LA 835;
Tyrone Hydraulics, Inc. (Murphy), 75 LA 672;
Kraft Foods, Inc. (Rose), 73 LA 493;
General Electric Co. (Craver), 71 LA 337;
Mobay Chemical Corp. (Weitzman), 74 LA 1113;
Transportation Labor, Inc. (Sheehan), 76 LA 1249;
Nickles Bakery, Inc. (Letson), 73 LA 801.

Notes to Chapter 16

1. *Ozark Lead Co.* (Belcher), 69 LA 1227; *Flat River Glass Co.* (Newmark), 76 LA 946.

2. *Clay Equip.* (Carter), 73 LA 817; *Bechtel Corp.* (Raffaele), 71 LA 1049; *United States Internal Revenue Serv.* (Edes), 77 LA 19.

3. *Hilo Coast Processing Co.* (Tanaka), 74 LA 236; *Kroger Co.* (Berns), 75 LA 290; *University of Mo.* (Yarowsky), 78 LA 417.

4. *Kroger Co.* (Sabella), 72 LA 540; *Bowman Transp.* (Goodman), 71 LA 342; *General Serv. Admin.* (Avins), 76 LA 118; *Alumax Foils, Inc.* (Hilgert), 73 LA 250; *Delaware River Port Auth.* (Raffaele), 76 LA 350; *Gateway United Methodist Youth Center* (Miller), 75 LA 1177; *University of Mo.,* supra, note 3.

5. *Chatham Supermarkets, Inc.* (Roumell), 71 LA 1084; *Monsanto Chem. Intermediates Co.* (Penfield), 75 LA 592; *General Elec. Co.* (King), 73 LA 1248; *Midland Ross Corp.* (Dallas), 65 LA 1151.

6. *Viewpoint Nursing Home* (Bard), 72 LA 1240; *Mead Packaging Co.* (Ziskind), 74 LA 881; *Godchaux-Henderson Sugar Co., Inc.* (Barnhart), 75 LA 377; *New York Air Brake Co.* (McDonnell), 75 LA 875; *Kaiser Found. Health Plan* (Herring), 73 LA 1057; *Alvey, Inc.* (Roberts), 74 LA 835; *University of Mo.,* supra, note 3.

7. *Southeast Container Corp.* (Seidenberg), 69 LA 884; *Perfection Am. Co.* (Flannagan), 73 LA 520; *W-L Molding Co.* (Howlett), 72 LA 1065.

8. *Perfection Am. Co.*, *supra*, note 7.
9. *Southeast Container Corp.*, *supra*, note 7.
10. *W-L Molding Co.*, *supra*, note 7.
11. *Chatham Supermarkets, Inc.*, *supra*, note 5.
12. *Kroger Co.* (Doering), 74 LA 785.
13. *Memorial Hosp.* (Sinicropi), 71 LA 1252.
14. *Bowman Transp.*, *supra*, note 4.
15. *Union Camp Corp.* (Hardy), 71 LA 886.
16. *LTV Aerospace Corp.* (Moore), 65 LA 195.
17. *Kaiser Found. Health Plan*, *supra*, note 6.
18. *Cavalier Corp.* (Haemmel), 75 LA 253.
19. *Alvey, Inc.*, *supra*, note 6.
20. *Tyrone Hydraulics, Inc.* (Murphy), 75 LA 672.
21. *Chatham Supermarkets, Inc.*, *supra*, note 5.
22. *Powermatic/Houdaille, Inc.* (Cocalis), 71 LA 54.
23. *St. Regis Paper Co.* (Kaufman), 74 LA 1281.
24. *Monsanto Chem. Intermediates Co.*, *supra*, note 5.
25. *Godchaux-Henderson Sugar Co., Inc.*, *supra*, note 6.
26. *University of Mo.*, *supra*, note 3.
27. *Rochester Methodist Hosp.* (Heneman), 72 LA 276; *Kraft Foods, Inc.* (Rose), 73 LA 493; *Mobil Oil Corp.* (Fox), 73 LA 993.
28. *Rochester Methodist Hosp.*, *supra*, note 27.
29. *Kraft Foods, Inc.*, *supra*, note 27.
30. *Welch Foods, Inc.* (Gootnick), 73 LA 908.
31. *Mobil Oil Corp.*, *supra*, note 27.
32. *Flat River Glass Co.*, *supra*, note 1.
33. *New York Air Brake Co.*, *supra*, note 6.
34. *Midland Ross Corp.*, *supra*, note 5.
35. *Perfection Am. Co.*, *supra*, note 7; *General Elec. Co.* (Craver), 71 LA 337; *Union Camp Corp.*, *supra*, note 15; *Alvey, Inc.*, *supra*, note 6.
36. *General Elec. Co.*, *supra*, note 5 (the arbitrator held that verbal provocation may be a reason for physical violence, but not a justification); *Mobay Chem. Corp.* (Weitzman), 74 LA 1113 (provocation does not exonerate the employee for his actions).
37. *General Elec. Co.*, *infra*, note 38 (both employees claimed self-defense; both provoked the fight; and both discharges were sustained); *Nitec Paper Corp.*, *infra*, note 38 (behavior might have been justified if for self-defense).
38. *General Elec. Co.* (Foreman), 72 LA 142; *Nitec Paper Corp.* (Goodman), 75 LA 1.
39. *Ozark Lead Co.*, *supra*, note 1.
40. *Monsanto Chem. Intermediates Co.*, *supra*, note 5.
41. *Gateway United Methodist Youth Center*, *supra*, note 4; *Ralston Purina Co.* (Brown), 75 LA 313; *Godchaux-Henderson Sugar Co., Inc.*, *supra*, note 6.
42. *VA Medical Center* (Ludolf), 74 LA 830.
43. *Gateway United Methodist Youth Center*, *supra*, note 4.

44. *General Elec. Co.* (Abrams), 71 LA 884.

45. *General Elec. Co., supra,* note 5.

46. *General Elec. Co., supra,* note 38.

47. *Mobay Chem. Corp., supra,* note 36.

48. *Transportation Labor, Inc.* (Sheehan), 76 LA 1249; *Nickles Bakery, Inc.* (Letson), 73 LA 801.

49. *General Elec. Co., supra,* note 35.

50. *Alvey, Inc., supra,* note 6.

51. *Nitec Paper Corp., supra,* note 38.

52. *Mobil Oil Corp., supra,* note 27.

53. *General Elec. Co., supra,* note 38; *General Elec. Co., supra,* note 5.

54. *Emery Indus., Inc.* (Gentile), 72 LA 110.

55. *See also LTV Aerospace Corp., supra,* note 16.

56. *Abbott & Co.* (Dworkin), 76 LA 339.

57. *Kroger Co., supra,* note 3.

58. *Russer Foods* (Grant), 75 LA 305.

59. *Ralston Purina Co., supra,* note 41; *Pioneer Transit Mix Co.* (Darrow), 72 LA 206; *Kroger Co.* (Doering), 74 LA 785.

60. *Union Commerce Bank* (Ipavec), 75 LA 1246.

61. *Clay Equip., supra,* note 2.

62. *Ozark Lead Co., supra,* note 1.

63. *Flat River Glass Co., supra,* note 1.

64. *Bechtel Corp., supra,* note 2; *Southeast Container Corp.* (Seidenberg), 69 LA 884.

65. *Kroger Co., supra,* note 4.

66. *United States Internal Revenue Serv., supra,* note 2.

17

Moonlighting

Issue: Whether an employee may be discharged or otherwise disciplined for moonlighting in the absence of a specific prohibition against outside employment in the collective bargaining agreement or in written company policy.

Principle: When the collective bargaining agreement or company policy manual is silent on the issue, an employee may not be discharged or otherwise disciplined merely because he or she has obtained outside employment. For discipline to be sustained, the moonlighting must have resulted in some independent grounds for discharge or disciplinary action. An employer may discipline an employee who has an otherwise unobjectionable outside job, however, if the employee has attempted to deceive the employer on the issue. The employer, nevertheless, cannot discharge an employee for the deception, except in extreme cases amounting to gross dishonesty.

Considerations:
1. Whether the outside job leads to excessive absenteeism, tardiness, or decreased work efficiency or otherwise interferes with the employee's duties at the workplace;
2. Whether the outside job places the employee in a position of competing with the primary employer or gives rise to a conflict of interest;
3. Whether the employee acts dishonestly toward the employer either to conceal his or her employment elsewhere or to enable the employee to perform the obligations of the other job.

Discussion: Generally speaking, an employee's off-duty activities are not open to question by an employer. Arbitrators consistently reaffirm the principle that, absent a prohibition against moonlighting in the collective bargaining agreement or in a policy manual, an employee who obtains outside employment cannot be discharged or otherwise disciplined for that fact alone.[1]

The primary focus in each case is on what, if any, was the adverse effect of the employee's second job on the legitimate interests of the primary employer. Discipline has been found to be justified where the employer has been able to show that a direct relation existed between the second job and the employee's absenteeism or lateness or in the employee's reduced efficiency or poor job performance. Or, the employer must be able to show that the second job is in competition with the primary one.[2] Discharge is the most common penalty imposed. As is generally the case with disciplinary measures, issues such as the prior record of the employee, prior warnings to the employee, and consistency in the employer's application of discipline for the given offense are important to arbitrators.

It is not uncommon for employees who hold two jobs to obtain a leave of absence or to take sick leave from the one employer, rather than simply not showing up for work, while continuing to work for the other. When the employer learns of such an employee's deception, it typically fires the employee. In cases of this kind which reach arbitration, an employee will be reinstated where it appears the employee is physically unable to work on his or her primary job but because of differing responsibilities is able to continue at the second job or where it does not appear that continuing the second job will prolong the employee's leave. However, if the employee has deceived the employer with regard to the secondary employment, a suspension rather than a discharge will be generally approved, absent prior discipline for similar causes which would justify discharge.[3]

An employer may unilaterally adopt a company policy against secondary employment by a competitor or against activities which might compromise with the company's best interests, so long as the policy is reasonable and not in conflict with the collective bargaining agreement. Violations of such rules generally will be considered "just cause" for discharge; however, the adoption of such a policy is not a prerequisite to a valid discharge when the employee holds a job which is in direct competition with the employer.[4]

Key Points:

1   *The outside job must have led to excessive absenteeism, tardiness, decreased efficiency on the job, or some other work deficiency.*

Examples:

Employee *A* obtained a second full-time job. His foreman reported that *A* is a good worker and appeared to be neither sleepy nor fatigued. Approximately seven weeks later *A* was involved in two incidents leading to spoilage of company goods. The employer admitted at arbitration that the incidents would not have lead to discharge were it not for the second job. The arbitrator reinstated the employee with full backpay, citing the employer's failure to establish a causal relationship between the moonlighting and the spoilage incidents.

Employee *B* operated a side business on his own which did not compete with that of the employer. During his six years of employment with his primary employer, *B* was absent from work 137 full days and 89 partial days. He was discharged following several warnings and one suspension for excessive absenteeism and tardiness. The grievance was denied by the arbitrator.

Guidelines

To sustain discipline, the employer must show that the action against the employee was for just cause due to a violation of some other rule of conduct. The fact that the precipitating cause was the employee's moonlighting can be used as a reason to deny mitigation on the grounds that the employee did not have the requisite loyalty to the primary employer or adequate concern for the job, which any employer may expect.

Relevant Cases

Gas Service Co. (Bronson), 63 LA 293;
W. R. Grace, & Co. (Boals), 62 LA 779;
Microdot, Inc. (Kelliher), 66 LA 177;
Randle-Eastern Ambulance Service, Inc. (Sherman), 65 LA 394.

2 *The employee cannot deceive the primary employer by misusing the benefits, such as sick time or leaves of absence, accorded the employee by the primary employer.*

Examples:

Employee *A* was a gravedigger and held a second job as a bartender. He called in sick to his gravedigging job, complaining of an injured arm, but worked that night as a bartender. He was discharged. The arbitrator reinstated A with full backpay, noting that the employee did, in fact, have an injured arm, which prevented him from doing his normal work but not from performing his second job.

Employee B received an annual leave of absence to leave town because of severe hay fever. One year he remained in town for part of the time and continued to work at a part-time job, but had lied to his employer about it. He was discharged. The arbitrator reinstated the employee, finding that the part-time job did not prolong the employee's leave of absence. Backpay was denied, however, because of the employee's deception.

Employee C was scheduled to work on Saturday because of a shipping emergency at the primary employer's plant. C called in sick but worked at his second job. He was discharged. At the arbitration C defended the deception by saying that he would have lost his second job had he not reported to work and that he did not seek to be relieved from his Saturday assignment for fear his primary employer would have fired him. The arbitrator reinstated the employee without backpay and warned him that a second incident of favoring the second job over the primary one would be cause for discharge.

Employee D had a second job in the evenings. He had told his primary employer that his wife was partially disabled and for that reason he could never work overtime. As a result, other employees were compelled to work more overtime than they desired. When the deception was discovered, the employee was discharged. The arbitrator sustained the discharge.

Guidelines

An isolated occurrence of an employee's deception may be a cause for discipline but not for discharge. However, a prolonged pattern of deception which has an adverse effect on other employees or which abuses a benefit, such as sick leave, may be cause for summary discharge.

Relevant Cases

Microdot, Inc. (Kelliher), 66 LA 177;
Rock Hill Printing & Finishing (Whyte), 64 LA 856;
Mercoid Corp. (Kossoff), 63 LA 941;

Rowe International, Inc. (Turkus), 55 LA 1298;
Cincinnati Tool Co. (Kates), 52 LA 818;
Harvard Mfg. Co. (Kates), 51 LA 1098;
Danbury Cemetery Association (Stutz), 42 LA 447;
United Engineering & Foundry Co. (Kates), 37 LA 1095;
Janitorial Service, Inc. (Whelan), 33 LA 902;
I. B. Goodman Mfg. Co., Inc. (Geissinger), 62 LA 732.

3   *The second job cannot place the employee in a position of competing with the primary employer or give rise to a conflict of interest.*

Examples:

Employee *A* operated a business in his home where he provided on a private basis the same services as his employer. The employer issued a warning to *A* to cease operation of his private business. The warning went unheeded, and *A* was discharged. The arbitrator denied the grievance.

Employee *B*'s primary employment was with a company which sold new machines. On the side, he purchased and repaired used machines of the same sort for resale. Following two warnings the employee was discharged. The arbitrator reinstated the employee with full backpay, stating that the employee was not in direct competition with the primary employer because the markets were sufficiently distinct.

An employer, engaged in the sale and repair of televisions, had attempted unsuccessfully to have inserted into the collective bargaining agreement a provision which prohibited employees from competing with the firm by working with other similar employers when not directly rendering services to it. It also had unsuccessfully solicited pledges from employees not to engage in similar activities either on their own or for another company in competition with it. Employee *C* was discharged for competing with the company by repairing televisions in his home for which he would charge. The discharge was sustained on the basis that the employee's conduct was so destructive to the employer that the prior unsuccessful attempts to obtain agreements were not indicative of an agreement by the employer to allow such conduct. The arbitrator held that there would have to be a specific and clear agreement to the contrary before the employer's primary interest could be overridden.

Guidelines

An employee may be discharged for taking steps to form a business which would compete with his or her employer, if the field is a highly competitive one or involves trade secrets.

Relevant Cases

Sperry Rand Corp. (Koven), 57 LA 68;
Heppenstall Co. (Shister), 55 LA 1044;
United Fuel Gas Co. (Whyte), 54 LA 942;
Utility Tree Service (Karasick), 53 LA 1176;
Philips Petroleum (Caraway), 47 LA 372;
Pipe Coupling Manufacturers, (McCoy), 46 LA 1009;
Janitorial Service, Inc. (Whelan), 33 LA 902;
Alaska Sales & Services Co. (Axon), 73 LA 164;
Jacksonville Shipyards, Inc. (Taylor), 74 LA 1066;
I. B. Goodman Mfg. Co., Inc. (Geissinger), 62 LA 732.

Notes to Chapter 17

1. *See Gas Serv. Co.* (Bronson), 63 LA 293; *Albertson's Inc.* (Christopher), 65 LA 1042; *Randle-Eastern Ambulance Serv., Inc.* (Sherman), 65 LA 394; *Rock Hill Printing & Finishing Co.* (Whyte), 64 LA 856.

2. *See Gas Serv. Co., supra,* note 1; *W. R. Grace & Co.* (Boals), 62 LA 779 (discharged denied); *Microdot, Inc.* (Kelliher), 66 LA 177.

3. *See Microdot, Inc., supra,* note 2; *Rock Hill Printing & Finishing Co., supra,* note 1; *Rowe Int'l, Inc.* (Turkus), 55 LA 1298; *Mercoid Corp.* (Kosoff), 63 LA 941; *Harvard Mfg. Co.* (Kates), 51 LA 1098; *I. B. Goodman Mfg. Co.* (Geissinger), 62 LA 732.

4. *See Sperry Rand Corp.* (Koven), 57 LA 68; *Heppenstall Co.* (Shister), 55 LA 1044; *United Fuel Gas Co.* (Whyte), 54 LA 942; *Utility Tree Serv.* (Karasick), 53 LA 1176; *Alaska Sales & Serv. Co.* (Axon), 73 LA 164; *Jacksonville Shipyards, Inc.* (Taylor), 74 LA 1066; *I. B. Goodman Mfg., Inc., supra,* note 3.

18

Poor Performance

Issue: Whether an employee may be discharged or otherwise disciplined for poor performance.

Principle: An employee may be discharged or otherwise disciplined for poor performance where the employer has established and communicated a reasonable performance standard prior to the date of the discharge or discipline, where there is evidence that the employee failed to meet the standard, and where the employee was accorded progressive discipline.

Considerations:

1. Whether the employer had established a reasonable performance standard prior to the discipline of the employee;
2. Whether the standard of performance was adequately communicated to the employee;
3. Whether the employer's performance failed to meet the standard;
4. Whether the employee was accorded progressive discipline.

Discussion: Generally, arbitrators will uphold discipline for poor productivity only if the employer had established a standard, prior to the disciplinary action, by which the employee's productivity can be measured. At least one arbitrator, however, has held that if the labor agreement does not require a standard, the employer may discipline an employee for poor productivity without showing that the employee failed to meet a pre-established norm.[1]

Arbitrators generally recognize that management has an inherent right to set reasonable production standards and to discipline an employee for failure to meet them.[2] Only clear language in the labor agreement prohibiting the establishment of standards or of quotas can prevent an employer from doing so.[3]

Arbitrators tend to prefer productivity standards which are based on objective, measurable criteria.[4] At least one arbitrator, however, has approved somewhat subjective standards: In *International Shoe Co.* Arbitrator Roberts noted that under the express terms of the labor agreement the employer could not establish production quotas for its employees, but he stated that the employer could, nevertheless, demand that its employees do an "honest, fair day's work."[5] Recognizing a need, however, for some objective way to judge an employee's performance, Roberts also stated that the employer could determine if an employee had put in a "fair day's work" by comparing that individual employee's production with the production of other employees (taking into account the normal variations among individual workers). Emphasizing that this method of measuring an employee's production was not the same as establishing a quota, he held that the employer had acted permissibly in concluding that an employee had not put in a fair day's work and, subsequently, suspending him for three days.

It should be noted that not all arbitrators approve of productivity standards based on the total average production of all employees. For example, in *Union Carbide Corp.*, the arbitrator refused to uphold such a standard, stating that the standard was invalid because it did not take into consideration individual work problems, such as those which employees had with machines or casings.[6]

Arbitrators will decline to uphold discipline for poor production, if the employee is unaware of the performance standard. The issue which has periodically arisen, therefore, is what constitutes the proper communication of the standard. In *A. P. Green Refractories* the employer conducted a time study after there had been a decrease in the productivity of a group of brick hackers.[7] After finishing the study, a supervisor met with the four-member hacking crew and told them that productivity had been set at 884 bricks per workhour. Four days later, the employer sent a letter to the union detailing the new standard. After an additional three days, the productivity level of the hacking crew did not improve, and the employer discharged all of its members. Despite the union's contention that the time study and the resulting production standard were not adequately communicated to the union, the arbitrator held that the company had properly communicated the standards to the employees and to the union and upheld the discharges. The arbitrator did not indicate whether the oral communication to the crew or the written notices to the union constituted the proper method of notifying the employees of such a standard.

As might be expected, arbitrators have an easier time upholding discipline where the employer can document, through extensive record keeping, an employee's consistent failure to meet productivity standards. For example, in *Florsheim Shoe Company* the company maintained a weekly "point system" indicating the amount of piecework done by employees, and the discharge of an employee, who had consistently failed to meet the standard each week for six and one-half months, was upheld.[8]

Other types of evidence, however, are considered to be less reliable. In this connection, one recurring problem is whether a supervisor's testimony constitutes sufficient evidence to support disciplinary action. The predominant view appears to be that whereas the judgment or opinions of supervisors deserve consideration, they are not of much evidentiary value without the support of accompanying objective evidence.[9] However, at least one arbitrator has upheld a discharge based solely on a supervisor's testimony that the grievant was the worst performer in the entire workforce.[10]

Several arbitrators have noted that where discharge or other discipline for poor production arises, not because an employee is guilty of fault or wrongdoing, but because the employee is not adequately efficient, it is incumbent upon management to warn the employee about his or her shortcomings.[11] Accordingly, in these cases, the issue often arises whether the employee has been adequately warned about his or her poor productivity. Generally, and particularly in the case of long-time employees, arbitrators insist that prior to being discharged, an employee must at least have been warned several times about poor productivity.[12]

One sub-issue which has arisen in these cases is whether the individual employee has been personally warned about his or her shortcomings. In *Canron, Inc.*, the employer sent two general notices in pay envelopes to welders, warning them that employees who made defective welds would be subject to discharge.[13] After an employee had made a defective weld, the employer discharged him. The arbitrator converted the discharge into a one-month suspension, holding that although the grievant had clearly violated the welding standard, he had been inadequately warned. The arbitrator stated that the general notice to all the employees did not sufficiently warn the grievant that he would be discharged if he made a defective weld.

In *Montague Machine Co.*, the arbitrator reduced a discharge to a suspension where the evidence showed several previous warnings about poor performance.[14] The arbitrator concluded, however, that these warnings could have been construed by the employee to have been nothing more than casual conversations. Accordingly, the arbitrator found that the employee had not been given sufficient notice of his poor performance to justify a discharge.[15]

A different view was taken in *City of Toledo*, where the arbitrator stated that a personal knowledge of shortcomings can be imputed to an employee.[16] In this case, the police department directed its accident investigation officers to issue more traffic citations, and when three officers failed to increase their number of citations, they were transferred. Although the arbitrator reinstated two of the transferred officers, concluding that they had been inadequately warned, he upheld the transfer of a third officer. That officer, stated the arbitrator, had issued so few citations that he had to have been aware that his performance was substandard.[17]

In only one recent case has an arbitrator held that notice of poor productivity need not be given prior to discharge. In *Tex-A-Panel Manufacturing Co.*, the employer discharged a machine operator without having previously warned him of his poor performance.[18] The arbitrator upheld the discharge, emphasizing that nothing in the labor agreement required previous notice of poor performance.

Several arbitrators have emphasized that in addition to providing adequate notice to an employee whose productivity is substandard, an employer must counsel the employee. The rationale is that the employee has committed no infraction and can be trained to improve his or her performance.[19] In one case, the arbitrator reinstated a discharged employee, finding that the employer had made no attempt to counsel and to rehabilitate the employee.[20]

In *City of Toledo*, the arbitrator found that one of the discharged police officers had responded to counseling, and noted that, although the officer had not quite met the established standard for the number of traffic citations to be issued, he had responded well enough to the counseling that discharge was unwarranted.[21]

Consequently, in order that disciplinary action for poor performance be upheld in arbitration, it appears vital that the employee be subject to progressive discipline. This, in part, follows naturally from the need to apprise the employee of the level of production expected of him or her. However, it is also necessary to put the employee on notice that if his or her production does not come up to standard, the employee will be terminated or otherwise disciplined. Arbitrators place great emphasis upon the need for progressive discipline, and they will often allow reinstatement of an employee, which they acknowledge is a poor performer, because of the lack of such discipline.[22] A feature closely related to progressive discipline is the arbitrators' consideration of the employee's prior work record. In this respect, a discharge may be upheld where there have been numerous prior problems—not necessarily all the same problems as that which caused the discharge—even though the final cause cited would not warrant discharge by itself.[23] Conversely, a lengthy record of good performance and conduct will make a discharge less likely to be sustained.[24]

Key Points:

1 *The employer must have established a reasonable performance standard prior to the discipline of the employee.*

Examples:

Employee *A* was disciplined for deburring 20 percent fewer gears than the average of the other employees in his work area. The discipline was sustained, when it was shown that, although there was no actual performance standard, the employee's substantial deviation from the norm had been noted for some time and had been a subject of discussion with the employee.

Employee *B* was disciplined for failing to meet an established productivity standard. At the arbitration, it was shown that the average performance of most of the employees was below the standard, and an expert testified that the level of production demanded by the employer exceeded the reasonable capabilities of employees working under the present conditions in the company. Although the performance of *B* was significantly below the average, the discipline was voided by the arbitrator on the basis that the standard was unreasonable.

Employee *C* was disciplined for failing to meet an established performance standard. The arbitrator sustained the grievance when the employer could not establish the objective and rational basis for the standard and could not show that the performance of the other two employees subject to the standard was not due to unusual or special abilities.

Employee *D* was disciplined for poor performance when he failed to meet an established standard of production. The arbitrator voided the discipline on the basis that the standard had been established only one week prior to the discipline and appeared to have been established for the sole purpose of justifying the disciplinary action. The arbitrator held that the employee was not given sufficient opportunity to bring his performance up to the employer's new standard.

Guidelines

The employer must be able to show that its performance standard has been based upon some rational determination of normal capabilities of other employees working under the existing conditions and that the standard is objective. Further, the standard must have

---

> **Guidelines**—contd.
>
> been established sufficiently in advance of its enforcement to permit employees to adjust their work habits and techniques to meet the standard.

Relevant Cases

Associated Grocers of St. Louis, Inc. (Dugan), 66 LA 55;
City of Toledo (Heinsz), 70 LA 221;
Great Atlantic & Pacific Tea Co. (Seidenberg), 68 LA 485;
Northern Telecom, Inc. (Sembower), 65 LA 270;
Allied Employers, Inc. (Hedges), 65 LA 405;
A. P. Green Refractories Co. (Williams), 64 LA 885;
Union Carbide Corp. (Jones), 70 LA 201;
General Electric Co. (Moore), 74 LA 1278;
Stoppenbach, Inc. (Lee), 68 LA 553;
Eaton Corp. (Kasper), 69 LA 71;
Houston Publishers Assoc. (Duff), 58 LA 321;
King's Command Meats, Inc. (Kleinsorge), 60 LA 491;
Varbros Tool & Die Co. (Kabaker), 42 LA 440.

2   *The employee must have been made aware of the standard.*

Examples:

Employee *A* was disciplined for having a production level 20 percent below that of other employees involved in deburring gear blanks. The employer had no published production standard, and *A* only learned of his below average performance at the time of his discipline. The grievance was sustained by the arbitrator.

Employee *B* was a pieceworker with a guaranteed base wage. Each week she was paid the higher of either her piece-based rate or her guaranteed wage and, when paid the guaranteed wage, was given a note with her pay indicating what her piece-based wage would have been. After receiving a guaranteed wage four weeks in a row, *B* was disciplined. The discipline was sustained. The arbitrator noted that the notice in the pay envelope was sufficient for any reasonable person to know that her or his performance was substandard and that such a performance could not be acceptable to the employer over a sustained period.

Employee *C* was given a three-day suspension for poor production. Although the employer did not have a published performance standard, the arbitrator sustained the suspension and held that, as the employee had received two warnings for low productivity before the suspension, she had received proper notice of her poor performance.

Guidelines

There must be a reasonable basis for an arbitrator to conclude that the employee knew or had to have known that his or her productivity was below what the employer reasonably expected.

Relevant Cases

County of Santa Clara (Concepcion), 76 LA 7;
VRN International (Vause), 74 LA 806;
Florsheim Shoe Co. (Roberts), 74 LA 705;
Lash Distribution, Inc. (Darrow), 74 LA 274;
Interstate Brands Corp. (Hamby), 73 LA 771;
Eaton Corp. (Kasper), 69 LA 71;
Associated Grocers of St. Louis (Dugan), 66 LA 55;
West Chemical Products, Inc. (Dykstra), 63 LA 610;
Canron, Inc. (Marcus), 72 LA 1310;
Midwest Telephone Co. (Witney), 66 LA 311;
Varbros Tool & Die Co. (Kabaker), 42 LA 440;
Uarco Co. (Gibson), 58 LA 1021;
Stoppenbach, Inc. (Lee), 68 LA 553;
Fort Wayne Community Schools (Deitsch), 78 LA 928;
Montague Machine Co. (Bornstein), 78 LA 172.

3   *The employee's performance must be proven to have been below the productivity standard.*

Examples:

Employee *A* was disciplined for poor performance when his production fell below the standard for the second week in three months. The arbitrator, stating that the poor performance of the employee was too occasional to justify discipline, voided the employer's disciplinary actions.

Employee *B* was disciplined for poor performance on the basis that his production in the polishing department of a striking-tool manufacturing plant was 20 percent below that of other employees in the department. Noting that there was a possibility that the tools polished by the grievant were significantly more difficult than those of other employees during the same period, the arbitrator sustained the grievance for lack of proof.

Employee C was disciplined for poor performance when her production records showed that in six of the prior eight weeks she fell below the standard by an average of 2 percent. Holding that the variance was *de minimis* and possibly due to legitimate reasons, the arbitrator voided the discipline.

Employee D was given a three-day disciplinary suspension when her production was shown to have averaged 2 percent below the standard in six of the prior eight weeks. The employee defended on the basis that the deviation was *de minimis*. The employer presented evidence that throughout her term of employment D's performance had always been marginal, and that the discipline had followed only after the employer had exhausted other remedial measures. Further, the arbitrator found that D spent an inordinate amount of time on the telephone and had an unsatisfactory attendance and tardiness record. The discipline was sustained.

Guidelines

Discipline may not be sustained if the poor performance was only occasional or was *de minimis*, except where other facts demonstrate that the employee had a poor attitude.

Relevant Cases

> United States Plywood-Champion Papers, Inc. (Amis), 56 LA 165;
> Houston Publishers Assoc. (Duff), 58 LA 321;
> King's Command Meats, Inc. (Kleinsorge), 60 LA 491;
> Florsheim Shoe Company (Roberts), 74 LA 705;
> Midwest Telephone Company (Witney), 66 LA 311;
> Jonco Aircraft (Merrill), 22 LA 1819;
> Pet Incorporated (Jason), 76 LA 292.

4   *The employee must have been accorded progressive discipline.*

Examples:

Employee A was discharged for insubstantial production. Previously, A had been warned and told to increase his production. When he did not improve within the month after the warning, he was discharged. The arbitrator reinstated the employee, because *A* had not been accorded the full progressive system.

Employee *B* was discharged after repeated warnings about poor production. The employee was reinstated without backpay on the grounds that his most recent warning did not adequately put the employee on notice that he would be discharged, unless his productivity improved.

Guidelines

The employee's discipline will not be sustained unless he has been warned, given an adequate opportunity to improve, and advised of the effects of not satisfying the employer's standards.

Relevant Cases

San Francisco Redevelopment Agency (Koven), 57 LA 1149;
Stoppenbach, Inc. (Lee), 68 LA 553;
Eaton Corp. (Kasper), 69 LA 71;
Bethlehem Steel Corp. (Harkless), 58 LA 363;
Varbros Tool & Die Co. (Kabaker), 42 LA 440;
Florsheim Shoe Co. (Roberts), 74 LA 705;
County of Santa Clara (Concepcion), 76 LA 7;
Midwest Telephone Co. (Witney), 66 LA 311;
City of Toledo (Heinsz), 70 LA 216;
Montague Machine Co. (Bornstein), 78 LA 172;
Fort Wayne Community Schools (Deitsch), 78 LA 928.

Notes to Chapter 18

1. *Eaton Corp.* (Kasper), 69 LA 71 (suspension upheld of employee who deburred clutches too slowly).
2. *City of Toledo* (Heinsz), 70 LA 216, 220; *Great Atlantic & Pacific Tea Co.* (Seidenberg), 68 LA 485, 488; *Allied Employers, Inc.* (Hedges), 65 LA 270, 273.
3. *See International Shoe Co.* (Roberts), 68 LA 444.
4. *See, e.g., Northern Telecom, Inc.* (Sembower), 65 LA 405 (assembly worker standards were based on a methods-time-measurement system developed at a university); *A.P. Green Refractories Co., infra,* note 7 (brick workers' productivity standard was established by long-term detailed study).
5. *International Shoe Co., supra,* note 3.
6. *Union Carbide Corp.* (Jones), 70 LA 201.
7. A. P. Green Refractories (Williams), 64 LA 885.

8. *Florsheim Shoe Co.* (Roberts), 74 LA 705.

9. *Midwest Tel. Co.* (Witney), 66 LA 311; *see also Jonco Aircraft* (Merrill), 22 LA 1819.

10. *Pet Inc.* (Jason), 76 LA 292.

11. *See, e.g., Florsheim Shoe Co., supra,* note 8.

12. *West Chemical Products, Inc.* (Dykstra), 63 LA 610 (the discharge of a 25-year employee was upheld where he had received at least six warning letters over a seven-year period); *Florsheim Shoe Co., supra,* note 8 (the discharge of a 10-year employee was upheld).

13. *Canron, Inc.* (Marcus), 72 LA 1310.

14. *Montague Mach. Co.* (Bornstein), 78 LA 172.

15. *See also Fort Wayne Community Schools* (Deitsch), 78 LA 928.

16. *City of Toledo, supra,* note 2.

17. *See West Chem. Prods., Inc., supra,* note 12.

18. *Tex-A-Panel Mfg. Co.* (Ray), 62 LA 272.

19. *See Florsheim Shoe Co., supra,* note 8; *County of Santa Clara* (Concepcion), 76 LA 7.

20. *Midwest Tel. Co., supra,* note 8, at 315.

21. *City of Toledo, supra,* note 2.

22. For example, *see San Francisco Redev. Agency* (Koven), 57 LA 1149 (a record which the arbitrator stated was "ordinarily a clear justification for discharge" did not support a discharge in that case, because there was a lack of progressive discipline); *Stoppenbach, Inc.* (Lee), 68 LA 553 (the arbitrator emphasized the employee's prior suspension and warning about discharge in denying the grievance over the discharge); *Eaton Corp., supra,* note 1 (the suspension was upheld, because the employee had been warned that he would face suspension if his production did not improve).

23. *Bethlehem Steel Corp.* (Harkless), 58 LA 363.

24. *Varbros Tool & Die Co.* (Kabaker), 42 LA 440.

19

Work Slowdowns and Stoppages

Issue: Whether an employee may be discharged or otherwise disciplined for engaging in a work slowdown or stoppage.

Principle: An employee may be discharged or otherwise disciplined for engaging in a work slowdown or stoppage where it is established that an interruption to production in fact occurred; that the employee participated in, led, or attempted to cause the interruption; and, that there are no mitigating circumstances which either justify the conduct or warrant a lessening of the penalty.

Considerations:
1. Whether the work slowdown or stoppage (or attempted work slowdown or stoppage) and the employee's participation is established to the extent that substantial weight is given the credible evidence;
2. Whether the employee was justified in participating in or causing the slowdown or stoppage;
3. Whether the employee was disciplined to the same degree as all other similarly situated employee-participants;
4. Whether there are circumstances which would warrant a lessening of the penalty.

Discussion: Most collective bargaining agreements explicitly prohibit the conducting of, causing of, or participating in a work slowdown or stoppage as part of the contract's No Strike-No Lockout provision. Nevertheless, a careful review of the arbitration decisions in this area reveal that the discharge of an employee for such conduct is not always simple.

Where there is no collective bargaining agreement and, under certain circumstances, even where such an agreement exists, this kind of activity is usually within the realm of concerted activity protected by the National Labor Relations Act. Violations of the NLRA are not within the scope of this discussion. However, a review of the bases upon which arbitrators have held that such conduct constitutes just cause for discipline is appropriate.

It appears that the participation in or stimulation of a work slowdown is generally accepted by arbitrators as a serious, direct assault on the essence of economic enterprise and, as such, warrants summary discharge, absent special circumstances. In most of the cases reviewed, the problem of proving the offense has been the dominant issue. Once this problem is resolved, the decision of the arbitrator appears, in most cases, to be a foregone conclusion. In this connection, arbitrators recognize a difference between employee discipline for poor productivity, the major element of which is a nonintentional failure to perform up to the employer's standards, and employee discipline involving a work slowdown, the major element of which is an intentional and concerted refusal to perform the work available. Consequently, the issue often arises as to whether the disciplined employee or employees exhibited the necessary intent. Also, where an employee has not acted in concert with others, the issue is usually restricted to a charge of insubordination and not of a work slowdown or a stoppage.

Obviously, where the employee or employees admit to the slowdown, the problem of intent does not exist. However, wherever the employee or employees deny the existence of a slowdown, or a scheme to conduct a slowdown, the issue of intent becomes central. On the other hand, it seems that in all cases where an arbitrator has construed the evidence as establishing that there was a slowdown, the intent of the employees ceases to be an issue. The inference, in fact, is quickly made and the subject of intent is frequently not discussed or even acknowledged; the occurrence of a slowdown is enough, apparently, to establish the requisite intent, and employee intent is assumed to be a part of the finding of a slowdown.

In *Mueller Company*, for example, the arbitrator upheld the five-day layoff of a drill press operator, whose productivity dropped for a month after new incentive rates had been introduced.[1] The operator had averaged 120 pieces per hour before the new rate was set, but only 72 pieces per hour afterwards. The arbitrator noted that "On its face, the sharp, unexplained, and long-continued drop in the grievant's productivity strongly suggests a conscious curtailment of effort" and held that the employer was justified in suspending the employee.[2]

In *United States Steel Corporation*, the issue of whether a group of employees had engaged in a slowdown was resolved through a similar analysis.[3] In that case, the company announced a "tightening" of production rates, and the output of an entire mill subsequently decreased from 50 to 20 units per hour. The decrease in output lasted for about a month, when the company decided to halt operations. The arbitrator rejected the union's contention that the company had caused a "lockout," finding that the employees had engaged in an illegal work slowdown. He stated,

> . . . Proof of the slowdown did not lie in overt acts, observed and recorded, so much as in the simple fact that output was running at about one-third the rate reasonably expected. [T]here was reason to believe the low output resulted from concerted action. . . .[4]

In at least one case, however, an arbitrator found that, although productivity was not what the employer thought it should be, the employees had not engaged in a slowdown. In another *United States Steel Corporation* case, the employer had suspended an entire shipping crew for engaging in a slowdown.[5] The suspended employees did not grieve at that time. For several days after the crew returned to work, its productivity increased, but not enough for the employer, which again suspended all of the crew members. The arbitrator set aside this second suspension and held that, although a higher level of production may have been possible, there was not enough evidence to establish that the crew members, who had substantially improved their production, had continued to engage in a slowdown.

Significantly, in cases of alleged slowdowns, arbitrators prefer that an employer show that an employee, or the employees, fell below an established productivity standard; but, there appears to be no insistence that the standard applied be a formal, implemented one.[6]

An important issue, akin to those found in cases involving concerted actions by employees and recognized as such under the National Labor Relations Act, is that having to do with an alleged justification for a slowdown. In this regard, the fact that the disciplined employee may be the union steward is central. While several arbitrators have stated that an employer has the right to discipline a union official who instigates or participates in a work slowdown, others have stated that union officials enjoy some degree of protected status and should not be harshly disciplined, if acting in good faith.

In *Inglis Limited*, for example, the employer discharged the grievant, a press operator and chief steward, for directing employees to produce pieces at a slower rate than that at which they were capable.[7] The grievant had been upset over the employer's new, but unofficial, production rate. Although he found that the grievant's behavior was unwarranted, the arbitrator nonetheless reinstated him, emphasizing that the grievant had been acting in his capacity as a union official and not out of self-interest. The proper penalty, the arbitrator held, was to strip the grievant of his union job and to reduce the discharge to a suspension, running from the day of the discharge to the day of the award.

In *Granite City Steel Company*, however, the employer discharged a crane operator with 21 years' seniority for engaging in a slowdown to protest the bumping of another employee.[8] Throughout the grievance procedure, the grievant never claimed that he had been acting in his capacity as a union committeeman, and the arbitrator, emphasizing this fact, declined to reinstate him. Rather, the arbitrator upheld the discharge, stressing that this was not a case involving the discipline of a union official, who had acted in that capacity.

In *Pullman, Inc.*, the arbitrator took a different view on the culpability of a union official.[9] In that case, the grievant was discharged for directing several employees to slow down so that more senior employees would not look bad. The labor agreement contained a "no strike" clause, which specifically prohibited slowdowns. The arbitrator upheld the discharge, emphasizing that a union official should be more familiar with the violations set forth in the agreement and should conduct himself or herself accordingly.

One rather strange, but noteworthy, case is *Stevens Air Systems*, which involved the reinstatement of a discharged shop committee member.[10] In that case, a production worker, who was a union committeeman, directed the other 24 members on his production line to slow down. The line was scheduled to be shut down, and he apparently wanted the job to be stretched out. The labor agreement stated, in pertinent part, "[N]o work stoppages, strikes or slowdowns shall be caused or sanctioned by the Union." Finding that the grievant had acted on his own and that the slowdown tactic had not been sanctioned by the union, the arbitrator held that the labor agreement had not been violated. The arbitrator also noted that the grievant had never been warned about engaging in slowdowns, and he therefore reinstated him.

A review of the dominant cases in this area indicates that the *Stevens Air Systems* case is not within the mainstream, which suggests that factors not appearing in the written opinion may have been operating which caused the arbitrator to rule in the fashion he did. For the most part, causing a work slowdown is generally recognized as a legitimate reason for summary discipline, regardless of the technicalities of contract language.

Typically, these cases involve groups of employees who act in concert. As a consequence, the employer's treatment of the entire group comes under scrutiny in many cases, especially when it is suspected that a single employee has been treated too harshly because of some alleged or actual leadership role. In this respect, several arbitrators have had to struggle with the problem of whether to uphold discipline for all or for many of the members of a group which has engaged in a slowdown, where it is difficult to determine the role each employee played.

At least one arbitrator has stated that where several employees participate in a slowdown, the employer must administer discipline on an equal basis.[11] A more difficult problem arises, however, where all employees may not have been equally culpable.

In *United States Steel Corporation* the employer placed written reprimands in the files of each of 26 employees in coke oven crews who had engaged in a slowdown.[12] The employer relied on a theory of "collective responsibility" in imposing discipline. The arbitrator rejected this theory, however. He concluded that similar discipline for all employees was unjustified, because the composition of the crews shifted from day to day and some crews performed worse than others. Further, the arbitrator held that, in order to reprimand individual employees, the employer did not necessarily have to produce evidence tying each employee to a precise slowdown action and that all the employer need do was to show that an individual grievant had worked regularly in crews which showed a consistent reduction in productivity. Accordingly, the arbitrator divided the grievants into four categories: those definitely not engaged in slowdown; those probably not engaged; those probably engaged; and, those definitely engaged. As to employees in the second and third groups, he considered evidence against individual grievants.

In the same case, Arbitrator McDermott upheld the suspension of several crew leaders, finding that they had contributed more significantly to the slowdown. Suspending the crew leaders and not other employees, he concluded, did not amount to discrimination.

A different approach was taken by Arbitrator Richard McIntosh in *Buddy L. Corp.* There, the arbitrator held that the employer had been justified in warning several employees and in suspending all the employees who had worked on an assembly line which suffered a slowdown.[13] Such a manner of punishment, he stated, does not amount to guilt by association where production amounts to joint effort by all employees.

In several cases, arbitrators have held that, although an employee was involved in a work slowdown, mitigating circumstances warranted a decrease in punishment.

In *Library of Congress*, for instance, the arbitrator found that a supervisor, who had wanted another supervisor to look bad, had condoned a slowdown and that not all employees who had engaged in the slowdown had been disciplined.[14] He, therefore, reduced a suspension from two weeks to five days.

In *Chromalloy American Corp.*, the arbitrator reduced the suspension of two employees from five days to two days, emphasizing that both employees—each of whom had been suspended for working too slowly—had good work records and had been told by the company president that their discipline would be light.[15]

However, in several cases arbitrators have found that there were no mitigating circumstances and have upheld discharges.[16]

Key Points:

1   *The work slowdown or stoppage must be proven by the substantial weight of the evidence to have been an intentional act.*

Examples:

Employee *A*, along with six other employees in the same department, was discharged for conducting a work slowdown. The employer presented evidence demonstrating that *A*, the shop steward, and all of the others in his department had been upset over the employer's decision to go onto a rotating shift the following month. The contract clearly allowed the employer to make unilateral shift changes. The employer also showed that, after the announcement of rotating shifts, within twenty-four hours production had fallen by 30 percent and stayed that way for three weeks, when the new shift schedule went into effect. The employees denied the slowdown but acknowledged the accuracy of the employer's production figures. They contended, however, that the loss in production was due to equipment failure and lack of raw materials. Finding that there had been a higher frequency of equipment failure, a shortage of raw materials due to breakdowns in lift trucks, and no proof that these malfunctions were due to sabotage, the arbitrator reinstated all employees with full backpay.

Employee *B*, along with six others, was discharged for engaging in a work slowdown. The employer asserted that production fell by 30 percent immediately after a rotating shift was announced. The employer also showed that production returned to normal levels after the discharges. The employees defended by denying that there had been an intentional slowdown and argued that numerous equipment failures and the lack of supplies had caused production to drop. The employer acknowledged the equipment failures; but it also presented evidence showing, in nearly all instances that the failures had been due to human failure, or acts of possible sabotage. The arbitrator sustained the discharges, noting the suspicious coincidence between the announcement of the rotating shifts and the questionable equipment failures.

Employee *C* was suspended, along with three of the other four employees on the same job crew, for engaging in a work slowdown. The employer presented to the arbitrator the production records of all employees for a one-month period. They were all roughly the same. The employer then presented the production record of a new employee for the same period. It was 30 percent higher. A supervisor testified that he had observed arguments between *C* and the new employee, although the supervisor did not hear the subject in dispute. He also said that none of the suspended employees had had anything to do with the new employee. However, about one month before the disciplinary action there had been an obvious attitude change toward the new employee, and the older employees appeared to accept and to include him as "one of the boys." The employer's records showed that the production of the new employee fell drastically one month before the discipline to a level about equal to that of the other employees. The arbitrator sustained the discipline and ordered that a time study be conducted on the job to determine an appropriate production level.

Employee *D* was discharged after a new employee had reported to his supervisor that *D* had told him to slow down to keep from making it "bad for the rest of us." The new employee refused to testify at the hearing. The production records showed the production of the new employee to be significantly higher than that of the others. A time study showed production levels of other employees to be below a reasonable standard. The arbitrator reinstated the employee, but without backpay. The arbitrator also suggested that the new employee should have been disciplined for refusing to testify.

Guidelines

An admission of guilt is not a necessary requirement for sustaining disciplinary action against an employee for participating in or causing a work stoppage or slowdown. Intent will normally be inferred from the absence of other factors explaining a drop in production.

Relevant Cases

Mueller Company (Porter), 52 LA 164;
United States Steel Corporation (Miller), 53 LA 1140;
Buddy L. Corp. (McIntosh), 49 LA 581;
United States Steel Corporation (Dybeck), 58 LA 977;
Inglis Limited (Shine), 66 LA 812.

2   *The purpose of the slowdown or stoppage cannot justify the act.*

Examples:

Employee *A*, a union steward, was discharged for calling for a work stoppage, after he learned that the employer had sub-contracted work in violation of the collective bargaining agreement. Noting that the issue in dispute was grievable and that a work stoppage was not justified, the arbitrator sustained the discharge.

Employee *B*, a crew leader, asserted that the working conditions were unsafe and urged the other employees to stop all work. Although the employer argued that the conditions were not unsafe, the crew stopped. *B* was discharged. The arbitrator found that the working conditions were not unsafe but also that *B* had been honestly mistaken. Consequently, he ordered that *B* be reinstated with three days loss in pay as discipline for not accepting the employer's evidence of safety.

Employee *C* was discharged following her statements to other employees that the employer's new production standards were unreasonable and that they should be disregarded. Finding that the employer's standards were a grievable issue, the arbitrator sustained the discharge. *C*'s lack of success in achieving concerted action did not change the fact that she had attempted to get others to join her and she had cut her own production.

Guidelines

A normally grievable or bargainable issue cannot be used as justification for a work slowdown or stoppage, absent an issue involving a threat to employee safety.

Relevant Cases

Inglis Limited (Shine), 66 LA 812;
Granite City Steel Company (Belshaw), 58 LA 69;
Pullman, Inc. (Dworet), 41 LA 607;
Stevens Air Systems (Stashower), 64 LA 425.

3   *All persons participating in a work slowdown or stoppage to the same or similar degree must receive the same disciplinary action, regardless of theoretic differences due to positions or responsibilities.*

Examples:

Following an announcement by the employer that rotating shifts would begin the following month in a particular department, production fell by 30 percent. Two years earlier, the employer had attempted to do the same thing. Following a wildcat strike, the employer had withdrawn the plan. The employer responded this time by discharging *A*, who was the union steward in the department, and by suspending all others in the department for ten days. The suspensions were sustained, but the discharge was reduced to a similar suspension.

Following an announcement by the employer that rotating shifts would begin the following month in a particular department, production fell by 30 percent. Two years earlier, the employer had attempted the same thing. Following a wildcat strike, the employer had withdrawn the plan. When the employer announced its plan this time, *B*, the department's union steward, told the production manager that he had stopped the company before, and he would stop it again. As soon as the slowdown became apparent, the employer discharged *B* and suspended all others in the department. The arbitrator noted the increased culpability of the steward and upheld the suspensions and the discharge.

Following the imposition of new shift schedules and production standards, all of the employees in the plant walked out on a wildcat strike. Following their return to work after an injunction under *Boy's Market*, the employer suspended six local union officers and discharged *C*, the local union president. The grievants argued that the employer was required to take the same disciplinary action against everyone the same or it could take none at all. The arbitrator rescinded the suspensions of two officers because their involvement in the walkout had been restricted to participation, and the arbitrator held that these two should have been treated like all of the other undisciplined employees. *C*, as well as the other officers, had instigated the walkout, and the arbitrator sustained their discipline with the exception of *C*'s, whose discharge was reduced to a suspension.

Guidelines

Where one individual is proven by independent evidence to be particularly culpable, more severe discipline may be justified.

Relevant Cases

Library of Congress (Rothman), 62 LA 1289;
United States Steel Corporation (McDermott), 49 LA 1236;
Buddy L. Corp. (McIntosh), 49 LA 581.

4   *Mitigation of a discharge is warranted only where the effects of the employee's action were minimal and where some other factor, such as a good work record or outrageous affront to the employee's principles, created an aura of injustice.*

Examples:

Employee *A* was discharged for leading a work slowdown to protest what he believed to be illegal subcontracting by the employer. Although the evidence was clear that *A* had endeavored to get other employees to reduce production, little, if any, production time was lost. The subcontracting was grieved, and the employer, at arbitration, agreed to discontinue the practice. The employee's work record was good. The arbitrator reduced the discharge to a suspension.

Employee *B*, a crew leader, had stopped his crew from working at the construction site, because *B* believed that some of the working conditions were unsafe. *B* had asked for an engineer to examine it; the request had been denied. *B* refused to allow the crew to continue to work, and *B* and the crew were discharged. Another crew was brought in and they completed the work without incident. The arbitrator held that, although the condition was clearly safe, the employer had no right to deny *B*'s request for an inspection, and the arbitrator mitigated the discharge to a warning.

Employee *C* was discharged after a new employee reported that he had been told by *C* to slowdown so "the rest of us won't look bad." The arbitrator, stating that discharge was too severe for the one isolated instance, mitigated the discharge to a suspension.

Guidelines

Generally, the stimulation of or participation in an unprotected work stoppage will justify discipline at any level chosen by the employer. The degree of discipline will not be subject to mitigation except in unusual cases.

Relevant Cases

Library of Congress (Rothman), 62 LA 1289;
Chromalloy American Corp. (Hon), 61 LA 246;
Universal Studios (Steese), 72 LA 84;
Granite City Steel Co. (Belshaw), 58 LA 69;
Collis Company (Doyle), 50 LA 1157.

Notes to Chapter 19

1. *Mueller Co.* (Porter), 52 LA 162.
2. *Id.*, at 164.
3. *United States Steel Corp.* (Miller), 53 LA 1140.
4. *United States Steel Corp., supra*, note 3, at 1142; *see also Buddy L. Corp.* (McIntosh), 49 LA 581, for a similar analysis.
5. *United States Steel Corp.* (Dybeck), 58 LA 977.
6. *See. e.g., Inglis Ltd.* (Shine), 66 LA 812.
7. *Id.*
8. *Granite City Steel Co.* (Belshaw), 58 LA 69.
9. *Pullman, Inc.* (Dworet), 41 LA 607.
10. *Stevens Air Sys.* (Stashower), 64 LA 425.
11. *See Library of Congress* (Rothman), 62 LA 1289.
12. *United States Steel Corp.* (McDermott), 49 LA 1236.
13. *Buddy L. Corp., supra*, note 4.
14. *Library of Congress, supra*, note 11.
15. *Chromalloy Am. Corp.* (Hon), 61 LA 246.
16. *Universal Studios* (Steese), 72 LA 84 (a steward truck driver demanded greater pay and caused many employees to stop work while he created an uproar); *Granite City Steel Co., supra*, note 8 (a discharged employee never invoked his union status); *Collis Co.* (Doyle), 50 LA 1157 (a union steward, upset about incentive pay rates, told the employees to "work accordingly").

20

Union Activity/Steward Abuse

Issue: Whether an employee, who is a union steward, may be discharged or otherwise disciplined for actions taken allegedly within the scope of his or her union duties.

Principle: A union steward may be discharged or otherwise disciplined for actions taken as a steward where the employee abuses the grievance procedure; disrupts production; abuses privileges accorded him or her as a steward; and is insubordinate in the exercise of a steward's duties; and, where there is no evidence of union animus on the part of the employer.

Considerations:
1. Whether the actions of the steward simply constituted a zealous representation of his or her constituents;
2. Whether the actions of the steward were inconsistent or otherwise clearly demonstrated an intent to harass the employer;
3. Whether the actions of the steward intentionally, and unnecessarily, disrupted production or operations;
4. Whether the steward had actual control over the employees or the situation when the disruption in production or operations occurred;
5. Whether the steward's action took place during a formal grievance, arbitration, or negotiation meeting;
6. Whether the disciplinary action taken against the steward was due to his or her position in that the steward was

held accountable to a standard different from that of other employees.

Discussion: Due to their concern about employer actions motivated by union animus, arbitra-
tors treat discharges and other disciplinary
actions taken against union officials with circumspection. The question of whether a steward was disciplined simply because of his or
her position as a union official or because of the steward's union
activity is properly treated by the National Labor Relations Board
under the Labor Management Relations Act. This issue, however,
can be deferred to arbitration, or "Collyerized." Nevertheless, there
are several circumstances where discipline will be considered independently of the union animus issue. Of necessity, however, the
question of whether the discipline was merely a subterfuge for discrimination based upon the steward's union activity is almost always
present.

Under some circumstances, a steward can be disciplined for abusing his or her authority as a steward. For instance, union officials
may be properly disciplined for abusing the grievance procedure. A
discharge of a union steward was upheld where he had filed many
grievances which were illogical and contradictory. He had also engaged in other actions whereby he harassed the company and its
management.[1] At least one other decision recognized that proper
discipline could arise from a union officer's use of the grievance
procedure for purposes of harassment. On the other hand, the arbitrator in *Carborundum Co.* sustained the grievance, because there
was no evidence that multiple grievances had been filed to harass
the employer.[2]

Interference with the employer's operations or production is a
more frequently cited basis for disciplining union officials. Within
this category one of the most common incidents is where the union
official instigates, encourages, or otherwise participates in a work
stoppage which violates a no-strike clause. In such cases, a discharge
will almost always be upheld in the absence of extenuating circumstances. Furthermore, a union official who merely takes part in the
strike will usually be found to have thereby encouraged the strike.[3]
In *Quanex*, however, the arbitrator ordered an eight-month disciplinary suspension instead of discharge, because after initially encouraging the wildcat strike, the steward tried to get employees to
return to work.[4]

Similarly, discharge has been held to be appropriate discipline for
union officials who failed to adequately discourage an illegal strike,
even if they did not originally instigate it. It is part of the responsibility of their positions to prevent the violation of the collective
bargaining agreement.[5] In such cases, the key to deciding whether

a union official encouraged, or failed to discourage, employees is whether the union official was in such a position that his or her actions would have the effect of leading the employees to illegally strike.[6] For example, in *Koehring Co.*, the arbitrator found that union trustees did not occupy such positions of leadership and ordered the employer to reduce the discipline to a suspension.[7]

Actions by union officials which are less likely to result in discharge, but will certainly result in discipline, are to encourage slowdowns, to refuse overtime, or to take other actions which interrupt production. Among these actions, the instigation of a slowdown appears to be the most likely to result in discharge. In *Dover Corp.*, the arbitrator upheld the discharge of a union steward who had encouraged the night shift to slow down production to comport with the day shift.[8] And, in *Inglis Limited*, the arbitrator reinstated a steward without backpay who had told employees to work more slowly.[9] The arbitrator cited extenuating circumstances and also stipulated that the steward could not hold union office upon his return. Encouraging employees to refuse overtime will also result in discipline. In *Central Illinois Public Service Co.*, the arbitrator noted that he would ordinarily have upheld the discharge of the steward, who had posted a notice for employees to refuse voluntary overtime, had it not been for extenuating circumstances.[10] Instead, the steward was reinstated without backpay. In *Zellerbach Paper Co.*, the arbitrator upheld the three-month suspensions of a local union president and recording secretary.[11] The arbitrator found that their encouragement of employees not to work voluntary overtime violated the no-strike clause.

Discipline has also been imposed where a union official directed an employee not to fill in at a nonunit position.[12] The arbitrator found that this did not constitute a work stoppage and, therefore, that discharge was too severe. However, the arbitrator reinstated the employee without backpay, which effectively resulted in a nine-month suspension. Accordingly, it is apparent that discipline can be severe when union officials interfere with the production operations of a plant.

Another set of circumstances which occasions disciplinary actions against union officials is where the officials have abused privileges extended to them by virtue of their position. However, these cases usually involve lesser penalties and discharges are rarely sustained. One typical scenario in this category involves a steward, or other union official, who exceeds time allotted to attend to union business or who does not return to work after attending a union business meeting. In these cases, lesser discipline has been sustained.[13]

In *Kay-Brunner Steel Products*, however, the discharge of a steward was sustained where he continued to argue loudly and insistently about the employer's use of a different canteen truck, even after his break had ended and after he had been ordered to return to work.[14] The steward's overly aggressive actions and refusal to obey his supervisor's order amounted to gross insubordination.

Similarly, discipline has been upheld where union officials attended to union business without asking for the time off or without having it granted. In *Greif Bros. Corp.*, the arbitrator reinstated without backpay a local union president who had been discharged for attending a meeting for which the company had denied him the time off.[15] The arbitrator stated that the obey and grieve rule did not apply here, because the employee's disobedience involved union business and, consequently, a discharge was not appropriate. In *Golden Foundry, Inc.*, a three-day suspension was upheld against a union vice president, who had frequently left his work station without approval.[16] The arbitrator stated that this conduct could not be condoned, whether it is characterized as insubordination or self-help.

Union officials can also be disciplined for using abusive language or for other actions taken in the course of performing their general duties. However, a different rule seems to apply to actions taken by union officials during the course of grievance procedures, collective bargaining negotiations, or the performance of similar duties.

Discipline, including discharge, has been sustained where union officials directed abusive language toward their supervisors in the presence of other employees while discussing disputes with the supervisors or employees. The fact that the union officials were acting in their capacity as union representatives did not immunize them from discipline for such actions.[17]

Frequently, overly aggressive representation by union stewards gives rise to disciplinary action. Stewards are expected to be aggressive in the performance of their duties, but arbitrators draw a line beyond which their conduct should not go if discipline is to be avoided. In *Kay-Brunner Steel Products*, a steward's discharge was sustained when he continued to argue past the time to return to work, refused to obey a supervisor's order to go to work, and created such a stir that other employees stopped work, or failed to go to their stations, while the arguing continued.[18] The arbitrator specifically identified the steward's conduct as overly aggressive and held the discharge to be proper.

In *Universal Steel Co.*, the issuance of a warning to a steward was found to be improper when his conduct, which consisted of finger pointing and arguing loudly in the presence of other employees, was not found to have been overly aggressive when taken in light of the employee's usual type of behavior.[19] However, in the same case, the arbitrator sustained a steward's discipline where the employee had threatened a supervisor, placing him in fear of his physical safety.

Profanity and verbal abuse figured also in *Jones & Laughlin Steel Corp.* In that case the steward protested his overtime assignment and the use of an outside contractor in a profane and abusive manner to a supervisor.[20] This conduct, found the arbitrator, was beyond the bounds of appropriateness, and a suspension was sustained.

When the union official makes the same abusive statements in the course of collective bargaining sessions or grievance arbitrations, however, discipline is usually not appropriate. In these situations, the representatives of the union and the company are equals and, therefore, there can be no insubordination.[21]

Discipline has also been applied for various other actions taken by union officials in their capacity as union representatives. In *Bakery and Confectionery Union*, a union steward was reinstated without backpay when he had refused to sign an evaluation form in an effort to bring the dispute over the evaluations to a head.[22] In *Potlatch Corp.*, the arbitrator upheld the discharge of a local vice president who had harassed other employees for not joining the union.[23] His actions exceeded the range of reasonable conduct. A similar standard of conduct was applied in *Union Fork & Hoe Co.* The arbitrator upheld the discharge of a steward who took an employee's time slip, which had been the subject of a meeting in the superintendent's office, and would not return it.[24]

Finally, a union official can be disciplined, up to and including discharge, for just cause, where there is no antiunion motivation on the part of the employer. Union officials have no special immunity from disciplinary action where the alleged cause is not just a pretext.[25]

Arbitrators will also look at the relative treatment of union officials and regular employees. If there is evidence of disparate treatment, arbitrators will assume that an antiunion motive exists and grant the grievance.[26]

Key Points:

1   *Where there is evidence of an intent to harrass an employer, as distinguished from an aggressive representation of the legitimate interests of the employees, a union steward may be disciplined.*

Examples:

Employee *A*, a union steward representing 250 employees, filed numerous grievances, most of which appeared to be clearly without merit and were withdrawn just prior to arbitration. A few proceeded to arbitration but were denied. Of the 100 grievances filed in one year, none was successful in arbitration: 86 were withdrawn prior to arbitration and 14 were settled. The employer discharged the steward after several warnings on the grounds that the steward had abused the system. The arbitrator sustained the grievance—giving the steward his first win—and ordered reinstatement with full backpay. There was no evidence of anything but a zealous representation of the employees.

Employee B, a union steward representing 250 employees, filed numerous grievances, most of which were of dubious merit and some of which had conflicting claims. Of the 100 grievances filed in one year none was successful in arbitration: 86 were withdrawn prior to arbitration and 14 were settled. After a single warning, the employer discharged the steward for misuse of the system and harrassment. Noting that on six occasions the steward had filed conflicting grievances interpreting the same contract provisions in opposite fashions, the arbitrator concluded that steward abuse and harrassment could be inferred from the facts, and the discharge was sustained.

Guidelines

The steward must be found to have done something more than merely file numerous grievances to sustain disciplinary action. There must be some evidence of actions which imply an intent to harrass the employer.

Relevant Cases

Robintech, Inc. (Block), 65 LA 221;
Carborundum Co. (Altrock), 72 LA 118.

2   *The steward must be found to have been in a position of sufficient control and/or influence over the employees to have been able to cause or to instigate a disruption of the employer's production.*

Examples:

Employee A, a steward, protested vehemently against the establishment of rotating shifts by the employer. A grievance over the right of the employer to institute rotating shifts was arbitrated and denied. After the arbitrator's award, the steward told the employer that this was not the last word on the issue. Immediately thereafter, the employees refused all overtime assignments, and production dropped 30 percent. The steward was discharged. The discharge was sustained.

Employee B, a steward, was discharged when he refused to "order" the employees to return from a wildcat strike. Noting that the steward apparently did not instigate the walkout and did not participate in the picketing, the arbitrator doubted whether the steward's order would have meant anything and reinstated him with backpay up to the day the strike ended.

Employee C, a steward, was suspended for one week for telling a new employee not to work in excess of a certain speed, because it would "make it bad" for the rest of the employees. The arbitrator found that this constituted an attempted instigation of a slowdown in violation of the labor agreement and sustained the suspension.

Guidelines

The evidence of the steward's improper conduct must show that the steward actually did, or attempted to, interfere with the employer's production for the purpose of obtaining a personal, or group, benefit or concession from the employer.

Relevant Cases

Dover Corp. (Kaut), 74 LA 675;
Inglis Limited (Shime), 66 LA 812;
Central Illinois Public Service Co. (Kossoff), 76 LA 300;
Clinton Corn Processing Co. (Madden), 71 LA 555;
Bucyrus-Erie Co. (Lipson), 69 LA 93;
Herrud & Co. (Keefe), 66 LA 682:
Dravo Corp. (McDermott), 68 LA 618;
Quanex (McDonald), 73 LA 9;
Zellerbach Paper Co. (Sabo), 73 LA 1140;
Mark Twain Marine Industries, Inc. (Guenther), 73 LA 551.

3   *The steward is expected not to abuse privileges accorded him or her as a union officer, and discipline will be sustained for proven abuse.*

Examples:

Employee A, a steward, obtained time off to travel into the center of town to confer with the union's attorney in connection with an upcoming arbitration. A supervisor saw A going into a theater four hours before the end of his scheduled shift. The steward was discharged. The arbitrator, while acknowledging that such abuse is just cause for discipline, mitigated the discharge to a disciplinary suspension.

Employee *B*, a steward, had been warned repeatedly that he was not to leave his work station to talk to other employees unless he had the prior permission of his supervisor and unless the subject was a grievance which had already been filed. The employer suspended *B* for not being at his work station because of union business. The steward's discipline was voided when the arbitrator learned that the business involved an employee emergency and that the supervisor had not been in the department when the issue arose.

Guidelines

Except as permitted by specific language in the collective bargaining agreement, the union activities of the steward cannot unreasonably interfere with his or her normal job duties.

Relevant Cases

Reichold Chemicals, Inc. (Hon), 73 LA 636;
Ward LaFrance Truck Co. (Levy), 69 LA 831;
American Hoechst Corp. (Purcell), 68 LA 517;
Greif Bros. Corp. (Flannagan), 67 LA 1001;
Golden Foundry, Inc. (Fitch), 67 LA 887.

4   *The steward cannot conduct himself or herself in a fashion which demonstrates contempt for supervisors or which is otherwise insubordinate.*

Examples:

Employee *A*, a union steward, discovered that a supervisor had offered overtime to a junior employee in violation of the negotiated procedure. Irate at yet another occasion of what he believed to be the third such mistake within the last month by the same supervisor, the steward ripped the assignment sheet off the bulletin board, stormed across the production floor, creating a commotion, and approached the supervisor, who was in the process of giving instructions to two other employees. *A* broke into the conversation and said, "You are a flaming a— h—. I don't know how someone so stupid could ever have become a supervisor. How many times do I have to show you how this system works?" The steward was discharged, and the arbitrator sustained the discharge.

Employee *B*, a union steward, was chairman of the grievance committee. During the course of a grievance meeting, *B* called the personnel director a flaming a— h— and told him he was too stupid to talk to. *B* was discharged. The arbitrator found that, while the conduct was reprehensible, it was protected in that the behavior occurred during the course of a heated argument over a grievance in a closed meeting between grievance committee members and company representatives. The discharge was commuted to a warning.

Guidelines

A steward's conduct is judged according to the same standards as other employees, except during collective bargaining sessions or formal grievance meetings. At these times, the steward is regarded as being equal to the company's representatives, and any behavior exhibited by the steward during these sessions is, therefore, incapable of being judged as anything more blameworthy than extreme rudeness.

Relevant Cases

Krauth & Benninghoffer Corp. (Imundo), 73 LA 1243;
Tobyhanna Army Depot (McLeod), 69 LA 1220;
General Electric Co. (Maroney), 71 LA 164;
Owens-Illinois, Inc. (Witney), 73 LA 663;
St. Joe Paper Co. (Klein), 68 LA 124;
Zell Brothers, Inc. (Mayer), 78 LA 1012;
Jones & Laughlin Steel Corp. (Cook), 78 LA 566;
Universal Steel Co. (Daniel), 78 LA 148;
Kay-Brunner Steel Products (Gentile), 78 LA 363;
Consolidation Coal Co. (Rubin), 78 LA 473.

5 *Although technically an issue to be treated under the National Labor Relations Act, discipline based on an employee's union status or on his or her union activities, rather than on the employee's conduct alone, will not be sustained by arbitrators.*

Examples:

Employee *A*, a union steward, was disciplined for poor production. The supervisor, when meting out the discipline, stated that he was disappointed in *A* because, as the steward, he should set an example for the others. In fact, the arbitrator found that A's production was no worse than at least one other employee who had not been disciplined. The arbitrator voided the discipline.

Employee B, a union steward, participated in a wildcat strike. When the strike was over, six of the employees were given two-week disciplinary suspensions. B was discharged on the theory that his culpability was greater than the others because of his position as steward. B's discharge was reduced by the arbitrator to a two-week suspension.

Guidelines

A union steward can be held to no higher standard of conduct than other employees, unless the steward's responsibilities are increased by specific language in the collective bargaining agreement.[27]

Relevant Cases

Sun Furniture Co. (Ruben), 73 LA 335;
Furr's Inc. (Leeper), 72 LA 960;
American Dairy of Evansville (Doering), 67 LA 1140;
Emery Air Freight Corp. (Darrow), 67 LA 541;
Bethlehem Steel Corp. (Sharnoff), 76 LA 480;
Humko Sheffield Chemical (Ross), 66 LA 1261;
Rock Creek Plaza, Inc. (Richter), 76 LA 1113.

Notes to Chapter 20

1. *Robintech, Inc.* (Block), 65 LA 221.
2. *Carborundum Co.* (Altrock), 72 LA 118.
3. *Clinton Corn Processing Co.* (Madden), 71 LA 555; *Bucyrus-Erie Co.* (Lipson), 69 LA 93; *Herrud & Co.* (Keefe), 66 LA 682; *Dravo Corp.* (McDermott), 68 LA 618.
4. *Quanex* (McDonald), 73 LA 9.
5. *Clinton Corn Processing Co.*, supra, note 3; *ITT Thompson Indus., Inc.* (Seifer), 70 LA 970.
6. *Koehring Co.* (Boals), 69 LA 459.
7. *See also John H. Fournelle v. NLRB*, ___ F.2d ___, 109 LRRM 2441 (D.C. Cir., 1982), and cases cited therein.
8. *Dover Corp.* (Kaut), 74 LA 675.
9. *Inglis Ltd.* (Shine), 66 LA 812.
10. *Central Ill. Pub. Serv. Co.* (Kossoff), 76 LA 300.
11. *Zellerbach Paper Co.* (Sabo), 73 LA 1140.

12. *Mark Twain Marine Indus., Inc.* (Guenther), 73 LA 551.

13. *Reichhold Chem. Inc.* (Hon), 73 LA 636 (warning); *Ward LaFrance Truck Corp.* (Levy), 69 LA 831 (three-day suspension); *American Hoechst Corp.* (Purcell), 68 LA 517 (one-day suspension).

14. *Kay-Brunner Steel Prods.* (Gentile), 78 LA 363.

15. *Greif Bros. Corp.* (Flannagan), 67 LA 1001.

16. *Golden Foundry, Inc.* (Fitch), 67 LA 887.

17. *Krauth & Benninghoffen Corp.* (Imundo), 73 LA 1243 (discharge upheld); *Tobyhanna Army Depot* (McLeod), 69 LA 1220 (discharge upheld); *General Elec. Co.* (Maroney), 71 LA 164 (upheld warning notice); *Jones & Laughlin Steel Corp.* (Cook), 78 LA 566 (suspension sustained). *But see General Elec. Co.* (Bridgewater), 72 LA 654 (grievance sustained where abuse provoked).

18. *Kay-Brunner Steel Prods., supra,* note 14.

19. *Universal Steel Co.* (Daniel), 78 LA 148.

20. *Jones & Laughlin Steel Corp., supra,* note 17.

21. *Owens-Illinois, Inc.* (Witney), 73 LA 663; *Tobyhanna Army Depot, supra,* note 17 (dicta). *See also St. Joe Paper Co.* (Klein), 68 LA 124 (suspension denied for official who wrote safety letter to management rather than grieve).

22. *Bakery & Confectionery Union* (Robertson), 74 LA 1297.

23. *Potlatch Corp.* (Leeper), 72 LA 583.

24. *Union Fork & Hoe Co.* (Ipavec), 68 LA 432.

25. *Sun Furniture Co.* (Ruben), 73 LA 335 (the arbitrator reinstated without backpay a steward who had disparaged the company and its product before a customer); *Furr's Inc.* (Leeper), 72 LA 960 (the arbitrator upheld the discharge of a steward, who had struck the manager, where there was no evidence of an antiunion motive on the part of the employer); *American Dairy of Evansville* (Doering), 67 LA 1140 (a steward was properly discharged for poor performance where there was no evidence of an antiunion motive); *Emery Air Freight Corp.* (Darrow), 67 LA 541 (the arbitrator upheld the discharge where there was no evidence of antiunion motive); *Bethlehem Steel Corp.* (Sharnoff), 76 LA 480 (the arbitrator upheld the discharge where the union officer accosted a foreman); *Humko Sheffield Chem.* (Ross), 66 LA 1261 (the arbitrator upheld a written warning for insubordination). *Compare Rock Creek Plaza, Inc.* (Richter), 76 LA 1113 (the discharge was reduced to a three-day suspension where there was evidence of antiunion motive).

26. *Boise Cascade Corp.* (Richardson), 66 LA 1302.

27. Recent Labor Board and Court decisions appear to create an additional requirement that the steward must also have a contractual duty to prevent or halt an illegal strike if he is treated differently from other participants in a strike. *See John H. Fournelle v. NLRB, supra,* note 7.

Table of Cases

A

AMF Harley-Davidson Motor Co. (Christenson), 61 LA 162   77

AMF Lawn & Garden Div. (Wyman), 64 LA 988   94, 97

A. P. Green Refractories Co. (Williams), 64 LA 885   32, 221, 225, 228

Abbott & Co. (Dworkin), 76 LA 339   201, 205, 213

Abex Corp. (Rybolt), 64 LA 721   152, 156

Acme Galvanizing, Inc. (Moberly), 61 LA 1115   188, 191

Acme Industrial Co. (Updegraff), 41 LA 1176   172, 177, 180

Active Industries, Inc. (Ellmann), 62 LA 985   131

Adair v. United States, 208 US 161 (1908)   42, 51

Adler v. American Standard Corp., 290 Md. 615, 432 A.2d 464 (1981)   43, 52

Advertising Publishing Co., Ltd. (Cobb), 32 LA 26   162, 167, 168, 169

Air Canada (O'Shea), 66 LA 1295   128, 129, 131

Alameda-Contra Costa Transit District
—(Koven), 76 LA 770   32, 58, 65, 68
—(Randell), 75 LA 1273   136, 137, 138, 140, 144

Alaska Sales & Service Co. (Axon), 73 LA 164   219

Alberto-Culver Co. (Grant), 66 LA 736   126

Albertson's Inc. (Christopher), 65 LA 1042   219

Alco Gravure, Inc. (Adler), 78 LA 368   125

Allied Chemical Corp.
—(Eischen), 74 LA 412   134, 137, 140, 144
—(Harkless), 76 LA 923   133, 137

Allied Employers, Inc. (Hedges), 65 LA 270   225, 228

Allis-Chalmers Corp. (Goetz), 73 LA 1230   191

Alumax Foils, Inc. (Hilgert), 73 LA 250   211

Alvey, Inc. (Roberts), 74 LA 835   197, 201, 206, 207, 211, 212, 213

American Broadcasting Companies, Inc. (Gentile), 63 LA 278   184, 191

American Dairy of Evansville (Doering), 67 LA 1140   250, 251

American Hoechst Corp. (Purcell), 68 LA 517   248, 251

American Motors Corp., 214 NLRB 455, 87 LRRM 1393   143, 144, 145

American Standard, Inc. (Biddinger), 64 LA 159   114

American Sugar Co. (Whyte), 52 LA 1228   177, 180

Anaconda Aluminum Co. (Erbs), 59 LA 1147   178

Anaconda Copper Co. (Cohen), 78 LA 690   72, 80

Apollo Merchandisers Corp. (Roumell), 70 LA 614   104, 108

D

Topical Index

About the Author

JAMES R. REDEKER is a partner in the law firm of Saul, Ewing, Remick & Saul with offices in Philadelphia, Pa., New York, N.Y., and Wilmington, Del. He is the chairman of the firm's labor department. Mr. Redeker received a B.A. degree, *cum laude* from the Central University of Iowa, an M.A. degree with honors from the University of Arkansas and a J.D. degree from the University of Pennsylvania School of Law. In addition to his direct practice of law and representation of clients in labor matters, Mr. Redeker has written and lectured extensively in all areas of employer-employee relations. He is listed in *Who's Who in American Law* and *Men of Achievement*.

DATE DUE

NOV 23 '87			
NOV 26 '88			
NOV 06 '89			
NOV 17 '91			
APR 24 '92			
	261-2500		Printed in USA